THE HARVEST GARDENER

GROWING FOR MAXIMUM YIELD, PRIME FLAVOR, AND GARDEN-FRESH STORAGE

By Susan McClure

A Garden Way Publishing Book

STOREY

Storey Communications, Inc.
Schoolhouse Road
Pownal, Vermont 05261

Edited by Gwen Steege
Cover design by Carol Jessop
Cover photograph by John D. Goodman
Text design and production by Carol Jessop
Line drawings by Judy Eliason, except for those by Elayne Sears on pages 3 (right), 6, 52, 78 (bottom), 80 (right), 87, 88, 113 (top), 114 (bottom), 138 (bottom), 147, 150, 183, and 243-277.
Indexed by Gail Damerow

Garden Way Publishing was founded in 1973 as part of the Garden Way Incorporated Group of Companies, dedicated to bringing gardening information and equipment to as many people as possible. Today the name "Garden Way Publishing" is licensed to Storey Communications, Inc., in Pownal, Vermont. For a complete list of Garden Way Publishing titles call 1-800-827-8673. Garden Way Incorporated manufactures products in Troy, New York, under the Troy-Bilt® brand including garden tillers, chipper/shredders, mulching mowers, sicklebar mowers, and tractors. For information on any Garden Way Incorporated product, please call 1-800-345-4454.

Printed in the United States by Courier
First Printing, January 1993

Library of Congress Cataloging-in-Publication Data

McClure, Susan, 1957–
The harvest gardener : growing for maximum yield, prime flavor, and garden-fresh storage / Susan McClure.
p. cm.
"A Garden Way Publishing book."
Includes bibliographical references (p.) and index.
ISBN 0-88266-798-X (hc) — ISBN 0-88266-797-1 (pbk.)
1. Vegetable gardening. 2. Organic gardening. 3. Vegetables. I. Title.
SB324.3.M38 1993
635—dc20 92-53951
CIP

Contents

To my husband, Ted, who got me started on gardening in a big way;
to my children, Scott and Eric; and to all the contributors
who shared their victories for this book — thanks.

one

An Introduction to Harvest Gardening

YOU MAY NEVER appreciate your garden more than in the middle of winter. Your fresh-frozen tomatoes will spare you from buying tasteless, leathery shipped tomatoes. A stock of endive roots for forcing or a cold frame full of chicories and Winter Density lettuce lets you scratch bland iceberg lettuce off your shopping list. In milder climates, a complete menu of cabbages, Brussels sprouts, and kales wait outside your door. Thank heavens for the succulent Purple Teepee beans and breaded eggplant in the freezer. You need not even consider the commercial Idahos and dusty cans of processed herbs — eat your own buttery heirloom potatoes, sprinkled with aromatic, emerald-green, home-dried parsley.

As spring approaches, you begin to finish up your stored goods and slip a few green things into the ground outdoors. Although the weather is far from reliably warm, the cold frame abounds with tender leaf lettuce, biting turnip greens, and crisp rainbow-colored Easter Egg radishes. Beneath floating row covers, zesty, succulent lemon sorrel is due to be picked for an excellent cream soup. The first crops of spinach and Swiss chard are ready for thinning, and the salad bowl is waiting for their tender leaflets sacrificed so that others will grow.

Late spring and summer burst on the scene with a riot of garden activity. This is a time of rich, sweet flavors. First strawberries, then to-

matoes and melons, soft and bursting with juicy ripeness, slip tenderly off the vine and into the kitchen. Within moments of being snapped off the stalk, corn is steamed and hits the dinner plate. Eating just doesn't get any better than this.

All these good vegetables don't grow gratis. A successful harvest garden takes advance planning, a good layout, some manipulation, well-educated harvesting, and safe, effective storage methods. This is what *The Harvest Gardener* is all about. I hope that as I share my own experiences as well as those of over fifty expert gardeners from all over the United States (for listing, see pages 283–286), this book can change your cuisine, your finances, and your outlook toward gardening. *Bon appétit!*

WHY SHOULD YOU GROW YOUR OWN?

You can grow better-tasting and more nutritious produce for a fraction of the cost of store-bought food. You will also find that gardening is a great stress-releasing hobby, and it provides exercise that keeps you fit and relaxed. Give it a try!

Home gardeners can harvest at the time of day crops are sweetest or at their most tender stage of development. The secret to the tastiest sweet corn, peas, and asparagus, for instance, is to pick them from the garden, cook them seconds later, and eat them immediately, before the sugars turn to starches. You can also custom harvest to serve your own needs. For example, I always grow a vine or two of Kuta squash, I pick the young golf ball-size fruit for salads, and let others grow mid-size for steaming and vinaigrette, or hard shell for storing or stuffing. If you just want to impress the neighborhood, you can let Kuta get as monstrously big as any zucchini. Show it off, then shred it, and use it like zucchini for bread.

This kind of flexibility is not possible for large commercial growers. Market demands and labor restrictions limit the crops most can raise. If they must ship their produce long distances, they are further limited to vegetable varieties with tough skins and firm consistency that can survive shipping. Whereas home gardeners pluck plump, soft tomatoes and melons off the vine, most large commercial growers harvest similar vegetable "fruits" before they ripen, resulting in a skimpy blend of acids, sugars, and aromas. Often these fruits are picked nearly green and gassed to color up enough to guarantee sales.

In addition, an assortment of

chemical sprays and preservatives are often required to bring uniform, blemish-free produce to the supermarket. We swallow fewer nutrients and more potentially hazardous chemicals. In short, flavor and nutrition take second place to the economy of large-scale agriculture.

You can grow better-quality vegetables and save yourself a bundle in grocery bills. An Ohio State University study showed that the average 10 x 15-foot garden yields 210 pounds of produce and even this can be upped by using some intensive gardening methods discussed in chapter 3.

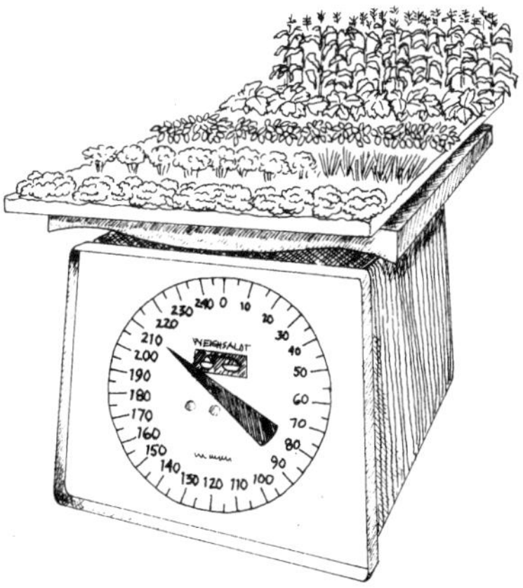

The average 10 x 15 - foot garden yields 210 pounds of produce.

I feed my family of four from the garden for about half the year. The rest of the time, I budget $3 a day to buy similar commercial produce (although I may soon have to up that amount). Presently, my garden saves me about $550, half of my annual produce bill. I estimate that for every dollar I spend on seeds and supplies I reap about $10 worth of food. I buy about $50 worth of vegetable garden seeds and fertilizers, supplementing that with plenty of free horse manure and leaf compost to enrich the soil. That leaves me with a big net gain — better than a savings account.

Growing your own fruits and vegetables can result in significant savings.

I can't help but feel smug when I browse through a grocery store. Snap peas at $3.99 per pound are such a snap to grow! A new green-headed broccoflower, identical to one that is filling out nicely outdoors right now, runs another $4. And then, just to make my day, I may wheel the cart around to the gourmet vegetables — chicories, endives,

Italian parsley, and raddicchios. This area is exotically and impressively iced and lighted. But what escapes all but a fellow gardener is that many of the items displayed are quite easy to grow. If you have gourmet tastes, an economical way to avail yourself of these or dozens of other ethnic or exotic plants is to get on the mailing list of mail-order seed houses that specialize in these products (see Appendix for addresses).

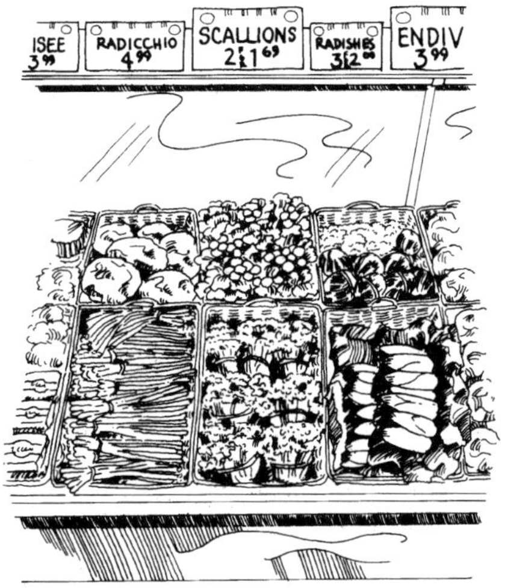

High-priced grocery-store gourmet vegetables can be grown at home for pennies.

But harvest gardening goes beyond good flavor and savings. Gardeners *like* growing things. I love to work the soil, although at times it can be strenuous. Gardening is an old-fashioned and earthy experience, yet I have a contemporary rationale as well. Gardening helps keep me physically fit and reasonably trim. Furthermore, it is interesting to watch the plants grow, to troubleshoot unexpected problems, and to create beautiful combinations of plants in the garden as well as on a plate.

I feel great satisfaction after weeding through the garden and sitting back in the lawn chair to see what my effort brings. Many of the rewards for gardening labors can be immediate. Others, like the first sweet tomato, are longer in coming but continue to pat you on the back as long as the plant produces. The fact is, I like to pick a bunch of greens or an eggplant and know that I worked with nature to produce this sustenance.

WHAT ARE YOUR FOOD NEEDS?

Growing good food and having it available when you need it takes planning. It is easy enough to get inspired to plant two dozen identical tomato seedlings when the warmth of spring rolls around. But you are likely to become discouraged a couple of months later when you harvest the five hundredth red tomato and don't know what to do with it. A more practical scheme would be to grow one extra-early tomato, a later big and beefy type, perhaps a white- or yellow-fruited type, and a few processing tomatoes for paste. Save the remaining space for basil and beans followed by lettuce and carrots. Plant lettuce every two weeks in the spring and fall and a sequence of snap bean crops in summer. Or grow cultivars that mature at different times. This technique is called *succession planting,* and it assures that you will always have something fresh for the supper table. For more on succession crops, see chapters 2 and 3.

When you are planning how much of any one plant you will need for the table, be sure to add in extras to can, freeze, or dry for later. Think about when you are most likely to take on these additional kitchen tasks and schedule their harvest time then. I am happy to escape indoors in the air conditioning and do some canning for a few hours a week in July and August, for instance, but everyone has a different schedule. To get the most out of the harvest, evaluate your schedule, and plan your garden accordingly.

Strive not for quantity but for quality. Especially when you go to the trouble to preserve produce, you should work with only the best specimens. If you save diseased, injured, half-ripe, or overmature crops, chances are good you will not eat them later and your efforts will be wasted.

Here are some food facts that may give you some idea of how much you should plant. According to United States government research, each American ate 78.6 pounds of fresh vegetables in 1987, averaging 21 pounds of lettuce, 14 pounds of fresh tomatoes, 55 pounds of processed tomatoes, almost 5 pounds of cucumber pickles, 32 pounds of canned and frozen vegetables, 42 pounds of fresh potatoes, and 22 pounds of frozen potatoes. (Statistics from the *Statistical Abstract of the United States,* U.S. Department of Commerce, 1990.)

Once you estimate how much produce you will need, the next big question is how much you can coax out of your garden space. You can approach this in several ways, some more exacting than others. Develop your own yield statistics, specific to your climate, cultivars, and growing methods. You could weigh what you harvest and keep records (although that seems like a lot of trouble to me) or you could refer to standard weight and volume tables for fruits and vegetables. Be sure to allow for the fact that different cultivars and varieties of any crop produce more or less than other cultivars and varieties of that crop, especially when given different growing conditions. In my opinion, your best evaluations will be based on your previous year's crop. If you had more beans than you could handle and your freezer is still packed with them, grow less this year. If you want more tomatoes for canning, grow a plant or two more.

INVENTORY YOUR SPACE AND TIME

A successful harvest garden really depends on whether you will make the long-term commitment to keeping the garden growing and producing all summer. Think about the size of your yard and the amount of time and energy you have to put into gardening. These factors are critical to planning the size of your harvest. When any of these resources are in short supply, stick with a diligently maintained collection of great cultivars in a small garden. A modest 10 x 10-foot bed can keep you supplied with vegetables all the growing season.

To get the most from a smaller garden may demand more time in the beginning. You may decide to build permanent raised beds and double dig the garden using biodynamic French intensive methods (see Jeavon in "Suggested Reading"). As compared to straight farm rows, these techniques let you grow two, five, or even ten times the amount of produce in a small space than conventional gardening methods. Or you may decide, for example, to build trellises to elevate vining crops and then plant shade-loving crops in their shadow (see chapter 2).

The simplest way to save space is to tuck a few edibles in existing beds, perhaps among shrubs around your foundation or in your flower garden. In a mixed island bed of hollies and pansies, for instance, I have tucked drifts of purple Rubine Brussels sprouts and purple-fruited eggplant, two colors that go beautifully together and blend with the Williamsburg blue shutters on the house. Many other edibles double as ornamentals, including ruby chard, cherry tomatoes, and blueberry bushes. Avoid those areas that have been exposed to toxic substances such as sprays that are not approved for edible plants. This might be the case near a rose garden, treated lawn, or areas exposed to automobile exhaust from a busy road.

Vegetables can make attractive — and practical — accents in your flower beds.

The way you harvest many edible landscape crops is important if you are to keep them looking attractive. Rubine Brussels sprouts, a long grower that forms a lovely upright silhouette, can wait to be harvested until September. I nip off the top shoot in late August and all the sprouts ripen at once, ready for the freezer. For example, if I plucked the sprouts one by one, I'd leave a barren stem with an awkward tuft of leaves on the top.

Just how much time your own garden will take depends a lot on your personality and management skills. Some people like to linger in the garden, watching birds and blossoms. Others hustle through hoeing and move on to something else. Management is important if you are looking for a fast-track, low-maintenance garden. You can employ a variety of products, plastics, and garden layouts to reduce your own physical labor and shrink the size of the garden without diminishing the volume of produce that comes out of it (see chapter 2).

My vegetable garden stretches a hefty 50 x 50 feet. Although I have room to expand on my 4-acre property, this is as much space as I can handle well. In fact, at the end of a good year, I have plenty of leftovers to share with the city food bank and other local charities. This means I could actually reduce the garden size without affecting our meals.

In winter, I spend a couple of hours a week browsing through garden catalogues, buying seed, and then starting the seeds indoors. Come spring, soil preparation, planting, and keeping up with the weeds takes me about six hours a week, plus the additional hours of heavy labor my husband Ted does. In summer, my garden time is spent irrigating, fertilizing, harvesting, and preserving. Of course, if a swarm of insects moves in or we suffer from a midsummer drought, I sometimes have to put in overtime. But weeks come along as well when all is calm and the garden needs no input.

HOW TO CHOOSE CULTIVARS THAT YOU WILL LIKE

When you are first thinking about what you want to grow, be conservative until you have some experience. A vegetable may sound good in a catalogue, but will you really eat it? If you are enthusiastic and talented in the kitchen, you will find a great dish for it. Less creative cooks, however, might put off the inevitable decision about what to cook until this stranger gets too old to use — so out it goes.

If you are growing something new, dig up a simple recipe well before the harvest. You can then give the plant a fighting chance and easily decide if it is worth growing again. After all, you can't eat hamburgers and beans every day of your life. Variety makes things more interesting.

Some gardeners have no interest in exotics. If you are a tried-and-true peas, potatoes, and corn eater, you can experience diverse flavors, however, and still stick with the vegetables you enjoy most. For instance, among the dozens of corn cultivars sold through seed catalogues,

A SPECIALIST IN SURPRISES

Dennis Keiser, who keeps an edible, organic landscape at his home in Mifflinburg, Pennsylvania, likes to surprise dinner guests. "It is neat to have unusual things to toss into a salad," Keiser said. "Our friends have come to expect the unusual — a blossom here, or perhaps miner's lettuce, a wild West Coast purslane that the forty-niners ate during the gold rush to prevent scurvy. It is fleshy and tender. One of those real treats." Keiser is also fond of tomatillos, a relative of the tomato that grows on a ground-creeping plant and is excellent for canned sauces.

you can grow Mandan Bride (Cook's Garden), a multicolor Indian corn used for cornmeal. Or, grow candy on the cob with new supersweet cultivars like How Sweet It Is. Yet another type, known as *sugar-enhanced corn,* maintains its sugar content for days in the refrigerator. Among the standard sweet corns are excellent cultivars like Silver Queen and Golden Bantam.

If you like peas, you can grow tiny French petit pois that will melt in your mouth, or sweet and productive edible-pod Sugar Snap types, or even peas to dry for split-pea and ham soup. The best place to start tracking the diversity of cultivars available is in the following sections of this book, as well as in seed and nursery catalogues (see appendix).

WHAT IS THE LENGTH OF YOUR GROWING SEASON?

The length of your growing season will affect your choice of plants. It is defined primarily by the dates of the last spring frost and the first fall frost. If you are growing perennial berries or herbs, you will want to know winter low temperatures as well. Your adventures in gardening should begin with a look at the United States Department of Agriculture zone map (page 282). Identify your zone number and refer to it whenever you buy trees or shrubs; if you live in an extreme northern or southern climate, consult it for vegetables and other annuals as well.

The zone map will give you a general feel for your regional statistics, but the conditions in your actual location may vary greatly from the regional norms. A home on a flat chaparral area with intense winds will be less hospitable to gardening than a less blustery site in the same vicinity. Locations near large bodies of water or in cities tend to be slightly warmer than outlying areas. If your garden site is sloped, the frosty air will tend to roll down the slope to rest in lower valleys, thus sparing early crops. If it also faces south and receives early spring sun, it will warm and begin sprouting earlier than average. Not surprisingly, north-facing slopes have the opposite characteristics.

In the South, where the summers are long, you have the luxury of cultivating crops and cultivars that take longer to mature. Your mammoth watermelons and pumpkins, as well as your pole lima beans, are the envy of the rest of the nation. Yet, you probably will never harvest broccoli shoots and early tomatoes at the same time. Your summers are too hot for cool-season plants to survive. Furthermore, you may have to take a vacation from your garden in the midst of the most intense part of summer. Excessive heat is hard on food crops. In dry southern climates, winter can be a good time for cool-season crops. Rains are lighter and more frequent, and the sun is not so intense.

Gardeners in arid areas of the West will have to plan their gardens around available rainfall or irrigation and times when the temperature is not too extreme. You may need to shade plants lightly to protect them from the beating sun.

Gardeners in frost-free areas of Florida, southern Texas, and California can delve into subtropical crops like citrus but will not have much luck with perennial crops like asparagus and rhubarb, which usually require a cold dormant period to grow well. You can, however, find berry cultivars that make do with very little cold.

On the other hand, if your summer is short or cool, you should specialize in long-growing cool-season plants, including sweet parsnips and flavor-rich rutabagas — two underdogs in today's market, but excellent producers in your climate. Sadly, you may not be able to coax long warm-season plants like peppers or eggplants to grow without the assistance of a greenhouse or artificial lighting. If you want to grow tomatoes, however, you have a friend in the Oregon State University plant breeder Dr. James Baggett. He has developed the Oregon Spring tomato, which produces crops in 57 days despite cool temperatures.

If you have a brief summer, you can choose to grow early varieties of corn or tomatoes in lieu of none at all, or you can squeeze in more growing days than the frost-free spell

A YEAR-ROUND GARDEN

Michelle Taylor, owner of Taylor's Herb Gardens, Inc., in Vista, California, has the perfect climate for year-round gardening. She grows herbs and vegetables all year without a greenhouse. Taylor says, "The nights get cool but never cold. In summer the temperature might reach 100°F for a couple of weeks but it drops fast, too. I grow the usual summer things then — peppers, tomatoes, eggplant, corn, and beans. But the greatest thing is that the humidity stays low, so there is not much of a disease problem and it still gets cool at night. In winter, the temperature can get down to 18°F for a short spell, but for the most part the season is fine for carrots, lettuce, peas, and cabbage."

in midsummer by using special cold-weather gardening techniques. Using cold-tolerant plants, along with protective row covers, cloches, and cold frames, you can start gardening as soon as the garden soil dries out enough in spring to walk on and hoe. Protect later-maturing crops so you can continue gardening until the soil freezes in fall or even longer.

VEGETABLES KIDS WILL EAT

I like to make the garden an experience everyone in my family, even the kids, will enjoy. When my son was two, he would burrow into a patch of caged sweet tomatoes and lose himself there, picking and eating in the shelter and shade of the walls of tomatoes. When he emerged, the front of his shirt would drip with seeds and juice, evidence of his healthful adventure. Of course, he didn't know it was good for him and I certainly wasn't going to tell him.

Neither was I ready to tell him that by watching plants as they grew

Feasting in the garden is a treat for any toddler.

in my garden, he was learning a lesson in life. Thus, he avidly followed a pumpkin growing from seed to sprout to running vine to tiny green button to mammoth orange jack-o'-lantern. He saw the flowers being pollinated by bees and the toads hiding in the cool shade of the foliage.

Now that he's a bit older, he has more lessons to learn. He can plant his own seeds, tend to the weeding, and tug up the proceeds. Of course, as a five-year-old, his attention span is still short. He stays happier gardening when he gets prompt rewards for his efforts. Thus, he grows the quick maturers like Easter Egg radishes, which turn a wonderful rainbow of pinks, reds, and whites. Although he doesn't care for their bite, he loves to share them with his father — another good lesson learned without a word from mother.

Kids are quick to become frustrated or discouraged when things go wrong, of course, so you need to troubleshoot for them in the garden. Stick with disease-resistant crops, and grow them when insects are least difficult (see chapter 3). Encourage your kids and their friends to help plants grow by keeping their feet off their roots. It's easy to make paths that clearly identify where kids can safely walk. With a little encouragement, even a one-year-old can learn not to tread on the flowers.

The following are good cultivars that kids can grow and enjoy, as long as you don't tell them they are good for them.

Sugar Snap peas. This relatively new class of peas have edible pods and are sweet. Since they grow on a trellis, they are easy to pluck and plop in the mouth, and, since they stay cleaner than low-growing kinds, it is not a disaster if a kid forgets to wash one occasionally (as long as you don't use garden sprays). I like the original Sugar Snap pea for its heavy productivity, but kids get frustrated by the strings. The most surefire snap pea is Sugar Daddy, which is stringless, but compact on 2½-foot vines.

Purple bush beans. If you tire of stooping to pick these beans, enlist the kids. It's easy to tell the bean from the leaf, and kids have a lot of fun collecting large piles of purple "treasure." The pods turn green while they cook, so they are not too exotic-looking to eat.

Beets. These sweet roots sprout and swell quickly enough to keep a child's attention. You will have to thin overcrowded seedlings for younger children, because they usually do not have the manual dexterity to develop ideal spacing. They certainly love to pull out the ripe, plump roots, however, which is an easy job, since beets grow near the soil surface. When cooked, beets are sweet and tender, another feast suitable even to finicky eaters. My family likes to boil young beets with hard-cooked eggs to turn the eggs pink and sweet.

Corn. This crop is a little trickier to bring to maturity, but the sweet reward is worth an effort. You will have to do the growing, fertilizing, watering, and pest control, but you can let the kids pick the ears, an easy chore. My kids top their list of favorite vegetables with sweet corn.

Cucumbers. Most kids like the crisp, wet texture of a fresh young cucumber. Make a game out of checking under the leaves to find all the fruit. A tiny new cucumber can plump up in a day — a surprise and delight for youngsters. In the kitchen, you can stuff cucumbers to make cream cheese boats or create a vegetable whale with raisin eyes and thin-sliced carrot fins.

Pumpkins. Mammoth pumpkins like Big Max would be a hit, I am sure, where the growing season is long. We have tried them with modest success, but in recent years the fruits have scarcely begun to yellow when the first frosts hit, which has been a big disappointment for everyone. So, in addition to the goliaths, I grow a more reliable but smaller pumpkin that is better tasting anyway. My favorites are Autumn Gold Hybrid, which is an early-fruiting All-America Selections Winner, and the meaty and sweet Small Sugar.

Cherry Tomatoes. Cherry tomatoes can grow as sweet as candy. Adults may prefer a richer tomato taste, but most kids adore the sweeter types. My favorite is Sweet 100 Hybrid, which has never let me down. One disadvantage, however, is that the tomatoes leave viable seeds wherever they fall, which inevitably happens. The next generation of tomatoes are quite variable and not nearly as tasty as their parents.

GETTING PRACTICAL ABOUT PLANTS: WHAT TO LOOK FOR IN CULTIVARS

Once you have inventoried the flavors you will enjoy and use, you need to consider the amount of space and level of care individual crops will need. You can cut down on the amount of work you have to do by planting compact, disease-resistant, and easy-to-harvest cultivars. All of

Look on seed packets for information about size, disease resistance, and harvest characteristics.

these qualities have been the emphasis of plant breeding in recent years in America. Here is a sampling of what you can find.

Compact Cultivars

Compact, bush-type cultivars let you plant a greater diversity of crops in a small garden. They have shorter vines than standard cultivars, but most produce full-size fruit, although there are fewer fruits per plant. On the other hand, if you can find the time and space to grow lanky cultivars, you can get a larger yield per plant. To save space in a small garden, you can train longer vines to grow vertically on a trellis.

Disease-Resistant Plants

Inbred resistance to disease is a crop saver wherever disease is a problem. I have a fair number of vegetable-loving diseases in Ohio, and this will be true anywhere the weather turns humid. These diseases can be especially troublesome when plants are stressed because of drought, excess heat or cold, or nutrient deficiencies. In southern states and mild climates, you can expect a number of soil-borne wilts and blights as well as nematodes, which thrive in the warm, frost-free soils. Tomatoes have more than their share of fungal and bacterial diseases. Thank goodness, breeders have developed plants with resistance for nearly all of these diseases. To date, early blight is the remaining holdout for breeders, and it can be a severe problem in my garden.

Disease resistance is especially important in berries, spinach, cucumbers, melons, and peas, although it is also available in many other kinds of plants.

Easy-to-Harvest Plants

Some vegetable cultivars are easier to harvest than others. E-Z Pick beans and Novella peas hold their leguminous pods high on the plant, so you can pluck them without having to dig through the leaves below. Purple Teepee, a rich burgundy-colored bean, requires some foliage ruffling, but the hunt goes more quickly because the fruits are so easy to see.

Other Improved Cultivars

Other improved cultivars tackle fruit splitting, a problem particularly when rain falls too close to harvest time. For example, Shepherd's Garden Seeds claims that the cherry tomato Sweet 100 Plus cracks less than its predecessor, Sweet 100. Park Seed's Musketeer cantaloupe is heavily netted for just this reason.

Among other breeding developments are changes in harvest time. Some cultivars are suited to a one-time harvest, a benefit for large mechanized farms, where harvesters are run through the field one time to get the whole lot. You, too, may prefer these cultivars if you like to freeze or can a winter's worth of beans or tomatoes on a single day. You can then reuse that garden space to grow something else. On the other hand, some crops are developed to re-sprout or reflower and thus give you a longer duration of harvest. Pole beans bear lightly but over a long season, if you keep picking them. Premium Crop broccoli bears only one large head, a sweet and tender accumulation of the entire season's productivity, whereas Bonanza and Green Comet sprout many smaller broccoli shoots over a long period of time.

Extra-early cultivars, ready for harvest a week or two before most others, give commercial growers a jump on the season and a chance to sell their crop and get some cash flowing. You may welcome early produce, too. Be forewarned, however: Early crops may not survive a taste test with later crops.

HEIRLOOM VEGETABLES

Some cultivars are popular simply because they taste better. A growing number of gardeners are buying their seeds and stock from small specialty companies that offer heirloom cultivars, which are appreciated for their rich flavor, or European cultivars, which are bred for taste instead of ease of harvest.

Part of the fun of gardening is knowing a bit about the plants' history. I like to grow a couple of heirlooms — plants used in past decades or centuries — every year so that I can amaze friends and neighborhood kids with their often odd shapes and sizes and their historical uses.

In nineteenth-century America, most gardeners saved seed from the plants that produced best in their yards or farms. Some growers favored unique eating qualities; others preferred differences in color, texture, flavor, or the shape of the fruit, leaf, or root. A great diversity of vegetable and fruit types developed, each of which was well-suited for a certain part of the country. Home seed saving came to a screeching stop in the mid to late 1800s, however, when seed catalogues began to flourish. Many American growers gave up saving seeds for the ease of buying them from someone else.

A few growers hung on to the old cultivars and traditions, however, and they are the source of many of the antiques that are now circulating through American gardens. Kent Whealy, founder of the Seed Savers Exchange (see box on next page), estimates that only 20 percent of the once-numerous early cultivars still exist today. Those 20 percent are looking at a brighter future as more gardeners become aware of their virtues. "We have found that serious gardeners are interested in trying

THE SEED SAVERS EXCHANGE

Much of the turnaround in heirloom variety loss is due to the Seed Savers Exchange, a network devoted to accessibility. This nonprofit group exists to educate others about the problem of heirloom cultivar extinction and to give gardeners easy access to cultivars not available commercially.

Seed Savers was founded in 1975 by Kent and Diane Whealy. Diane's grandfather gave the couple seeds of potato-leaved pink tomatoes, pole beans, and purple morning-glories that had come with the family to America from Bavaria and had been passed down for four generations. The gift opened Kent's eyes to the fragility of such hand-me-down systems. He envisioned a nationwide organization dedicated to preservation of open-pollinated crops, noncommercial cultivars, antique fruit and nuts, and old-fashioned farm animals.

Members of the Seed Savers Exchange can swap seeds, and nonmembers can order seed for about a dollar per package with higher costs for heavier items like seed potatoes. Members also have access to Seed Savers publications like the *Fruit, Berry and Nut Inventory* and a book on open-pollinated crops, which are carried by some 220 American seed companies. As companies suffer economic pressure or are taken over by others, such stock may be eliminated.

At this writing, you can join Seed Savers for twenty-five dollars a year, with a ten dollar discount for low-income families. This entitles you to three publications a year. The most vital is the January yearbook, which lists member names and addresses and what seeds they have to share. The 1991 issue included 910 growers and six thousand varieties of rare fruits and vegetables.

The Exchange's 140-acre Heritage Farm features thousands of vegetable varieties, a historic orchard, and heirloom lifestock. You can write to Seed Savers Exchange at RR 3, Box 239, Decorah, IA 52101; send one dollar to receive their informational brochure.

really good garden varieties that are not available commercially," Whealy says.

Some of the cultivars that seem almost unreal in historic catalogues are still around today. Fords Seeds (late 1800s) listed the Purple Peach tomato, which was the size and color of a peach and also had fuzz. A variety called Garden Peach Fuzzy is still carried by Seeds Blüm, a mail-order heirloom seed specialist in Boise, Idaho. Jan Blüm assures me that it really is fuzzy and that people do indeed order it.

Perhaps the most widely accepted heirlooms are the antique potatoes. Inside and out they can be violet, pink, or yellow with buttery, waxy, creamy, or moist flesh.

The heirloom corns also are gaining recognition, even among commercial growers. The blue corn used for chips that sell at bonus prices in most local grocery stores is probably related to Black Mexican sweet corn, which Kallay Seeds described this way in 1895: "Probably the sweetest of all the sweet corns [which at that time was far from today's sugar levels]. The ear is mottled with black and white grains, the darker grains becoming a violet shade when cooked." Nichols Garden Nursery and the Abundant Life Seed Foundation offer a similar Black Aztec corn, which matures to this unusual color and is recommended for grinding into flour.

Another perk associated with growing heirloom seeds is that you become one of a network of American growers who are saving both crop genes and our gardening heritage. By taking things into their own hands and growing open-pollinated plants (see page 19) year after year,

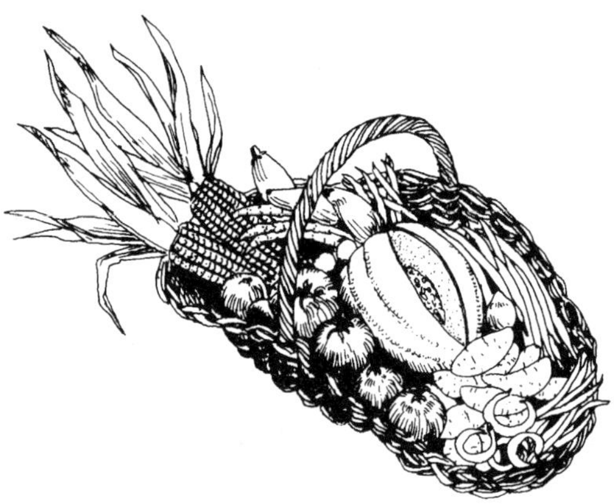

they are saving seed that may be needed in the future. Breeders may someday require traits carried in historic plants to battle disease or improve yields of contemporary selections. If you decide to become part of this network, you will find it is fun, you will make friends, and you will be doing something to improve the world.

Among such growers is school teacher, Suzanne Ashworth, curator of eggplant, tomatillos, cardoon, and other lesser-known plants for the Seed Savers Exchange. Ashworth grows hundreds of cultivars of eggplant and recommends two especially beautiful ones that have returned to commerce in recent years: Listada de Gandia, a medium-size pink-and-white-striped fruit listed in many catalogues, and a 1903 rediscovery called Rosita, a full-size fruit with lavender-pink skin. In addition to the really handsome types, Ashworth grows a perennial eggplant with clumps of grapelike fruit and another with fruit the size of a pearl.

In a 1½-acre garden at her home and 2½-acre gardens in another county, Ashworth grows plants of every variety included in the Exchange list and sends that seed back to be preserved in the Exchange's freezer.

"About five years ago, we had a problem with things disappearing over time. People were not growing certain plants. In effect, we were losing things we had found," says Ashworth. So the Exchange established curators as a way to keep a seed reserve always on hand. In addition to this time-consuming task, Ashworth has further helped the cause with her book, *Seed to Seed,* a detailed guide to growing and saving quality seed from open-pollinated crops. It is available through the Exchange and other mail-order seed companies.

If you get involved with heirloom seeds, either by saving your own and swapping with others or through buying them from catalogues, it is best to stick to types that grow well in your own vicinity. Remember, these are not modern hybrids but rather individuals with specific climatic preferences. You may be

HELPING HEIRLOOMS CATCH ON

Elizabeth Berry, a market gardener in Gallina Canyon, New Mexico, battles to increase acceptance of heirlooms. Berry trials dozens of unusual and heirloom cultivars and attempts to sell local chefs on the best of them. Berry writes this about her work:

"People have begun shipping me loads of seeds that they have saved. I got some great heirloom tomatoes from Italy and chili peppers from Spain. I grow all these things. Then once a year, I have huge tastings with all the chefs who buy from me. I blindfold them so they won't be influenced by appearance, but let them see everything later. I keep track of the results. Then I grow what is really palatable, even if it is an odd color. I keep the chefs involved in the whole process and can convince them to get away from ordinary crops, like Black Beauty eggplant.

"To keep these heirlooms going, chefs have to use them to create dishes people want, and then people will begin to demand these vegetables. You can't just start with what grows on the land. You have to begin with a dream and go the other way. It is working."

back to battling with long vines, long harvest seasons, and diseases. On the other hand, Whealy points out that at Heritage Farm they grow twelve hundred open-pollinated crops without any particular problems. As he explains, "When a cultivar has been grown in a particular area for 150 years, it naturally becomes acclimatized to the climate, insects, and diseases in that area."

Once you find a cultivar you like, do your part in the preservation effort by saving the seeds. Because heirlooms are open pollinated, they do not produce identical offspring even though they are quite similar to the parent. You will need to follow a few pollinating guidelines to keep certain lines pure. Melons and corn will hybridize with neighboring crops, for instance, and the resulting seed will be changed. To avoid this occurrence, isolate these by planting them at different times or places. Other plants, such as peas and beans, self-pollinate most of the time and are therefore much easier to keep pure.

SEED CATALOGUES: WHAT SHOULD YOU LOOK FOR?

Once you have decided what kinds of cultivars you need — those with disease resistance, ease of growing, a long harvest, or good flavor, for example — you can find just the cultivar to suit you in seed catalogues. These range from glossy, one-hundred-page magazines with detailed descriptions and color pictures to simple photocopied lists of seeds with economical prices. It is easy to get on mailing lists. Many catalogues are free, and you can simply send a postcard or call and ask for one. Some companies charge a dollar or two but take the price off your seed order total. I like to order an assortment of catalogues so I can compare offerings, information, and prices. Some companies are geared toward supplying the commercial grower; others specialize in heirlooms, home gardeners, European cultivars, or regional adaptations.

You can also find many good seed cultivars conveniently stocked in the seed racks in garden centers and even department stores, although those cultivars are often limited to what sells best nationwide — they may or may not be the best varieties for your particular climate. Also, few seed companies display seeds that cost more than two dollars per package. They just don't sell. If you want something special, out of the ordinary, or more expensive, you will need to peruse the seed catalogues.

No matter which company you deal with, you should feel confident that it will stand behind its products. Seedling plants and even seeds can carry insects or diseases, or they may not grow into the cultivar you ordered. In any case, reputable companies have developed management practices that minimize complications and will stand ready to rectify errors of their own making.

You can find a great deal of information in a quality catalogue. Remember, however, that they are sales tools. The advantages of a particular plant will be highlighted, and the disadvantages will be downplayed or not mentioned at all. Also, you may find the same plants listed under slightly different names in different catalogues. This can be confusing.

Seed Catalogue Terminology

To help you understand seed catalogues better, here is a glossary of terms you may come across.

Cultivar and variety. A *cultivar* is a group of similar plants that occurred and is maintained under cultivation. The term *variety* refers to a group of plants that originated in the wild (or as a sport of a cultivated plant) though they may also be cultivated. Their names are capitalized and are often descriptive — for instance, Provider green beans and Easter Egg radishes.

Hybrid(F1). A hybrid is the offspring from two dissimilar individuals. Modern breeders use hybridization extensively to produce new cultivars. You cannot reproduce the same combination of traits, however, if you save seed for another generation. The seedlings will be a mishmash of all the assorted genes in both plants and will often be inferior to the parent.

Hybridizing is done by hand, so you can expect to pay more for hybrid seed. It may earn its fee, however, because hybrids tend to grow particularly vigorously and uniformly and are fine-tuned to offer high-performance qualities.

Open-pollinated seed. The plants in any one of these cultivars or varieties have similar but not identical genes, and thus their offspring are similar but not identical. They can freely interbreed within the same cultivar. Some species also can outbreed, which limits the purity of the line.

Days to maturity. Most seed catalogs count the number of days from sowing the seed to harvest for fast maturers like beans and radishes, and the number of days from transplanting seedings to harvest for plants like tomatoes, peppers, and Brussels sprouts. This varies according to climate and weather, so expect it to be approximate at best.

Treated seed. Growers sometimes treat fleshier seeds, such as beans, peas, and corn, with a fungicide to reduce the chance of rotting in cool or wet soils.

Germination percentage. This figure represents the percentage of seeds that sprouted in controlled germination experiments. Higher percentages usually indicate higher-quality seed. Under home conditions, however, you may not duplicate commercial results. Germination percentages decrease as seed ages.

Disease resistance. The ability of a particular cultivar to avoid contracting a bacterial or fungal disease.

Disease tolerance. The ability of a cultivar to grow despite the presence of disease.

Compact. Varieties bred specifically for smaller gardens; these bear full-size fruit on shorter branches.

AAS Winners. All-America Selections (AAS) is a nonprofit organization that evaluates new cultivars in trial gardens across the country. A winner must be widely adapted and high performing.

Evaluating Catalogue Information

In addition to learning about disease resistance and other characteristics of cultivars you are considering, you can also study seed catalogues to make some interesting price comparisons. For instance, you may learn that one company that offers Cylindra beets sells a packet of 375 seeds for $1.15, while another offers 100 seeds of the same cultivar for 45¢. If you need a large quantity, you will want to purchase the larger packet. If you want to sample only a few plants of this cultivar, however, you may decide on the smaller packet, even though it is not as good a value. Sometimes you will find the same number of seeds of a cultivar offered at widely varying prices in different catalogues. You may even notice that one company offers more seeds at a lower price than other companies. Germination percentages differ, as well.

While you are comparing prices of individual cultivars, be sure, too, to study the shipping and handling costs of various companies.

A SAMPLING OF SEED COMPANIES

A list of some of the companies that I like to patronize follows, as well as those recommended by organic market gardeners and avid home gardeners who contributed to this book.

Specialty Companies

Abundant Life Seed Foundation. This nonprofit organization sells open-pollinated seed, many of which are heirloom varieties. Located in the maritime Northwest, Abundant Life carries seeds that excel in the cool weather common to its local trial gardens. Abundant Life collects seed from its own gardens and members or buys it from organic growers. It conducts germination experiments with most varieties and does not use fungicides.

The Cook's Garden. This small company offers over 350 cultivars, and specializes in salad greens and mesclun. The owner, Shepherd Odgen, is a former market gardener and has grown many of his offerings. He seeks out new varieties in Europe and from heirloom seed savers. Some listings do not include days to maturity, and seed packets are just beginning to include planting instructions. There is a fee for the Cook's Garden catalogue.

Johnny's Selected Seeds. A small company in central Maine, Johnny's caters to northern gardeners with short seasons. It trials its offerings and develops hybrids that do well even in Maine. The catalogue listings include hybrids and heirlooms for home and commercial gardeners.

Le Jardin du Gourmet. This modest catalogue offers a limited selection of quality varieties for lower prices. You can buy sample packets for twenty-five cents, an unheard-of price, or large packets for eighty cents. The catalogue lists French seeds, heirloom and modern varieties, herbs, and food.

Pinetree Garden Seeds. Pinetree puts out a thick black-and-white catalogue that specializes in smaller packets of seeds at lower prices. Pinetree emphasizes contemporary cultivars for home gardeners with a scattering of European, regional, and heirloom varieties.

Plants of the Southwest. This small company specializes in plants from arid climates in the American Southwest. It offers older Mexican and Native American varieties, as well as a few modern and heirloom vegetables.

Seeds Blüm. This company is operated by Jan Blüm, who has produced a catalogue worth reading whether you buy anything or not. She lists offerings by botanical affiliation and includes detailed information on how to save top-quality seed. She offers heirloom and other open-pollinated varieties. There is a fee for the Blüm catalogue.

Shepherd's Garden Seeds. This mail-order company offers European- and Oriental-bred as well as open-pollinated and hybrid seed; a limited number of varieties may be treated with fungicides if not otherwise available. The company owner, Renee Shepherd, trials new offerings in her own garden and has developed recipes that she includes in the catalogue and in small cookbooks offered through the catalogue. The seed packets contain a wealth of information, valuable when you are ready to plant and do not have your catalogue handy.

Large Seed Companies

W. Atlee Burpee and Co. A formerly family-owned company that set the pace for early American seed companies, Burpee has developed many fine varieties of vegetables through its decades-old breeding program. The business has been sold several times in recent years and presently is owned by Ball Seed, which is a commercial distributer. The new owners have limited the number of varieties offered, but they still carry the mainstays in both hybrid and open-pollinated varieties.

William Dam Seeds. This Canadian company carries European selections uncommon in the United States, as well as the best-liked American cultivars, both hybrid and open pollinated. The catalogue is easy to use because it shows the best qualities of each variety. Varieties are marked "Early," "Market," and "Freezer," in bold to indicate specific usefulness.

Harris Seeds. This is another granddaddy among American seed companies that specialize in vegetables. Harris develops many of its own varieties in Rochester, New York. The catalogue lists and pictures many popular hybrids as well as some novelties. Some seeds are treated with fungicides.

Park Seed. This is the last remaining large family-owned seed company. The catalogue is nicely produced, full of color pictures. It contains an extensive listing of varieties, some of which are sold exclusively by Park. They emphasize hybrids, low-maintenance, and compact plants.

Thompson and Morgan. This is a large British seed company with a branch in America. Although they have a limited number of vegetable varieties, many are uncommon in this country. The prices tend to be a little higher; order early to avoid sell-outs or substitutions.

Other seed companies. Garden City Seeds sells open-pollinated vegetables for the valleys of the Rocky Mountains and the Northern Great Plains. DeGiorgi Seeds and Goods has an inventory of traditional, open-pollinated, and hybrid seed. Nichols Garden Nursery sells herbs and rare seeds. Stokes Seeds, Inc. carries open-pollinated and hybrid seed especially for commercial growers. Vesey's Seeds, Ltd. specializes in varieties for short seasons.

SAMPLE HARVEST SCHEDULES

To make the most of your local growing season, plan ahead before you plant. Identify the amount of time each crop will need and decide whether you can follow an early crop with a later one. You can estimate when each vegetable will begin production and how long you can expect to continue picking. Of course, the exact timing will vary depending on weather and other factors beyond your control. Make sure that the entire garden will not ripen during the same week. If you expect to have some simultaneous harvesting, leave a couple of days on your calendar free so you will have time to freeze, can, or dry the excess produce for winter. Here are some sample schedules for different parts of the country.

Cleveland, Ohio

I have come to expect the following out of my own garden. Of course, there are always a few surprises, brought on by the weather, the pests, or the experimental cultivars I slip in every year. We are in zone 5, where winter temperatures drop to –20°F. On average, the last spring frost can be May 20, and the first frost returns in autumn about October 20. Summer may reach 90° or 95°F, but not usually for more than a few weeks. Evenings are generally cooler. We often have a drought in July and August.

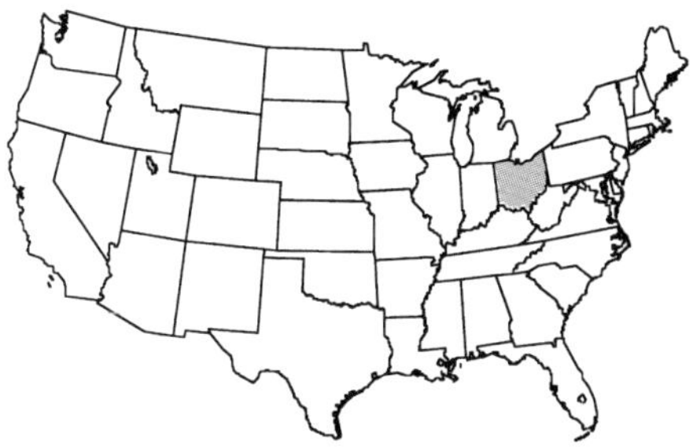

April. If the spring is not too frigid or too wet, I can pull my first radishes from the cold frame by April 1. Lettuce, spinach, and Swiss chard follow soon after.

May. If the season remains mild, I may pluck a few early peas in May. Late in this month, the quick-growing root crops, like beets and turnips, are beginning to swell and may make a meal as baby vegetables.

June. June is a month to eat peas and strawberries out of hand, and to harvest broccoli.

July. July marks the start of some freezing as cauliflower matures and the first planting of beans and tomatoes needs picking.

August. August is for freezing beans and tomatoes and eating eggplant and then breading and freezing the rest. We eat as much summer squash as we can stand, freeze some more in breads and casseroles, and give a lot away.

September and October. In September and October we welcome the winter squash and pumpkins. We eat some right away — usually those that the kids dropped or that have a soft spot. The rest we save for a rainy day when they taste even better. The cool-weather greens, coles and peas, are back again. We eat leafy things, may try a batch of sauerkraut, and freeze the extra peas, broccoli, and cauliflower. By late October the first frost has passed and everything else is relatively still, so I begin to harvest late roots, cabbages, and Brussels sprouts. I sometimes hold cabbage heads, cold-season greens, and peas outside until this time, but keep them under a floating row cover to protect them from frost.

Winter. Kale plants last outdoors until the temperature drops in January. The cold frame is my only source of leafy green plants. The hardier lettuce cultivars keep going gamely until about Christmas. Chicories may fall dormant but are the first to emerge in February or March.

Gallina Canyon, New Mexico

Elizabeth Berry's market garden in Gallina Canyon, New Mexico has frosts that usually end May 28 and begin again around September 1. The canyon is at a 6500-foot elevation. Although growing season daytime temperatures may get up to 85°F, nights remain between 50° to 60°F. Unusual greens like arugula grow beautifully all season in sunken beds that conserve moisture. Here is her schedule:

May. Plant corn; it can take a little cold. Harvest greens.

June. Plant tomatoes, chili peppers, and eggplant, all started indoors ahead of time. When the ground is really warm, plant beans. Harvest greens.

July and August. The Santa Fe tourist season begins and restaurants have peak demand for produce. Harvest all plantings.

September and October. Harvest dried beans and popping corn. After frost, dig fingerling potatoes.

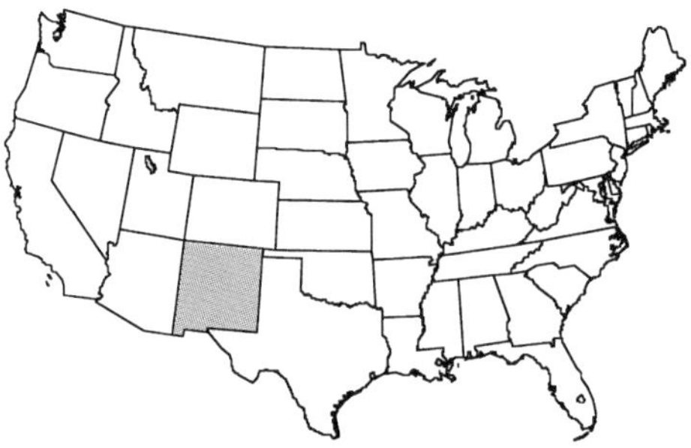

South Carolina

Park Seed, which is located in Greenwood, South Carolina, offers this advice in their direct seed sowing schedule: In South Carolina, trial gardeners direct-sow cool-season items such as peas and leeks in early to mid February. In early March and again at the end of August, they plant seedlings of herbs and parsley and the seeds of beets, carrots, chicory, radishes, spinach, and turnips. Summer vegetables such as corn, beans, and more peas are planted in the garden in early May. Peas return again for a final sowing at the end of August.

GETTING STARTED WITH SOILS

While you are planning your garden, look closely at the soil. There should be as much activity below ground as above. In a healthy soil, roots burrow, drawing in moisture and nutrients and establishing mutually beneficial relationships with microscopic organisms. Earthworms tunnel through the soil, bringing up nutrients from the depths and opening avenues for air to enter from the surface. Bacteria and fungi turn decaying plant and animal matter back into humus, which holds moisture and nourishes this complex subterranean community.

Clay, Sand, or Silt?

In an unhealthy, compressed clay soil, oxygen levels are low, there are few microbes, and roots are stunted. These factors slow organic decay and prevent soil enrichment, and the crop struggles. Equally unproductive are overly sandy soils, which have plenty of oxygen but which lack nutrients and moisture. Roots must dig deeply and scavenge what they can or perish.

Clay, sand, and silt — the natural mineral components of soils — are defined by their sizes. Clay is the finest particle — one thousand times smaller than sand and one hundred times smaller than silt. It captures nutrients but may be slow to release them to plants unless the soil chemistry is right. Clay stays wet and cold longer in spring, and readily compacts so that oxygen is withheld from roots. When gardening in clay, you can circumvent some difficulties by physically raising planting areas above the surrounding ground level. Water will then drain to lower areas. Another advantage of raised beds is that you can walk around the edge without compacting the clay with your weight. Clay soil is pervasive in some areas of the country, most notoriously Georgia. Elsewhere, you are likely to find clay or similarly compacted soils in the topsoil-depleted, equipment-compacted area immediately around a new home or other construction locations.

Areas near existing or former lakes, rivers, oceans, or deserts may have looser soils with more sand. Coarse sand, the largest soil particle, is devoid of nutrients. You must add a substantial amount of organic matter to sandy soil to bring it up to reasonable fertility. While sand allows air to permeate roots, it also lets moisture run freely through the spaces between the soil particles.

Silt, the medium-size particle, is ideal for gardens, especially when blended with a little sand and clay. Such a mix holds some nutrients and moisture but also lets excess water percolate through.

Most soils are actually loams, blends of some sand, silt, and clay.

You can identify the size and quantity of the different mineral components in your loam soil by having it tested by your local Cooperative Extension Service or a private laboratory. You also can make a couple of tests at home. Shake up 1 cup of soil in a quart jar of distilled water. The soil that settles within 5 minutes is sand. Silt settles during the next hour, while clay settles about 24 hours later. Do a quick test by grab-

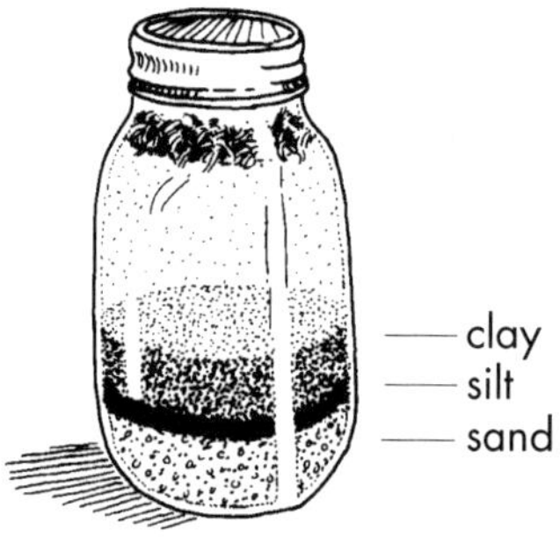

Home-test soil composition by observing a sample mixed with water in a glass jar.

bing a handful of soil and squeezing it into a ribbon. If the ribbon breaks up immediately, the soil is mostly sand. If it falls apart before it is ¾ inch long, it is silt. Ribbons up to an inch long are silty clay, and anything over 1 inch is clay.

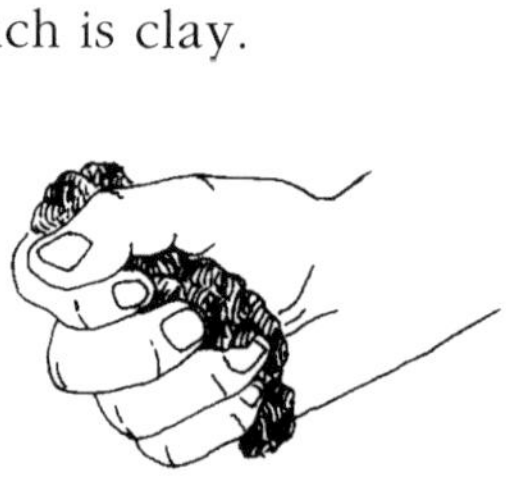

Another quick soil test: squeeze a handful into a ribbon and observe how it holds together.

Organic Matter in Soil

Having evaluated the mineral elements, inspect the biological component — the humus or decaying organic matter. Most soil tests will indicate levels of organics in the soil. An experienced gardener can tell when those levels are high by the success of the crops. Humus lets air penetrate to roots, even clumping fine clay particles so they resemble silt. It holds moisture and nutrients, releasing some as it decomposes, and storing others so they are readily available to roots. Humus is what makes a healthy, living soil.

You can steadily improve any soil by adding organics such as compost, decayed manures, and peat moss, as well as by providing your own organics by planting a cover crop. You should note that different soil amendments can have different effects on the soil. For example, sheep, poultry, and rabbit manures are high in nitrogen — too high for most crops, unless the manure is thoroughly aged. Horse manure often comes complete with weed seeds and woody bedding. The bedding absorbs nitrogen as it decomposes and can stunt the growth of nearby plants. Cow manure, which has been twice digested, is usually free of weed seeds and, once decayed, offers a small dose of nutrients.

A homemade compost is usually ideal, especially if you blend seed-free weed scraps, grass clippings, shredded leaves, and herbivore manures. Sandwich different substances in layers, keep the pile moist, and turn the mixture occasionally with a pitchfork to aerate it and speed decomposition. When the pile decomposes to a dark-colored humus, it is ready for the garden. You can compost in ditches, plastic bags, or, to make the process easier, prefabricated composting bins or barrels.

Contributor Wilfred Wooldridge has found one of the easiest ways to add humus to the soil. "Last fall, we layered 4 inches of ground-up leaves on the garden and innoculated it with Ringer's Winter Restore [a product containing nutrients and microorganisms]. Then we turned it all under. By spring, the soil was in beautiful shape and seemed to need no extra fertilizer. What a great way to use leaves!"

If you don't want to make your own compost, you may be able to buy it. The city of Cleveland sponsors a leaf ecology program that uses leaves collected by two dozen communities to make compost. Locals can buy it by the truckload or bag. The price is not cheap, but it is competitive. With the shortage of landfill space, your community or local landscapers may be doing something similar.

Some Cover Crops to Try

Cover crops add humus to your soil, but that is just the start of their value. When you carpet the vacant parts of your garden with beneficial greenery like timothy or fall rye, you protect the soil from erosion, nutrient leaching, and weeds. At the appropriate time, add a little extra nitrogen, turn under the tender greenery, and in a few weeks the plants will decompose into organic matter to nurture the next crop.

You can choose from quick-growing, short-term cover crops or longer-growing perennials. To hold the soil over winter, start fall rye in the late summer or very early spring, and till it in when you prepare the garden. To fill a gap, perhaps between a spring and fall crop or between sparce pumpkin vines, use quick-growing timothy or buckwheat.

Helen Atthowe, a consultant to organic orchards in New Jersey, uses buckwheat as a green manure and soil enricher for the sandy loams typical of the region. She recommends that fruit tree growers disk or till every other row in the orchard in the spring and plant buckwheat there. Since buckwheat is an annual crop, it flowers, attracting beneficial insects as it does, and then goes to seed and dies. Atthowe says if you leave the crop alone, it will decompose into an organic mulch while clovers and grasses creep in to cover the soil. If the summer is especially wet or if the area is irrigated, seed set by the first crop may germinate and grow 6 inches or so before fall frosts.

For cover over a longer time, try

legume crops, which can capture nitrogen and enrich the soil. Vetches, relatives of the broad bean, are usually grown as annuals. You can till many of the perennial clovers and deep-rooted alfalfas in while young or let them hold garden space for a year or more, if you want to leave a section of the garden fallow.

Kathleen Fenton, co-owner of Peaceful Valley Farm Supply in California, points out that there are over one hundred cover crop varieties available and the best one for a particular situation depends on such factors as the specific soil and weather conditions and the desired goal. However, Peaceful Valley offers a generic cool-weather green manure mix that includes bell beans, Austrian winter peas, and vetch, both with and without rye. This mix works well in most areas of the United States, except where there is severe frost.

Fenton advises, "The legumes can fix up to 150 pounds of nitrogen per acre. But you need to innoculate the seed with *Rhizobium* bacteria. These will grab nitrogen right out of the air and collect it in little pink nodules in the roots. When the nodules slough off from the roots, the nitrogen becomes available to the plants. Then, when the cover crop is in about three-quarters bloom and before it sets seed, till it in to release even more nitrogen in the top growth. Let the garden sit and digest a week or two before you plant."

For more information on improving soils, see John Jeavon's *How to Grow More Vegetables* (see Suggested Readings in Appendix).

What To Do for Faster Results

Organic or mineral amendments can steadily improve a soil's productivity over a period of years. For faster results, however, you can simply replace the soil if it is not suited to the crop you want. This is hard work the first year, and it can be expensive to find or blend the right kind of soil. The resulting soil will be ready, however, to grow great crops instantly.

Since herbs do best in a reasonably sandy soil and I have heavy clay, I used the following technique in my herb garden. I decided to plant my herbs in a bed near the south-facing wall of my garage, where the sunlight is the most intense. I dug out the old soil as deep as I could

Build a raised bed and fill it with improved soil.

with a shovel — an average of 6 to 8 inches. It took about an hour a day for a week, to empty the 25 x 12-foot garden. I raised the perimeter of the slightly sloping area with a 1-foot-high dry stone wall. I then filled the bed with a mixture of 35 percent sand and 40 percent leaf compost. The remaining 25 percent of the soil came from clumps of clay blended in with the rototiller.

Right from the start, the garden grew sturdy and flavorful herbs. I know their roots are healthy. I once followed a parsley root 7 feet. The garden warms and dries early in spring. I can step in and out of it when my vegetable garden would suck the boot right off my foot. However, heavier-feeding plants sometimes flounder because the area is drier and more nutrient-poor than surrounding areas.

Soil Tests and Adjusting Soil pH

The acidity or alkalinity of the soil is measured on a pH scale. Most vegetables prefer a slightly acidic soil (pH 6–6.9), which chemically frees most nutrients in the soil and makes them available to plants. At a more acidic pH, you can grow blueberries, huckleberries, and scab-free potatoes. Beets prefer more alkaline soils.

You can get a general feel for soil pH with a home pH test kit, available in many garden centers. For more specific information, have your soil tested professionally.

Armed with information on the condition of your soil, you can adjust soils according to what specific crops need. Add slow-working ground limestone, quick-acting hydrated lime, magnesium-releasing dolomitic limestone, ground oyster shells, or wood ashes to make a bed more alkaline. To make a garden more acidic, add sulfur, peat moss, and/or pine needles. Two effective but more expensive additives that moderate alkaline soils are ferrous sulfate and aluminum sulfate.

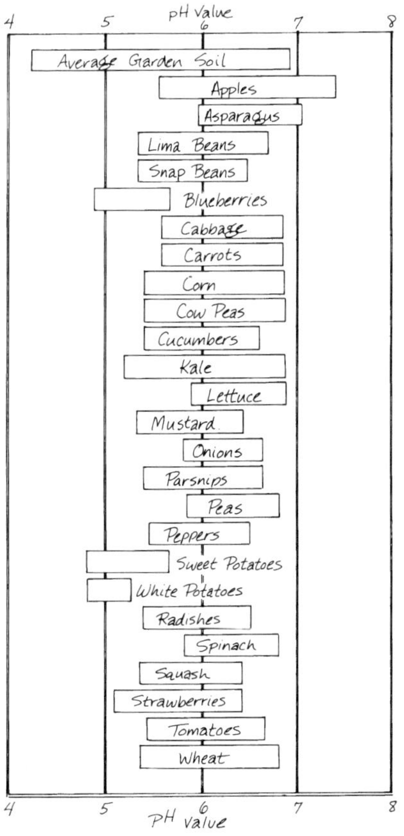

pH value preferred by some common fruits and vegetables

HOW TO EVALUATE YOUR SOILS WITH SOIL TESTS

In a new, troubled, or intensively cultivated garden, you will want to know the chemistry and physical structure of the soil so you can plan your soil-amending strategy and decide which crops to grow. You can get a good idea of soil fertility, pH, fertilizer needs, nutrient-holding capacity, and organic content from your county's Cooperative Extension Service, usually listed in the telephone book white pages under "County." Call the Service and ask for a test packet. In Ohio, a soil-test kit includes instructions and a small cloth bag for a sample. The fee is usually under ten dollars.

If you are after a more exhaustive report, you may pay a little more to have the soil tested by a private laboratory like A and L Eastern Agricultural Lab (see Appendix for address). Their report will give you all of the above information, plus micronutrient levels, cation exchange capacity, base saturation, and explanations of the findings.

Test results can come as a surprise. One woman I know discovered the soil in the planter boxes she had used for years was pH 5.5 — so acidic that many essential nutrients were locked up. The only reason her crops continued to grow was that she applied water-soluble fertilizer every week. The plants absorbed some of the fertilizer before the nutrients were caught up by the soil chemistry.

You may notice a difference between the reports from different labs or even from the same lab at different times. Such variability occurs as soils naturally change with what you are growing, when you last fertilized, and pH, organic matter, and moisture levels. It also depends on the sensitivity of the instruments the lab uses. Results from a home testing kit are pretty ambiguous. A modern lab with the latest analytical equipment will be much more specific. For more on nutrients, see chapter 4.

two

Organizing Your Garden

WHEN IT COMES to putting in a new garden, think in general terms first, then work down to the details. Ask yourself where in the landscape a garden will look good and perform well. When we first bought our house and debated where to put our vegetable garden, we went back and forth between different sites. Should we squeeze it close to the house or spread it out further back? Should we center it in the middle of the lawn to be alone in full sun, or tuck it off to one side against a shade-casting hedge? It was almost as difficult to decide as agreeing on a name for our first baby.

THE SITE: BASIC CHARACTERISTICS

To come to a final choice, we sat down and objectively rated possible locations according to how well plants would grow and how well the site would mesh with the rest of the landscape. Our first priority was plenty of sun and clean, well-drained soil. Beyond these basics, we balanced lesser concerns such as slope, cold air drainage, wind, and nearby tree roots.

Sun. Strive for over six hours of sun a day, although the exact duration will vary with the season. The more sun you have, the more productive, diverse, and flavorful your harvest will be. If your yard is shady, remove lower limbs from nearby trees or cut

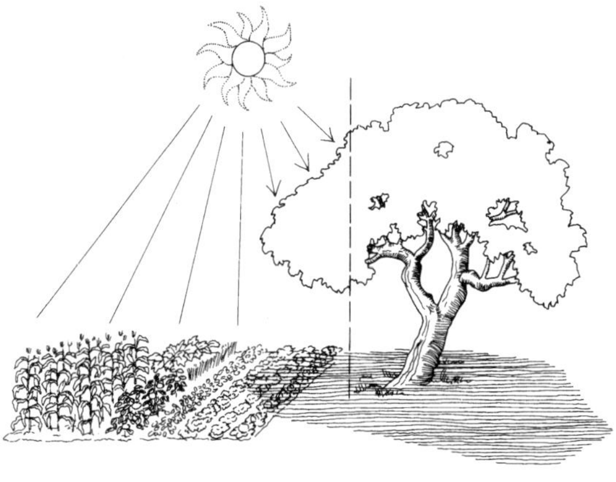

You may have to prune nearby trees to ensure at least 6 full hours of sun each day for your garden.

them down altogether. Thin or shorten shrubs. Move structures that cast shade to another part of the yard.

Root competition. Woody plants will steal moisture and nutrients from herbaceous plants you attempt to grow nearby. Trees, like food crops, root primarily in the top 12 inches of soil, especially if there is clay below. Maple and beech trees are particularly shallow rooted. You can see their actual rooting area during a dry summer if the grass around lawn trees browns-out where the two root systems compete for moisture. To avoid competition, establish a garden well beyond a mature tree's branch tips. Young trees, of course, will continue to extend both roots and branches. Take that into account.

Place gardens beyond the area of tree roots, which compete for moisture and nutrients.

If you have no alternative but to set up your edible garden near tree roots, you can till the soil and remove woody roots that you kick up. It is a sure bet that they will return, however. Slow them down by installing a vertical, nontoxic plastic, wooden, or sheet-metal barrier 3 feet deep at the perimeter of the garden.

Drainage. Plants need to breathe oxygen with their roots as well as their leaves. This is impossible for most plants if the soil is under water. If you have a low spot where you intend to start a garden, therefore, add drainage tiles or a drainage trench around the perimeter to percolate away the excess moisture. You also can raise the area so it is level with or higher than surrounding soil.

On the other hand, a low-lying garden can be a blessing in a dry climate. It will collect any rain or irrigation runoff, supplying the plants, even temporarily, with moisture. Be aware that it can also collect chemicals sprayed on your lawn or your neighbor's lawn.

Toxic chemicals. Newspapers everywhere are filled with news of toxic spills and chemical dumps found on old farm sites, city property, even suburban yards. Sometimes such accidents are not too far from our own backyards. When we bought our present home, we were surprised to find mercury and arsenic sitting on the shelf in the garage. You can't know everything that has been in the soil before you begin working it, but you can have the soil tested for heavy metals and other contaminants if you suspect foul play. It is better to find out whether or not the site is clean *before* you bother to prepare it.

Slope. If you plant on a slope, you can garden as if you lived a couple climatic zones to the north or to the south. A southern slope, which receives maximum sun exposure, warms quickly in spring, stays hotter in summer, and remains temperate to the last possible moment in fall. You can thus start gardening there earlier in the spring and keep going later into autumn. The hot days of summer will be even hotter, however, a special problem in the South. Crops may suffer if not lightly shaded.

North-facing slopes, the last to warm in spring, have certain advantages as well. If you live in an area with wide spring temperature fluctuations, you may have better success planting early-flowering gooseberries, currants, or June-bearing strawberries on a north slope. They may stay dormant long enough to escape frost damage. Likewise, rhubarb and asparagus may emerge later and thus have an extended harvest season.

Regardless of the direction it faces, a slope will drain cold air and frost. You may notice freeze damage puddling in dips along the slope and collecting in the valley at the bottom, while the top stays frost-free.

Winds. Although the top of the hill may escape frosts, it is more likely to be swept by winds that reduce winter low temperatures and accelerate the effects of summer droughts. Winds can also be a problem near flat plains or fields, where they gust unimpeded and can knock plants over. Because wind steals the protective coating of humidity on plants and increases evaporation, few grow well in windy areas.

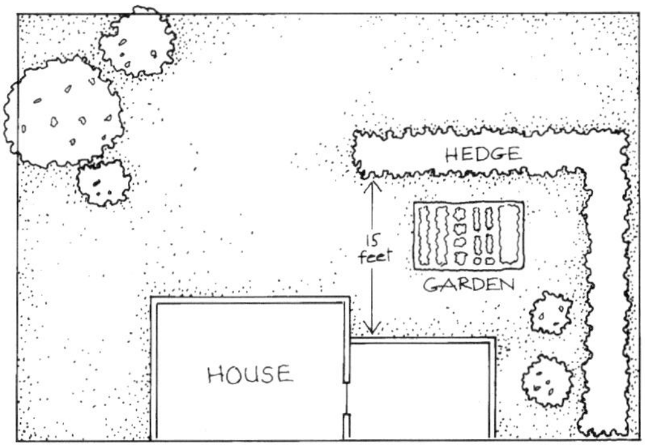

A low-growing hedge can serve as a windbreak to protect your garden.

To make the most of a windy location, build or plant some sort of wind block — a row of low-branched trees or shrubs, a solid wooden or stone fence, or an open fence covered with vines. The higher the blockade, the more area it will protect from strong wind. Don't wall the garden in on all sides, however. Plants do need gentle breezes to fight off fungus diseases.

THE SITE: WHAT IS PRACTICAL FOR YOU

When you are thinking about locations for a garden, don't forget to

If you enjoy keeping a picture-perfect garden, plant it where you can see it often.

consider your own convenience. If you have the garden close to the house, you can dash out there in a moment to harvest or pull dandelions before you pick up the kids at school. A readily accessible garden, however, will be readily visible as well. Can you commit to keeping it attractive and or to putting in the time to maintain it? If so, make the most of it. Set the garden outside your kitchen window or near the patio so you can look out and gloat over your accomplishments. Be sure to plant it with a green cover crop so it will look reasonable in wintertime, too.

On the other hand, if you don't mind a few weeds and know that you will let your garden go from time to time, you should not put it where it will be a landscape focal point. Consider it a service area, just like a tool shed or garbage bin. Site it behind the garage, or wrap it in a picket fence. Plant a cluster of blueberry bushes as a screen to limit your view of the garden from the house.

Where space or time is limited, you may decide simply to put a few gourmet or particularly attractive crops into existing ornamental beds or to grow them in containers on a porch, patio, deck, walk, driveway, or whatever open space you have. If you have a small yard, you may have to squeeze vegetable and fruit beds into whatever nook and cranny you can find. If your yard is large and open like mine, you have many choices. You can pick and choose shapes and schemes. The following pointers will make your garden look as good as the produce from it will taste.

Integration. Try to line up the perimeters of your garden with some existing feature — like a walk, the garage, the back patio, or the kitchen window — so that it is integrated into its surroundings. If you can tie the garden into the landscape, it will enhance the overall effect and may even increase your property value.

Create unique shapes. Consider using a different shape from the standard

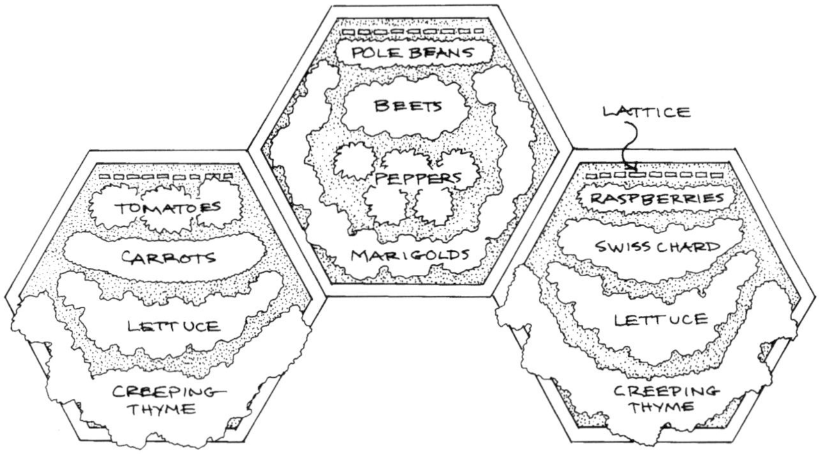

Hexagonal raised-bed vegetable gardens could form a strong design element in your landscape.

rectangle or square that has become common. Neither choice is the only option.

Donna Swansen, past president of the Association of Professional Landscape Designers, thinks an edible garden can make a fashion statement: "I think we should get away from the rectangular vegetable garden. I think a garden would be handsome in hexagons." She imagines linking three hexagonal raised beds in a sunny corner of a yard. She would frame them with railroad ties and back them with upright latticework trellises for tomatoes, purple pole beans, melons, blackberries, and raspberries. The front of the bed would be draped with cascading herbs, such as creeping thyme, which would emit their fragrance when brushed by passers-by, and edged with *Tagetes patens,* a marigold species with a rich orange or lemon fragrance that may deter rabbits.

You might add an apple tree or a seedless, thornless honey locust in the center of the arc made by the three vegetable beds. The light shade could extend the growing season for cool-season vegetables and serve as a retreat for the gardener and visitors. Encircle the tree trunk with benches for seating or a staging area for pots of ornamental plants.

An idea for a round vegetable garden comes from Michelle Taylor,

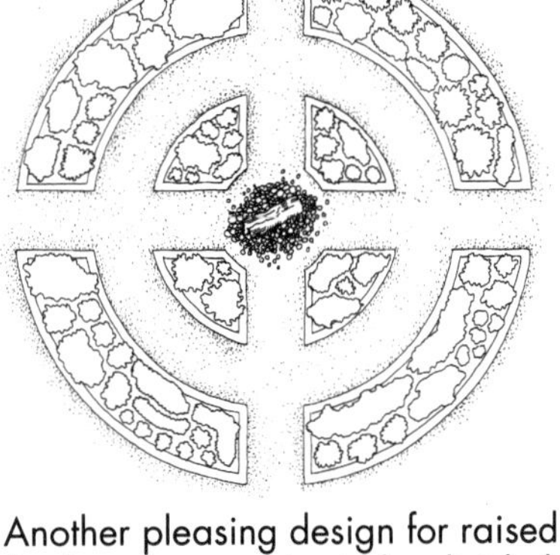

Another pleasing design for raised beds — concentric circles divided by grass paths.

MY GARDEN

We decided to put our vegetable garden behind a white garden shed at one edge of our property. The garden stretches close to a large maple on the south end; a wind-breaking hedgerow of viburnums to the east, the shed to the north, and a grass path to the east divides it from a half-moon-shaped perennial garden. The grass path has become the focal point for the backyard. It leads from the breezeway glass doors, past both gardens, through a row of maple trees, to a children's play area and a path leading into the woods.

When we added a new master bedroom to our house, we positioned a glass picture window to face toward the garden area. In season, the view was wonderful, but during the winter, it was barren. To have something attractive to gaze at, I screened the front corner of the vegetable garden with a mounded rock garden, a miniature replica of a mountain. It is the first thing I see when I look out the window. Blue Maxim Marina pansies, which make an edible garnish for salads or desserts and tolerate cold weather, reside there all year round and bloom even in midwinter. An evergreen weeping dwarf hemlock is my prize specimen, surrounded by alpine perennials and strawberries. For summer color I plant creeping annuals. This garden was fun to create, and the result is quite satisfying.

who grows her vegetables in concentric loops. Each 3-foot-wide loop is raised and double dug. The loops are separated by grass paths; and grass paths also cut an X straight to the center. At the heart of the garden is a petrified log surrounded by beach rocks.

Give it polish. Paths make the garden look more sophisticated. Paved paths give a sense of permanence, while mulched or graveled ones project a more natural look. Angle the paths so they take a longer route if you want to make the garden seem longer, or make them direct to minimize the appearance of length.

Add an entry. Put an ornamental entry on the main path into or out of the garden. This could be an arbor, rock garden, or wrought-iron gate, anything wide enough to squeeze your wheelbarrow, rototiller, and tractor through.

Create raised beds. Raise the beds with railroad ties, boulders, rock walls, driftwood, brick, or cement. Plants will have more rooting room and better drainage. You will also have something nice to look at all year.

Make it dramatic. Make a big splash in a small area by planting several varieties of a single kind of plant, such as tomatoes, but use assorted cultivars, so that you have different colors, sizes, and shapes of fruit. For example, let some yellow and red determinate tomatoes (those with limited growth) sprawl on the soil in the foreground, then build progressively taller staked, caged, or trellised plants with pink, orange, lemon, and crimson fruit in pear, pearl, beefsteak, and egg shapes. You can do the same with heirloom eggplant, leaf lettuces, and peppers. Try to hold yourself to two or three primary colors for some sense of unity.

THEME GARDENS

Have some fun — give your garden a theme. If you are a beginning gardener, a focus will also get you off to a better start. The produce you grow will mean more to you if you know its lore and legends, and you will be less tempted to plant every seed you can — a quick way to get overwhelmed.

My husband loves to eat salad and hot peppers. He would need

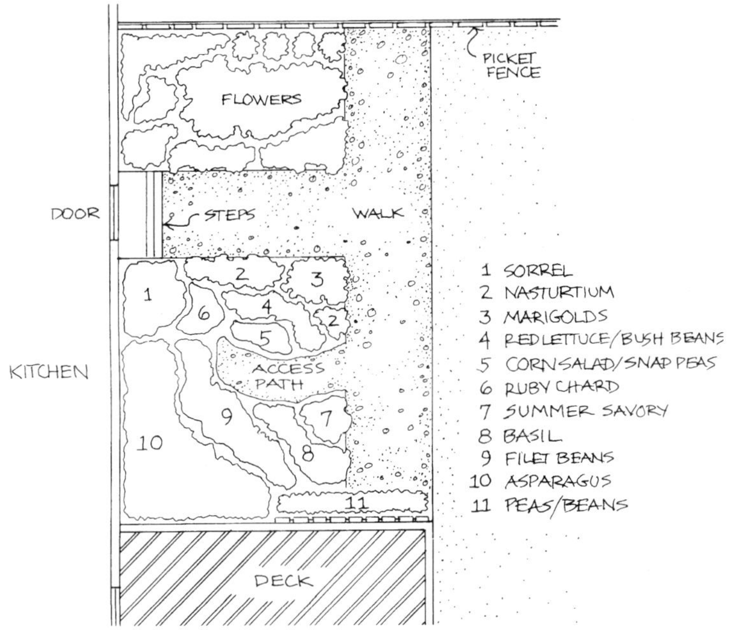

A kitchen garden planted close to the house makes it easy to watch and tend your crops.

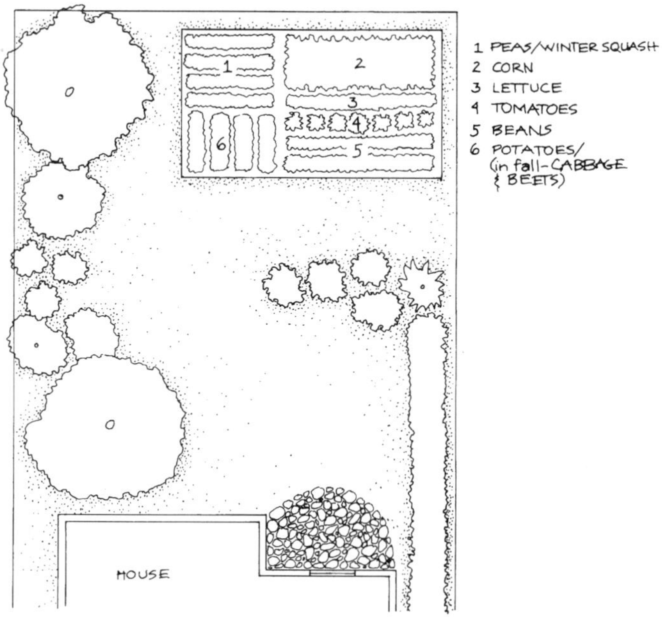

An "outback garden" can hold larger, more utilitarian crops.

only a cool-and-hot garden of greens and chilis to be satisfied. For suggestions of other ideas to build your garden around, check out preplanned theme gardens in seed and nursery catalogues. Adapt the size and shape, as well as the cultivar selection, to your part of the country. Here are some specialty gardens that may catch your interest.

Kitchen gardens. The small kitchen garden is traditionally located near the kitchen door, and generally devoted to produce like peas, asparagus, filet beans, and tender greens like sorrel or corn salad, which taste best eaten right after harvest. Placing the garden close to the house makes it easy to keep an eye on your crops and pick them at peak times.

Outback gardens. This garden is for the avid gardener or cook, or perhaps someone who aspires toward moderate self-sufficiency. The outback garden occupies a larger space in the rear of your yard and might not be as intensively tended as the kitchen garden. Here, you can grow enough long-storing vegetables to keep your family fed all winter. You can include unusual varieties of potatoes, popcorn, sweet corn for freezing, tomatoes for freezing, sauce, and juice, winter squash, and for the root cellar, beets, carrots, and cabbages. Be sure to include lettuce, beans, peas, and corn for in-season eating.

Container gardens. These gardens can serve as conversation pieces, ornamental gardens, and sources of ultra-fresh edibles. When you have limited space, you probably will use a container garden to grow only what you cannot buy. To make them more decorative, organize the pots in pyramids, clusters, or rhythmic lines on a patio, step, walk, or drive. Use regular nursery containers, buckets, or garbage pails, or get fancy with decorative containers made of terra-cotta, wood, metal, or other material. If you use the same type of pot for all plantings, the effect will be more uniform and orderly.

Group the pots in some interesting way, perhaps in the corners of a sunny patio with the shortest plants in front and the tallest in back. In spring, the small pots, 6 to 8 inches in diameter, might contain red-leaf lettuces, red mustard, and arugula interplanted with baby carrots. The next tier of pots, 10 to 14 inches in diameter, could grow purple cauliflower, followed in summer by pink and white eggplant and Butterblossom summer squash, which is grown for its edible flowers. Forty-gallon garbage cans might hold trellised yellow tomatoes with purple basil. Fill the empty pockets of a strawberry pot with everbearing strawberries and thyme.

Plant in a synthetic soil mix consisting of a blend of peat moss, vermiculite, and perlite, enriched with your own compost (1 part compost to 3 parts soil mix). This blend will not compact into a bricklike block as the summer progresses. It will dry out quickly, however, and need fertilizing often.

Herbs, vegetables, and even strawberries make handsome container plants.

Window gardens. You may want a few pots of something edible to spruce up your kitchen windows or to turn an empty bedroom into a garden room. The plants receive less light indoors, but a south-facing window can sustain some shade-tolerant crops. In winter, when the furnace causes humidity in the house to plummet, mist the plants occasionally, or set them on top of pebbles in a tray of water.

You can grow various lettuces, chard, parsley, basil, and radishes with a few marigolds to perk things up. In the winter, you could devote this garden to saving marginally hardy plants like tarragon, lemon thyme, variegated sage and rosemary, and those plenty hardy and useful extras, parsley and chives.

Edibles in the ornamental area. Blend edibles with your flowers, shrubs, or trees. Asparagus makes a nice backdrop for a perennial border. Bold rhubarb, with its huge leaves and ruby stems, makes a splash planted in a highly visible location. You can also find more flamboyant ornamental rhubarb species, but they are not necessarily edible. Burgundy-fruited okra, tall and boldly flowered, fits in an informal bed of country flowers. You may find, however, that you would rather look at these plants than eat them.

Salad gardens. Keep salad gardens near the kitchen and devote them to greens that will come and go throughout the spring, summer, and fall. Plant green and red lettuce varieties every two weeks throughout the summer. Put heat-tolerant cultivars in shady spots in midsummer. For spring and fall, add radicchio, endive, spinach, red mustard, arugula, and orange calendula. In late spring, plant Swiss chard, sorrel, opal basil, and New Zealand spinach for summer harvests.

Seasoning gardens. These can be quite beautiful. You could, for example, site one on a rocky slope with herbs growing amid clusters of submerged boulders and stepping stones. The bed might sweep into a lower loop where the taller herbs can grow on relatively flat land. On the bank, you might plant winter savory, lemon thyme, French thyme, parsley, and dwarf basil, with the lower area devoted to lovage, tarragon, and bush basil.

Winter gardens. Create a hard-working garden for growing winter crops in a cold frame. Combine a raised bed that drains well with graveled all-weather paths. Use it to overwinter cabbage, leeks, root crops like carrots and parsnips, and cold-hardy greens.

Growing-up gardens. These gardens make the most of a limited amount of space and create an interesting architectural effect as well. Let peas twine up a picket fence in the front, then have pole beans grow on three-pole tepees; let melons and cucumbers clamber on inverted Vs you have built of 2x4s; and add more pole beans to share a corn and Jerusalem artichoke patch.

Wagon-wheel garden. Use this design to spruce up a garden, filling the spaces between each "spoke" with a different vegetable: spinach followed by summer squash, bush peas followed by bush beans, lettuce followed by cucumbers. Let two paths intersect in the center where a mammoth tomato plant and four pepper plants cluster as a focal point.

Gourmet garden. Enter through a wrought-iron gate into an enclosure made by 2½-foot-high clipped alpine currant hedges. A brick path leads through the center of the garden past slightly raised rectangular beds with brick edging. Another path forms a T with the first and leads between the sets of gardens to a small fruit tree on one side and a bubbling fountain at the other. Each bed has a purpose — for instance, one might be devoted to heirlooms, another to tropicals, and others to European and Oriental crops.

Fruit gardens. Use a foundation planting close to the house to blend the house into its natural surroundings and produce food, as well. Soften the vertical lines of the house with a horizontally branched, vase-shaped peach tree at one end and a cluster of blueberry bushes at the other. Use everbearing strawberries as a ground cover. Edge the garden with fragrant herbs, such as bush basil and winter savory. Let thyme creep between the flagstones in a path to the front door. Their aroma may help keep pests away from the fruit. Balance the landscape with another, later-fruiting peach tree on the other side of the driveway.

RECORD KEEPING

While you are trying different garden layouts and vegetable varieties, make a point to take some notes on

Vegetable/Fruit ____________________
Cultivar ____________________
Supplier ____________________
Packet Size __________ Price __________
Features ____________________
____
Planting Date __________ Date Planted Outdoors __________
Condition When Planted Outdoors ____________________
____
Pest Problems ____________________
____
Comments ____________________
____
____
____
____

Create your own recordkeeping system for your personalized garden notebook.

what you have done. Before I began to keep a fairly detailed notebook of plant lists and observations, I was sure I could remember just what had and hadn't worked well. I was right, to a certain point. I still do remember the screaming failures and vivid successes. But the intermediate things — the crops that never really got started, the varieties that performed pretty well, and the interplantings that were adequate — have grown quite dim. Put the vitals down on paper and you can easily avoid past difficulties and repeat the triumphs.

I keep several kinds of records. During the winter when I make my plant orders, I give each cultivar its own sheet of notebook paper and put the sheet in a loose-leaf notebook divided into headings, like *Peas* or *Strawberries*. I note what cultivar I bought, the size of the package, the supplier, the price (if it was outstanding in some way), the advertised features of the plant, and anything else that enticed me to buy it. I keep this sheet up to date as I start seeds or plants indoors, noting such things as planting date and how the seedlings were doing before they were set outdoors. If I buy the same cultivar several years running, I can compare performance.

Once the spring gardening season is upon me, however, I don't have time to write everything down. So I use a day-by-day calendar to note when I plant certain things, when pest problems arise, and general weather facts (rain and temperature, for instance). When I am not as busy later in the season, I can transpose this information into my garden notebook.

You may want more or less detail. Try storing information about cultivars on individual index cards, or build a big file with catalogue or seed packet descriptions and illustrations. Load vital information on a computer data base. But whatever you do, organize the system so you can use it easily next year. If you can't find the information, it won't be much good to you.

ORGANIZING THE INSIDE OF THE GARDEN

Once you select your garden site and you have thought through potential themes, you will have to get down to the nitty gritty. How will you lay out your rows? What spacing and grouping will work best?

Organizing your garden is like decorating your living room. Just as you choose and arrange furnishings to suit your taste, you will want to choose and arrange plants. You need some diversity in both cases: a couple of chairs, a couch, a coffee table, and a rug on the one hand — a couple of sweet fruits, such as strawberries and melons; some tomatoes, beans, and peppers; greens like lettuce and spinach; and a few root crops like carrots and radishes on the other.

Put each plant where it can grow most effectively. You wouldn't block a window with a bookcase or set a chair in the middle of a doorway. Likewise, you shouldn't plant a tomato in the shade of a blackberry trellis. Develop a layout that gives crops the right combination of soil and sun. Group them so they are easy to plant, tend, and pick. Establish some traffic patterns — paths you can walk on without interfering with the plants.

Exactly how you go about arranging everything will vary with your circumstances and needs. Just as no two living rooms are exactly alike, neither will two gardens be the same. You can organize your garden by season, life cycle, soil and sun needs, culture (maintenance requirements and techniques), and even harvesting method. You should also consider how interplanting, companion planting, and crop rotation fit into the scheme of things. Let's look at some of your options.

Succession Cropping: Organizing for Season after Season of Harvesting

Succession has become the popular buzzword among gardeners who want to harvest a lot from a limited space. Instead of growing just tomatoes, you may be able to get in three seasons of crops by using the same space to plant spring peas, summer tomatoes, and fall cabbage. In the South, you may be able to squeeze four seasons — fall, winter, early spring, and summer — in a single space.

To be successful, such planting takes plenty of precision planning and some special soil care. Identify how long a plant takes to mature and how much time you will spend harvesting it. Crops like indeterminate tomatoes (which keep on producing fruit as they grow), peppers, and beets can continue to mature over a fairly long period, prolonging your harvest but reducing the potential for future crops. Radishes, turnips, broccoli, cabbage, salad greens, bush beans, and English peas are generally ready to harvest all at once. Some may resprout with a second flush of leaves or pods, but the harvest will not be as bountiful as the first. Instead of waiting for the next harvest, you could replant with something different and well suited to the present season.

If you want to put aside a certain amount of produce for freezing and canning, you can use this method to bring in a freezer's worth of a crop all at once. You can pick and freeze on Saturday, and then till, fertilize, and replant on Sunday.

Crops that take longer to mature or have an extended harvest period can still be included in your succession plan. However, they will not

SUCCESSION CROP POSSIBILITIES

Crop	Days to Maturity	Comment
	COOL SEASON	
Beets	50 to 60 days from seeding	
Broccoli	55 to 70 days from setting out plants	
Cabbage, Chinese	45 to 60 days from setting out plants	
Cabbage, early	40 to 50 days from setting out plants	
Carrots, baby types	50 days from seeding	
Carrots, large cultivars	70 days from seeding	
Cauliflower	45 to 60 days from setting out plants	
Leaf lettuce	45 days from seeding	Harvest all at once or leaf by leaf
Spinach	40 to 50 days from seeding	Harvest all at once or leaf by leaf
	WARM SEASON	
Beans, bush	45 to 60 days from planting seed	
Corn, early sweet	60 to 70 days from seeding	
Squash, summer	45 to 50 days (harvest can be extended)	
Tomatoes, early or determinate	50 to 60 days from setting out plants	

bring you the same harvest diversity (and perhaps less quantity) as other areas that are planted successively.

Crop Rotation

Whether you are rapid-firing crops into the soil or not, you need to take special care that you do not deplete nutrients or let insects and fungal spores build up. The secret is to change to a different type of crop each time you replant. Avoid replacing one plant with a relative or a plant with similar growth habits or nutrient requirements. For instance, follow heavy feeders with light feeders or renewers; follow tomatoes

SLOW-MATURING OR EXTENDED-HARVEST CROPS THAT LIMIT SUCCESSION PLANTING

Crop	Days to Maturity	Comment
	COOL SEASON	
Brussels sprouts	90 to 105 days from setting out plants	Harvest can continue for another 60 days
Kale	65 to 70 days	Harvest possible all winter
Onions	80 to 100 days	
Peas	60 to 70 days from seeding	Harvest can continue for another 30 days
	WARM SEASON	
Beans, bush lima	65 days	
Beans, pole lima	90 days from planting seed	
Beans, pole snap	60 to 70 days from seeding	Harvest extends 30 days or more
Cantaloupes	65 to 90 days from setting out plants	Harvest extends another 30 days
Corn, standard sweet	75 to 90 days from seeding	
Cucumbers	45 to 60 days from seeding	Harvest extends all summer
Eggplant	50 to 70 days from setting out plants	Harvest extends until frost
Peppers	65 to 75 days from setting out plants	Harvest extends until frost
Pumpkins	90 to 100 days from planting seed	Harvest can continue 30 or more days
Squash, winter	70 to 85 days	60 days of harvest
Indeterminate tomatoes	70 to 80 days from setting out plants	

AN IN-DEPTH ROTATION PLAN DEVELOPED BY ELIOT COLEMAN

When planning rotation, Eliot Coleman, author and Maine market gardener, divides crops into several groups: root, vine, fruit, green, brassica, or grain. He also considers botanical family. He notes which make the most of available nutrients, which draw heavily from the soil or leave nutrient-rich residues, and which can crowd out weeds. He then tries to find crops that will benefit each other when grown in succession. Hypothetically, his system works as follows:

Coleman manures one-third of his garden and plants it with refined plants, such as cool-season lettuce and warm-season cucumbers, that have high nutrient requirements but are less aggressive about extracting them. These might be followed by more nutrient-aggressive extractors, like cabbage. The following year that site would be perfect for root crops and potatoes. The fourth year in the cycle is devoted to re-enriching this soil with nitrogen-fixing legumes, such as peas and beans, or deep-rooted plants, like alfalfa which loosen the lower soil and release nutrients extracted from soil depths when they decompose.

When rotating crops to different parts of the garden from one season or year to the next, Coleman considers individual crop peculiarities. He has found that legumes, onions, lettuces, and squashes generally benefit later crops. Potatoes yield best when grown in a former corn site but they can suffer scab when grown after peas or soybeans. Carrots, beets, and cabbages generally are detrimental to whatever follows.

In a larger garden with several rotating beds, the system can get complicated. Coleman divides his garden into ten sections. These can be different sizes to accommodate the amount of each crop he needs. He puts the names of bigger crops on one index card and cuts other cards into proportional pieces to fit together later and share a bed. Usually shared beds go to plants from the same family or with the same growing conditions. One exception is potatoes, which he keeps separate from tomatoes and peppers.

Like a jigsaw puzzle, he can piece together potential neighbors as well as succession crops. When he feels the combinations are right, he assigns each one of the ten beds. Then in following years, he moves the cards in systematic order, from heavy feeder to less aggressive, root crop, and then rebuilder. Finally, he remanures.

According to Coleman, "This is only one of the many possibilities for a small garden. It should not be intimidating. Any sort of variety in succession crops would be beneficial. I've taken a group of city kids, told them these ground rules, and made a game of mixing the cards and making up new sequences. They really had fun."

Coleman has written about his rotation plan in a 1989 *Harrowsmith Country Life* article and in his book *The New Organic Gardener.*

that died of wilt diseases with beans or carrots, crops that will not succumb to the problems of tomatoes. Understanding botanical relationships will help you decide which plants to choose.

Just as you may look like your mother or laugh like your Uncle Bob, plants share similar traits with their relatives. Members of the Bean Family include snap, lima, dry, soy, and fava beans, as well as peas and some cover crops, like alfalfa. These plants may be able to "fix" or capture nitrogen in the air and use it for growth. Thus, they can be good soil builders.

The Mustard Family includes cabbage, collards, Brussels sprouts, broccoli, cauliflower, kale, arugula, kohlrabi, turnip, mustard, rutabaga, radish, Chinese cabbage, and the cresses. These siblings tend to be more aggressive in nutrient consumption than other families and need calcium and boron to prevent deformed growth. Many can develop club root, a soil-borne disease, or can come under attack by cabbage loopers, flea beetles, and other pests.

The Nightshade Family embraces tomatoes, peppers, eggplants, husk tomatoes, and potatoes. While they vary in their nutrient requirements, all can be susceptible to wilts, blights, aphids, tomato hornworm, and other common problems.

The Cucumber Family includes summer and winter squash, cucumber, pumpkin, cantaloupe, and watermelon. These need a great deal of easily accessible nutrients to support their succulent vining growth. All members can fall prey to similar wilts, beetles, or borers.

Other family groups to rotate include onions, garlic, and leeks; corn and popcorn; parsley, parsnips, celery, celeriac, and fennel; and beets, Swiss chard, and spinach.

SINGLE ROWS OR WIDE BEDS?

Until recently, most gardeners planted their vegetables in long, parallel rows of single plants. This layout is not necessarily the most efficient for the home gardener, however. Those nice straight lines allow mechanical planters, cultivators, sprayers, and harvesters to sweep up and down a field. Even in a home garden, the single row is useful if you have plenty of space and a rototiller to maintain the open areas between crops. Many gardeners, however, have found another technique more effective: planting in blocks or in wide rows where plants are staggered to provide an open square of rooting space for each. The amount of space required between plants varies according to plant. The reason is simple: Wide beds let you grow more produce in less space. With wide beds, you can prepare thoroughly, maintain better quality soil, and plant more efficiently. These beds are usually from 3 to 6 feet wide, 4 feet being the standard. This is wide enough to hold a double- or triple-row arrangement of plants, but narrow enough so that you can reach the center without stepping on the bed. You can mound the soil up to 12 inches high for good drainage and deeper rooting.

Raised wide beds fail only in arid or extra windy climates where moisture is limited. In these places, depress the beds to collect most water runoff. Even under average conditions, however, raised beds may require more watering in the summer.

You can make raised wide rows permanent or temporary. If you change the garden scheme often, rototill the entire garden. Next, rake all the loose soil into a central mound, and then flatten it out to whatever width you want. The naked subsoil to either side is perfect for paths. If you make permanent beds that are elevated with timbers, bricks, blocks, or other supports, you can develop better soil by amending it regularly over several seasons or years.

I combine both systems in my garden. I raise planting mounds in new locations every year and have one permanent bed stretching across the lower end of the garden. Before we put the bed in, nothing grew well in that area. I contained the soil with 8-inch-high railroad ties, borrowing some topsoil from surrounding areas and enriching it with an abundance of cow manure. Like magic, it has become fertile. I vary plantings of squash, cucumber, and melon with corn, and I plan to try potatoes and other root crops. The bed width lets me stagger two, one, and two of the longer vining squash and later maturing corn. Or I can fit two, three, and two of compact cucurbits and early corn.

These staggered planting arrangements give each plant a block of space in which to root. For a large yield, squeeze most root crops, beans, and peas quite closely — about a 4-inch square for each bush bean plant. Studies have shown that planted like this in a double row, bush beans will produce two or three times as many beans as any single row containing the same number of plants. Eggplants need a space about 18 x 18 inches and caged tomatoes, about 36 x 36 inches. Viners and bramble berries will need the most room of all, unless you grow them up on a trellis. You can also use wide beds to interplant a row of lettuce on either side of cucumbers, bush basil around tomatoes, calendula with radicchio.

Wide beds do require hand weeding until the crop plants grow large enough to squeeze weeds out. Don't neglect weeding or the closely spaced seedlings will suffer.

Intercropping

If you want to make the most of your garden space, you can intercrop — plant two different vegetables in the same bed. Not just any two will do, for they must not compete with one another. The best pairs combine tall plants with shorter ones, deeper-rooted plants with surface rooters, quick maturers with slow starters.

Lettuce intercropped with pole beans is partially shaded from the heat of the sun.

To do justice to both plants, intercrop only in deep, fertile soils, especially if you are growing two heavy feeders like lettuce and cucumbers. Enrich the soil well before planting and use water-soluble

SHARON CARSON'S INTERPLANTINGS

Sharon Carson relies on interplanting to make the most of her intensively cultivated garden. Watermelon mingles with buckwheat, a soil-improving green manure that matures to an edible grain. Sunflowers interweave with tuberous-rooted Jerusalem artichokes, which have sturdy enough stems to support the sunflowers in strong winds. Chinese cabbages share the asparagus bed. Carson harvests the cabbages as the asparagus ferns fill in and shade the area. The light shade discourages nearly mature cabbages from bolting.

Interplanting is not always perfect. "I have tried interplanting spinach, carrots, lettuce, and beets," Carson says, "but I gave it up. It was too hard to control the spacing on each and the radishes often took over."

fertilizers such as fish emulsion or Rapidgro as the plants mature, especially if growth slows or the leaves begin to yellow. Keep an eye out for any aggression by one of the varieties. At the start, the quicker grower may easily overwhelm the slower unless you step in and reconcile numbers or sizes. I learned this lesson the hard way when vigorous pole beans toppled my young corn.

Sometimes, one crop will benefit the other. If you combine carrots with radishes, the radishes will sprout much earlier, loosening the soil so the delicate carrot seedlings can emerge. If you grow leaf lettuce and cabbage, the lettuce is long gone by the time the cabbage heads swell. Plant summer lettuce or spinach with tomato, eggplant, pepper, or pole beans. The shade of the warm-season plant helps keep the young greens cool. If you let pole beans climb up corn stalks, give the corn at least a two-week head start so the root system is large enough to support the weight of the beans.

No discussion of intercropping would be complete without adding the dimension of companion planting. In the study of biodynamics (the intricate interworkings of closely spaced plants) researchers have found that certain neighbors seem to thrive together while others quarrel.

Just how companions benefit or abuse their neighbors is not well understood. The interactions may be chemical, spatial, or both. The degree of influence may be impressive or, more often, subtle. Despite the unknowns and inconsistencies of companion planting, many organic gardeners consider it important enough to include in garden planning. Eliot Coleman writes in *The New Organic Grower* that companion interactions may account for only a small change in productivity, but over time small changes can accumulate enough to make a significant difference.

I avoid certain unneighborly combinations like beans and peas with onions, chives, garlic, leeks, or shallots; cabbages, broccoli, Brussels sprouts, and cauliflower with strawberries; carrots with dill; and cucumbers, pumpkins, squash, and tomatoes with potatoes. According to texts and my own experience, these combinations just don't grow as prolifically when planted together. On the other hand, I often do mix fragrant herbs like basil, oregano, and thyme with any vegetable crop. Their aroma helps repel insects.

Grouping Plants by Soil Type and pH

Different types of crops require different soils. Determine what conditions you have, and select crops that will grow there or amend the soil to fit the crops you have chosen. (See chapter 1 for more on soil preparation and chapter 9 for soil requirements for individual crops.)

Light soils. Blueberries and herbs, as well as root crops like carrots and parsnips, thrive in light, sandy soils. The root crops need to dig deeply without interference from rocks, soil clumps, or compacted clay. If your soil is heavy, fluff it up with peat moss and some coarse sand, and then mound the loose soil 6 to 12 inches high to give the plants extra growing space. Even then, a shorter-rooted cultivar may prove most adaptable, as it will not have to tangle with

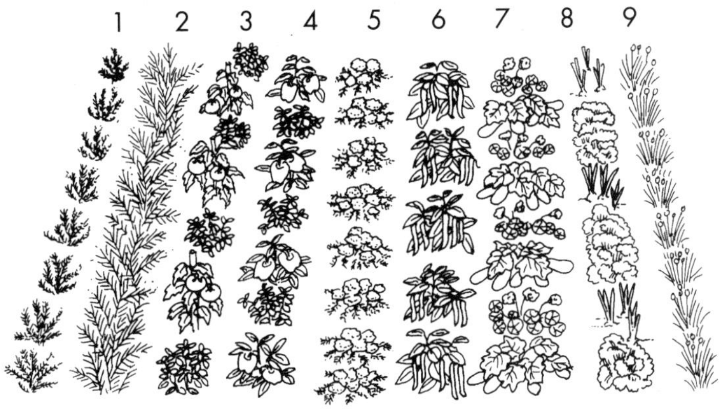

A garden plan based on companion planting: (1) savory, (2) asparagus, (3) tomatoes/basil, (4) peppers/basil, (5) marigold, (6) beans, (7) squash/nasturtium, (8) lettuce/onion, (9) chives

the stiffer soils further down.

Parsnips, especially, will not tolerate anything but free and easy downward access. To ensure this, make a hole into the earth with a crowbar and refill it with fine soil, free of rocks and clumps. I once experimented with planting in elevated plastic drainage pipes, but found the soil in the pipes dried out too quickly for even modest seed germination.

In addition to a light soil, root crops need some fertility to maintain a steady growth pace. A delay in fertilization makes the roots woody and tough. On the other hand, too much nitrogen encourages these crops to grow a huge above-ground leafy portion at the expense of the root. Recently manured soils can inspire the root to fork or put out a network of tiny hairlike feeding roots.

Forked roots may develop if carrots are seeded in recently manured soil.

Heavy soils. Some crops tolerate heavy soil as long as it has enough organic matter to allow air penetration down to the roots. In my garden, bush snap beans, bush lima beans, tomatoes, sweet corn, Brussels sprouts, and kale all have made a good showing where the rooting is tough. Gooseberries and currants also excel in heavy soils.

Wet soils. These appeal to few crops — rice, water chestnuts, and watercress.

Soil pH. When grown in acid soils, potatoes will not be affected by scab, a disfiguring fungus disease on the tubers. Blueberries and huckleberries need even more acidity, about pH 5.5. Beets prefer slightly alkaline soils, which also discourage the disease club root from attacking the *Brassicas* and sweet alyssum.

Grouping Edibles by the Care They Need

Certain vegetables require the same kind of cultivation, fertilization, pest control, and harvesting. It's natural to put these crops together and handle them as a unit.

Group plantings that need protection from cold or insects under floating row covers. Keep all the perennials, biennials, and lategrowers in one corner so you can clean up or put a cover crop on the rest of the garden. To streamline tying up vines, pruning off suckers, and supporting swelling fruit, combine all crops that will grow on a trellis and position them in a part of the garden where they will not shade neighbors. Group crops that need mulching or irrigation, and those that have the same fertilizer requirements.

Caution: Grouping by care can make you more efficient, but it also may attract more pests. You may find yourself grouping related plants together, since they often take similar care. They also can attract similar pests in large numbers, which creates bigger-than-usual problems. In nature, large-scale insect attacks are uncommon, because wild plants grow in small groups widely scattered from their relatives and surrounded by other types of plants unpalatable to a particular pest. The smorgasbord is simply not there.

Grouping by Sun Needs

Nearly all vegetables do best in full sun. Light is the fuel that powers their growth and development. In general, a plant basking in a full day's sun is using racing fuel and will produce the biggest and best harvest. Don't let any one crop hog the sun. Group taller plants together on the north end of the garden so the shade does not fall on shorter ones.

The exception to this rule is in hot climates where the blazing sun combines with excessive heat. In this case, many plants will prefer lesser amounts of sun in exchange for the coolness of shade. Likewise, light shade can keep cool-season crops producing longer or give them a better start in summer. If plants are prone to wilting, burning, or bolting in heat group them together in light shade.

Grouping Crops by How You Will Harvest Them

If you need to thin, spade, cut, or pluck certain crops, you can group them together. You will make fewer mistakes, such as pulling up something you should have thinned or thinning something you should have pulled, and you will switch tools less, as well. For more harvest organization information, see chapter 5.

Living on the Edge — Decorative Borders

One of the secrets to having a good-looking garden, be it vegetable or flower, is a handsome border — the place people look first. They may gaze back into the interior, but not with the intensity of their first preview along the edge.

Do something interesting, neat, or exciting to edge your garden and invite people in or encourage them to stay out. Make the border a focal point for your yard, or at least keep it colorful enough to distract from a few weeds or empty spots between harvests. The following are some borders that can be useful as well as beautiful.

Calendulas make a decorative accent in your garden and may also repel certain insect pests.

Sunflowers. Use these to form a tall hedge around the north side of the garden and partially wall it in, rather like a room. Have the entrance toward the rear for more privacy. Or try the 2-foot-high Sunspot sunflower, which has huge, 10-inch-wide heads — a hit with kids *and* the wild canaries.

Marigolds. Bright gold, yellow, and russett marigolds cheer even a gloomy day. America's favorite is the petite French marigold, Queen Sophia. My favorites are the orange- and lemon-scented species with smaller flowers on a mound of feathery foliage. Marigolds provide another bonus: They release chemicals from their roots that repel nematodes and perhaps other pests as well.

Calendulas. Pot marigold, or calendula, is similar to marigold but thrives in cool spring and fall seasons. Calendulas may fade, even die, in summer, but they usually self-sow and return in fall. This is an edible flower with a unique taste that is fun to add to a salad.

Pansies. The newer weatherproof pansies will last most of the summer and well into winter in Cleveland. My favorite is the new blue-flowered, All-America Selections Winner, Maxim Marina. Pansies make pretty, edible garnishes, though I do not find them too tasty.

Ornamental cabbage and kale. Heads of colorful frilly leaves form on these plants when weather turns cool in fall. They look great until about January here, perhaps all winter long in the South, cheering up gardens that may otherwise be idle.

Globe basil. Forming neat and fragrant emerald balls, globe basil gives you a trim culinary herb edging. Shear them with clippers to keep them rounded and use the trimmings for cooking or vinegars.

three

TRICKS OF TIMING

TIMING WHEN YOU plant and pick has a lot to do with how successful your garden will be. I think scheduling your harvest is a little like readying a colt to run the Kentucky Derby. For a race, you have to get the animal fit, break fast at the starting gate, cover ground in midseason, and then sprint for home. In the garden, you have to condition the soil, set the plants out when they can grow like crazy, and keep them going through the season. Should the crops (or horse) suffer delays at any point, a super cultivar (or really talented colt) may pull you through, but most contestants will fall behind the field.

With enough experience in the garden, you will see timing begin to fall into place, just like a good horse trainer knows when his colt is ready to race. You will learn from your mistakes and successes. You will become more sensitive to weather and learn how to correct conditions that are less than ideal. You can make the most of advice from others and avoid some of the most basic failures. Together, these experiences develop your sense of intuition, which will get your garden through most tough spots.

Some gardeners turn timing into state-of-the-art clockwork, while others take a seat-of-the-pants approach. I tend to do a little of both and still come up with some pretty good results. When, on occasion, a crop does fall through, simply try again with the same or a different crop. Fortunately, says contributor Rachel Snyder, "The garden is very forgiving of mistakes."

You will have to be a little forgiving, too. Irma Dugan writes, "Because my husband, Dave, and I are both retired and finally able to have time for adventuring, un-horticultural hobbies, and home projects, our vegetable gardening efforts are not terribly disciplined. When the bunnies made off with all of our broccoli plants this spring, we said 'Oh, well,' and sowed some more beans." Each year brings its own surprises!

WHERE DO YOU FIT INTO THE EQUATION?

Consider your own preferences when you are timing the planting of your garden. When do you like to be outdoors most? I enjoy early spring, especially, because I cherish the excuse to work outdoors after a long winter. You may prefer to occupy yourself in other affairs until the summer is good and warm and you can garden in shorts and a tee shirt. Maybe you'll postpone the garden until the kids are out of school in the summer or squeeze it in before the yard turns into their summer stamping grounds.

The planting schedule you devise will vary according to what you want from the garden. Growing enough to feed your family for the entire summer or year will take a longer season of continual activity than enjoying a few sweet tomatoes and strawberries.

With a little creative timing you can tie gardening into other activities. Rather than eating sweet corn until you turn yellow, how about timing its harvest so you can have the neighborhood over for a Labor Day cookout with fresh-picked corn on the cob? Or have the kids' play group over in fall to pick pumpkins and make jack-o'-lanterns. Plant enough simultaneously ripening tomatoes and cucumbers so you can invite the family over to spend a day canning and pickling. Entice them by dividing up the bounty at the end of the day.

TIMING CROP NEEDS

Develop your own personal planting strategy, and then play your garden as you would a poker hand. You have cultivars and techniques that you hold in your hand and can control in the garden. Yet there are unknowns in the deck waiting to be dealt — elements of surprise that emerge during the growing season. A winning hand — or garden — need not be a full house or flush. It could take succession planting, staggered plantings, interplanting, avoidance of overload, vacation time out, and tricks to extend the season. You choose your bet. Play conservatively or go for a bluff. Here are some of your choices.

Finding the Right Temperature

Just like people, individual plants prefer warm or cool weather. You might compare a lettuce plant to a Minnesota resident who thrives at 60°F but shrinks from 90° and above. An okra, on the other hand, would be paralyzed at 35°F, but swells with vigor when the summer swelters. The middle-of-the-roaders take a wide range of moderate temperatures but suffer at either extreme.

ANOTHER PERSPECTIVE ON TIMING

Raquel Boehmer, resident of an island off the coast of Maine, wrote in *National Gardening* magazine about how she has adapted to the long frost-free season. Although it begins April 15 and ends September 30, the weather never gets hot enough for good tomato growth.

Rather than fight the weather, Boehmer relaxes through the spring, planting a few lettuce and cabbage plants, but otherwise enjoying herself with other interests. In May, she adds a few plants of rhubarb chard, summer squash, and edible-pod peas, as well as successions of lettuce and other peas. Once July approaches, she gears up for a major planting of crops for winter storage — parsnips, winter squash, beets, Daikon radish, turnips, carrots, kale, mustard, Chinese cabbage, and shingiku (edible chrysanthemum).

Boehmer notes that although spring is relaxed, come July there is no time to delay. Days are getting shorter. Crops must grow quickly or they will not reach harvesting size. Fortunately, summer-started seedlings are not bothered by cutworms or damping off, problems common in cooler spring soils. She can keep the crops in seed beds moist by watering through a newspaper mulch. The cool-season crops continue to develop late into the fall, supplying much of her off-season produce.

To match a crop with the weather it prefers, take stock of the length of spring, summer, and fall in your region, as well as the average high and low temperature. When is the weather humid, rainy, or dry? Your county Cooperative Extension Service or a local botanical garden may have this information.

As you study your weather, you should begin to see what will limit your garden. Northern areas have a moderately short frost-free period. In the Pacific Northwest and parts of New England, summer weather is cool. In northern New England and the northern plains, winters can be bitterly cold. In the South, there is excess summer heat and high humidity. In the Southwest, summers can have searing sunshine and inadequate rainfall.

You can do little to change the weather, although you can moderate cold temperatures, block out some excessive sunshine, and irrigate dry roots. But your easiest and possibly best successes will come from growing what naturally thrives under the local conditions. Author and horticulturist John Bryan, who lives in Sausalito, California, writes, "Many gardeners set out their plants too early in the season. It is far better to wait until the right temperatures are consistently correct for the type of plants being grown. No advantage is gained by setting plants out early. They suffer checks from colder nights and then do not have a long and steady growth pattern."

Likewise, Mike McGrath, editor of *Organic Gardening* magazine, writes in a July 1991 editorial that the peas and spinach he rashly planted in February germinated at the same time as those he planted in March. "The moral of this story? You can plant on March 1 or you can plant on May 1, but you'll probably eat your first spinach on the same day either way," McGrath wrote.

To get you started, here are some crop temperature preferences:

Hot. Arkansas Traveler 76 (a tomato bred for the South), black-eyed peas, eggplant, lima beans, okra, peanuts, peppers, Tepary beans (*Phaseolus acutifolius*), tomatillo, Smokeylee-SSE watermelon (bred for hot, humid, disease-prone areas)

Warm. Basil, beans, corn, cucumbers, dill, melons, squash, summer savory, tomatoes

Cool. Arugula, broad beans, cauliflower, Chinese cabbage, kohlrabi, lettuce, peas and quick-maturing peas, radishes, spinach, storage onions, turnips

Crops That Bridge Seasons. These may mature in a different temperature range from the range they were planted in. They include beets, Belgian endive, Brussels sprouts, berries, carrots, collards, corn salad, fennel, hardy perennial herbs, Jerusalem artichokes, kale, leeks, parsnips, radicchio, rutabaga, sorrel, sugar snap peas, Swiss chard

For Cooler Than Ideal Weather

Crop	Cultivars
Bush green beans	Provider, Venture, Royalty, Purple Pod
Bush lima beans	Geneva, Eastland
Corn	Early Sunglow
Pepper	Hungarian Hot Wax
Tomato	Oregon Spring, Siberian

Adaptability: What Is a Plant's Comfort Zone?

The time inevitably comes when a freak cold snap or a surprise tropical heat wave blows into town. When this happens, different plants react differently to temperature stresses.

With unseasonal cool temperatures, seeds might not germinate. In too much heat, cole crops tend to button, leaf crops and celery may bolt, and root crops can devote their energy to leaves instead of roots. Other plants may become more susceptible to damage from insects and diseases. Yet, the more complacent crops or cultivars may survive with no apparent damage done. You'll find some season stretchers in the charts on page 58 and at the right.

You can find these and other cultivars featured in catalogues that cater to cool-season climates or warm-season climates. Among those that specialize in cool-season seeds are Johnny's Selected Seeds, Garden City Seeds, and Veseys; those that carry warm-season seeds are Hastings, Southern Seed Exchange, Native Seeds/ SEARCH, and Plants of the Southwest (which carries seed for arid as well as for warm-season areas). (See Appendix for addresses.)

For Warmer Than Ideal Weather

Crop	Cultivars
Red raspberry	Bababerry
Broccoli	Saga
Collards	Georgia Southern
Fennel	Fennel Fino
Lettuce	Victoria French Crisp, Red Sails, Mantilia
Spinach	Nordic, Tyee

How to Succeed with Timed Succession

Among the tricks of timing is succession cropping, described in chapter 2. The goal is to keep crops coming and going, rather like a revolving door. Here are some different approaches to take.

You might plant one-third of the contents of a lettuce seed packet every two weeks. You will have fresh greens longer and less likelihood of mass bolting or other disheartening failures when you have waves of younger plants as well as mature ones. Adapt the schedules on page 60 as needed to jibe with your regional temperature variations and culinary preferences.

Another way to work in an earlier or later succession crop is simply to fill an unexpected gap. For example, when seeds don't come up, pests consume a plant, or a small section of the garden fails, you can shuffle back through your seeds or

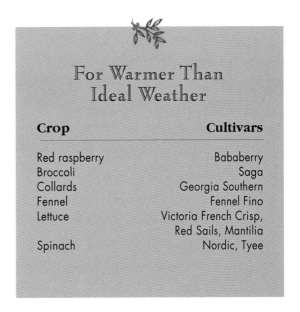

Fill in gaps that occur in your garden rows with extra seeds.

TIMED PLANTINGS

Vegetable	Plantings
Bush beans	2 weeks apart in summer
Broccoli	3 weeks apart, twice in spring and again (central-headed type) in late summer
Carrots	1 to 2 weeks apart in spring and fall
Coriander	2 weeks apart in spring and fall
Corn, sweet	2 weeks apart in late spring and early summer
Cresses and Oriental greens	2 weeks apart in spring and fall
Dill and summer savory	2 weeks apart in summer
Peas	2 weeks apart in spring and fall, and possibly summer
Radishes	1 week apart in spring and fall
Sunflowers	2 weeks apart in summer
Turnips	2 weeks apart in spring and fall

find an extra seedling to take up that space. Replant the same crop or another that is in short supply. The newcomer will grow and mature later, under different conditions, and if you're lucky, flourish where the original failed. (See also chapter 2 on rotation.)

You can also start new crops around the perimeter of aging ones, so the young ones can spread into the space vacated by yesterday's harvest. As the cool season ends, replace roots, greens, and coles with warmth-loving tomatoes, peppers, corn, and beans. When fall approaches, do the reverse.

AVOIDING OVERLOAD

One year, the gardening season had been particularly long and prolific. I had worked hard and put enough food in the freezer to last most of the winter. I figured I had done everything right. There were still tomatoes and peppers out in the garden, but I decided they could just stay out there. One day when a frost was expected, however, my husband picked every morsel and left it piled in the sink and on the counter for me "to take care of." It was a big mess, and I was not too pleased.

Imagine if you had that kind of surprise awaiting you throughout the summer! Dealing with mounds of suddenly ripe producc is not an uncommon experience, and one that can make even an avid cook swear off gardening. There are many alternatives to the old ton-of-tomatoes-in-the-sink trick, however. One is succession. You can also extend harvest times by planting early-, mid-, and late-maturing cultivars, as well as by mechanically manipulating the planting.

How to Plant an Extended Harvest

Rather than returning again and again to the garden to plant new waves of crops, you may find it easier to plant the entire garden at one time using two or more cultivars that take different amounts of time to mature. This strategy works well with head and leaf lettuces, baby and full-size carrots, and Early Girl and late beefsteak tomatoes. The result is an extended harvest time and a greater variety of flavors and textures for a longer time.

Extend your harvest by planting a variety of lettuces that mature at different times.

For this method to succeed, you need to do a little extra planning with seed catalogues to find out the number of days to maturity for different plants. For instance, in the 1991 Burpee catalogue you could easily identify three seasons of cabbage cultivars. Earliana, with 60 days to maturity, reaches a diameter of 5 inches and weighs 2 pounds. The midseason Copenhagen Market takes 72 days to reach maturity and can become 6 inches across and 4 pounds or more. The late Danish Roundhead takes 105 days, but swells to 8 inches and 7 pounds. You can buy the seeds and start the plants yourself, or look for these cultivars at local greenhouses. If you are not armed with a list of suitable plants before you shop, you may have difficulty identifying maturity time and will not get as wide a range in harvest dates as you otherwise would.

How to Pluck an Extended Harvest

Once you have done all you can from the planting end, you can stretch the harvest period even more as crops begin to ripen. Here are some options:

Pick young. You can thin young vegetables or some herbs to enjoy for a month or two before the main crop comes in. Try this with beets, lettuces, onions, turnips, spinach, squash blossoms, tiny pickling corn or onions, and green tomatoes for sautéing with brown sugar and cinnamon or pinch out a few new potatoes after the vines flower.

The secret here is to grow a

cultivar that you can pick small or large. Not just any crop will do. Check seed catalogue descriptions for vegetables that taste good immature. For example, Shepherd's Seeds carries the carrot Caramba, said to develop flavor at 3 inches and to continue to grow and remain sweet to 5½ inches long.

Delayed-harvest tolerant. Grow cultivars that keep their quality for extended periods. A patient group of vegetables reaches prime harvest stage and then can wait on the vine or in the soil for a few days or even a few weeks. Try at least a few of these for the busy times when you simply cannot pick, freeze, or can everything at once. Try cabbages that are less prone to splitting, such as Johnny's Primax or Lasso early red cabbage, and roots that won't get woody or bitter with a short wait, such as Shepherd's Bolthardy beet, Garden City's Nantes Fancy carrot and Minicor, one of the few baby carrots that can survive delayed harvest. Pic Red tomatoes, bred for shipping, also last on the vine longer than thinner-fleshed cultivars. Garden City's Delicious cantaloupe remains sweet with a good texture for a week, and their Mickylee watermelon is less likely to get mushy than Sugar Baby. Winter squash and pumpkins are the ultimate in harvest versatility. You can leave them to mature and cure out in the field until just before a heavy rain or frost.

Corn has traditionally been a crop that required picking as soon as it became ripe and required immediate freezing or cooking. New sugar-enhanced and supersweet types last on the stalk longer, however, and store in the refrigerator for up to 2 weeks. Normal sweet corn, which is labeled "Su" in catalogues, loses sweetness from the moment of picking. "Se" (sugar-enhanced) types convert sugar to starch more slowly than normal sweet corn. These are easier to grow than other supersweet types because they tolerate cool soil and don't require isolation. The "Sh2" supersweets have much more sugar than normal sweet corn and convert it to starch extra slowly.

Some crops will not wait and must be picked and used quickly. If you wait too long, they will spoil, lose flavor and tenderness, or prevent new fruit from forming. Eggplant, cucumbers, summer squash, and snap beans will get tough if you do not get them while immature. Once seeds are set, these plants will stop producing. Small-fruited strawberries, raspberries, and blackberries need to ripen on the vine as long as possible to develop maximum sweetness and flavor, but they do not keep well thereafter.

Manipulations. You can delay or speed up harvest times by strategic pruning of roots or shoots. Cut the roots on two sides of a mature cabbage to reduce the amount of mois-

To reduce splitting, cut the roots on two sides of developing cabbages.

ture the plant draws in and thus the chance of the head splitting. Pinch out the tip of pole beans and Brussels sprouts to encourage existing fruits or sprouts to mature faster. Pinch some plants and leave the rest to their standard season. To pull in an earlier crop of tomatoes, limit their vegetative growth by pruning

Pinch out the growing tip of Brussels sprouts to encourage sprouts to mature.

to just two shoots and tying each to an upright trellis. The plant will produce larger and earlier tomatoes, a good complement to a couple of other unpruned, caged tomatoes.

STARTING EXTRA EARLY OR FINISHING EXTRA LATE

Earlier in this chapter, we discussed keeping every crop to its season. Now, you will learn how to break this rule — if you dare. You can pull a few tricks on the weather to keep your garden growing longer in fall and starting earlier in spring. Don't plant anything that you do not mind risking. Experiment with extra plants that you start from seed yourself.

For example, in the spring of 1991, I planted a half package of Daybreak peas and a sprinkling of turnips, spinach, Swiss chard, and beets in early March in my especially well-drained raised garden. My previous attempts at this early a start either drowned in the super-soggy vegetable garden or were frozen flat. But for some reason, that year was different. As luck would have it, the weather was mild, neither swampy nor parched, and temperatures for the next two months were quite seasonable. I got my earliest harvest ever. My family consumed all the peas and spinach by mid May. The turnips and beets were perfect by mid June. We then enjoyed the next waves of plants from my remaining seeds, which had provided insurance in case this risky early crop fell through.

In keeping with these spring successes, I decided to set out some cucumber and tomato plants a month and a half before the usual frost-free date near the end of May. I put the cucumbers in hot caps and the tomatoes in Reemay-covered trenches or in Wall O' Water, but in the end needed neither. There were no frosts at all. The tomatoes were ripe at the end of June, a month before those I set out at my traditional planting time.

You can minimize potential failure by evaluating the status of the garden when you plant. Monitor soil temperature as well as air temperature. To encourage the earth to warm more quickly, raise a bed or just mound up some soil in the garden. Speed its absorption of sun rays by covering a particular area with different plastic mulches (see pages 65–66). You may be able to evaluate whether the soil is warm enough for a particular crop by feeling it at the surface and several inches below. But like touching a child's forehead to evaluate whether she has a fever, relying on touch alone can be deceiving. If you like to go for the gusto and expect to push your luck with every garden, you probably should invest in a soil thermometer. You will then know without a shadow of a doubt that the seed or plant

WHEN SHOULD YOU STICK TO TRADITIONAL TIMING?

New gardeners, newcomers to a climate, and people who are not prepared to take a few losses should stick with traditional timing. Until you make a pretty good guess what the weather, soil, and local cultivars will do, you probably won't have much luck growing extra early or late. I made this goof the first spring I lived in northern Ohio. As I had done for the past five years in the Cincinnati area, in early May I went out and bought tomato, pepper, and eggplant seedlings. They didn't even last through the first night. Frost struck and caught me completely unaware and unprepared to protect my twenty dollar investment. I had forgotten, in my zest over the fine sunny day, that northern Ohio evenings can stay frosty until late May. It was a great disappointment but a good lesson.

can grow rather than simply moldering before its time.

Increase Your Odds: Protective Tools and Techniques

If you decide to chance an extra-early or -late crop, you can up the odds of success if you protect the plants. If you are watching weather forecasts and see a brief snap of cold weather coming, you can simply cover the plants with inverted clay pots, buckets with a hole in the bottom, or bushel baskets. Or, erect a ring of straw bales around the bed and drape clear plastic over the top. This should keep the plants safe for a couple of days until the weather improves. If a crop will be facing a week or more of temperatures below (or above) its tolerance, however, you will need to create an artificially warm (or cool) microclimate for it. The following are some of the more commonly marketed means.

British author Eleanour Sinclair Rhode advocated using twiggy growth over a cold frame to protect cauliflower. She noted that cauliflowers need to be the plants nearest to light in a cold frame or they will grow drawn and sickly. But if grown out in the open, "Even a few leafless boughs laid over them will keep out many degrees of frost," she wrote.

Rhode recommended sowing parsley outdoors in a cold frame or cloche but picking just a leaf or two at a time, so you don't check the growth. "It is worth a little trouble to secure fresh parsley through the winter, for it is one of the few culinary herbs that dries so badly that it is hardly worth doing," Rhode wrote.

Eleanour Sinclair Rhode, 1938

Place straw bales around a bed and drape clear plastic over the top.

Plastic mulch. You can use sheet plastic to warm or cool soil, as well as to reduce weeds and soil evaporation. After the soil is ready to plant, cover it (and trickle-irrigation tubes, if you use them) with the plastic sheeting, and secure the edges under rocks or soil. Make slits or round openings in which to set plants.

Not all plastics are the same. The biggest factor when it comes to adjusting soil temperature is color. Clear plastic works the fastest, raising temperatures as much as 20°F, which actually can be too much in warmer climates or for cool-season crops. Another disadvantage of clear plastic is that it lets sunlight through and thus encourages weed growth. In hot weather, though, the soil can super-heat and kill weeds, weed seeds, insects, and some pathogens. In this case, clear plastic can be an option for sterilizing particularly weedy or unproductive soils.

The new infrared-transmitting (IRT) plastics are dark green, opaque enough to reduce weed growth, and specially engineered to transmit heat to the soil.

The more common black plastic also warms the soil, but not as much as clear or IRT plastics. The black color holds the sun's warmth instead of passing it directly through to the soil. You may want to remove black plastic when frost threatens, so the soil will reradiate enough heat to reduce freeze damage to low-lying crops.

Light-colored plastics reflect sunlight and keep the soil cool, a benefit for southern gardens and for starting cool-season crops in midsummer. They also maximize sun exposure in partially shady locations. You can even find plastics that start out black and fade to white as the season heats up.

All of these plastics will gradually grow brittle and ragged when they are exposed to sunlight. Newer biodegradable types are designed to fall apart within the span of a year, so you don't have to worry about disposing of them.

Floating row covers. This is a new breed of lightweight spun sheeting sold under a number of brand names. Cover your plants with it, leaving enough extra fabric to allow the plants room to grow. Secure the edges under rocks or soil. It puffs up around the developing foliage, keeping the plant several degrees warmer than the outside air and also sealing out insects. (It is important to note that pollinators, as well as pests, are excluded. Once plants like squash or melons show buds, remove the sheeting to allow pollination by bees and other insects.) These fabrics also slow the speed and strength of rainfall, thus limiting the amount of soil and disease spores that splash on plant leaves. Plants grow healthier and are less troublesome to wash off.

Floating row cover

Hot caps. These are individual plant covers, modeled after the old-fashioned bell jars used by gardeners centuries ago. You can buy prefabricated versions (Hotkaps, for instance) or make your own. One popular option is a 2-liter soda bottle. Cut off

Hot caps

the opaque bottom and set the transparent part over the plant. You can unscrew the cap to let more air in on a hot day. For a larger plant, use the top portion of a clear plastic umbrella that has been set prongs-down into the soil. These tend to be lightweight and very temporary, and not particularly useful for windy locations.

Plastic tunnel. To grow long rows of small vegetables very early or late in the season, stretch clear or transparent milky plastic over metal hoops or some similar kind of framework. You can buy these tunnels as kits or improvise your own with wood scraps, crouquet wickets, coat hangers, or other household items. Tunnels trap sun heat like an unheated greenhouse, but they can also overheat unless riddled with ventilation doorways, and it's hard to thin or weed plants grown under them unless you remove them altogether.

Plastic tunnel

Trenching. In dry climates or areas with well-drained soils, you can start crops early in a trench topped with clear plastic. Dig a long, narrow trench, about 12 inches deep, and set the seedling stem inside sideways, burying all but the top few leaves with soil. The leaves will begin to grow upward but will be slow to emerge from the trench. The buried portion of the stem will root, creating a strong foundation for

Trenching

future performance. Watch the temperature inside the trench. It can rise to 30° above ambient temperatures and may require ventilation. Where high temperatures are not necessary, substitute a naturally ventilating floating row cover for plastic.

Cold frame

Cold frame. While the previous techniques tend to be temporary, a cold frame is a more permanent structure with a lid that can be opened, making it easier to work in. I set mine in the garden facing south, backed up against a white-walled shed. Thus, it receives full sun plus reflected light. It is 8 feet long, 3 feet high and wide, and made of transparent, corrugated plastic. I use it to grow salad greens from September until January, and again from early March to May. It also houses perennial seedlings, root crops, and anything else that can take a little cold. Thankfully, it keeps out many flying and crawling insects and other creatures, though not as well as floating row covers.

A cold frame ordinarily is not airtight, but unless you ventilate the interior when the sun is bright, the plants may overheat. If you don't have the time to do this manually, you can invest in an automatic, temperature-sensitive opener.

Make your own cold frame out of cement blocks and window frames, corrugated plastic, or fiberglass, or buy premade models.

Hot bed. You can use a cold frame and outfit it with a thick layer of fresh manure for a short (3- to 6-week) shot of warmth. Or, for a more permanent heat source, use a heating cable or even an incandescent light bulb. Like using a greenhouse (but without the expense), this lets you grow many out-of-season crops.

Shade cloth

Shade cloth or lath house. To stretch cool-season crops like lettuce and other salad greens into the summer season, or to protect warm-season plants from intense sun or heat, you

SOME HOME TRIALS OF PROTECTIVE DEVICES

Here are some thoughts on a few different methods of protecting plants:

◆ Smith and Hawken Hotkaps work very well for cucumber plants. The Hotkaps trap enough heat and humidity to let the warmth-loving cucumbers grow with vigor. Unfortunately, however, the cucumbers may overflow these none-too-large protectors. Furthermore, the lightweight green plastic is easy for the kids or wind to tug off and send sailing over to the neighbor's yard.

◆ Wall O' Water protectors, used for tomato plants and marigolds, are trickier to set up than Hotkaps, but they are heavy and thus stable. They seem to do an adequate job of keeping the plants warm, but they do not let in much water or air and may need to be watered by hand.

◆ The best method for tomatoes is a floating row cover (Reemay, for example) and trench system. Mound up soil about 10 inches high and make a trench about 6 inches deep. Lay three tomato seedlings in the trench and cover the stems with soil so that only a few sets of leaves show. All of the foliage remains below the soil walls and under the Reemay. The combination traps some heat and lets most of the sun and rain in. In six weeks, tomatoes will be bushy and lively.

can block part of the sun's rays and create an artificially cool climate. Rachel Snyder does this on a very small scale by setting a shingle beside newly transplanted seedlings to block the sun. You can shade larger beds of young plants or cool salad crops with open snow fence set on cement blocks. You can also try shade cloth, a woven green plastic. Choose from tightly woven, dense cloths, which shade out as much as 80 percent of the sun, or a range of looser weaves that block less sun, down to about 30 percent.

TIMING A VACATION BREAK

For some of us, a week at home in the garden *is* a vacation. For others, a week off work is not complete without getting away from every-

FALL PROTECTION

As fall approaches, protect warm-season crops from frost and keep cool-season plants growing actively with methods similar to those used in spring.

Warm-season crops slow their growth as temperatures grow cooler and days get shorter. The flowers suffer first and probably will stop producing fruit well before they fail from cold or frosts. Corn and beans will begin to decline when the temperature goes below 50°F; for tomato and squash, the critical temperature is 55°F. Since many parts of the country are blessed with a few weeks of warm Indian summer in late autumn, however, it is worthwhile to keep these plants alive, in the hopes they will return to productivity in the final weeks of warmth.

Lettuce, beets, cauliflower, celery, radish, peas, and potato tubers can survive 33°F and Brussels sprouts down to 25°F. But low temperatures are not the only deciding factor to consider. Very wet weather can encourage the rotting of roots and of open, leafy vegetables that puddle the water near their hearts.

Sam Forbes, an organic market gardener in Oklahoma City, stores some of his carrot crop out in the fields until December and January. To keep the roots market-perfect, he mulches the carrot tops, which are particularly vulnerable to freeze damage, with a heavy layer of seedless grass. This protects the shoulders and keeps the ground from freezing, so he can dig them regardless of the weather.

Some growers use dilute seaweed sprays for a couple of weeks before a frost and on the day of the frost to raise mineral levels in the leaf tissue enough to prevent freezing. You may also be able to save a crop from frost by watering it lightly all night with a fine-mist sprinkler. If the water freezes on the plants, however, it is likely to crush them.

thing. Before you expect to leave town, calculate incoming harvests so they won't produce their first crop of luscious beans when you are at a cabin in a far-off woodland. By the time you get home two weeks later, the beans will be mealy and their plants will have shut down their future production. The same is true of cucumbers and summer squash. Other crops can take some picking delay without harm (see chapter 6).

You may also plan garden care into your vacation scheme. Vacation after turning a cover crop into the soil and before replanting with something else. Vacation when the tomatoes are about finished and the winter squash, pumpkins, and roots are not yet ready. Vacation after you plant the new lettuce seedlings but before they are ready to pick; they will not wait. Vacation after you spray for bugs and before you pick.

I have had some jaw-dropping returns from summertime vacations, so I am continually striving to correct my timing in this department. Occasionally, we depart after the spring harvest and summer planting but before the summer harvest starts. June generally proves a safe month for this, as long as I cut back on successions of lettuce, spinach, and radishes. This is ideal growing weather, however, and the weeds skyrocket. Controlling them is not always easy. I once layered straw around the entire crop-free footage and left with high hopes. The weather that week was wet, unfortunately, and slugs crept under that moist blanket of straw by the thousands. I returned to find all of my carefully planted seedlings eaten down to the quick, my work wasted, and my garden bare.

My most recent experience has been more successful. I mulched young corn and squash plants with black plastic. These plants suffer greatly if you yank large weeds out around their tender young roots. I layered straw on paths between raised rows to reduce weeds in areas devoted to transportation alone. I left the rest of the garden open to the elements. Double rows of beans fared well, for they had spread wide enough to shade out most of the weeds. Where carrots and peas were struggling for a foothold, however, a strong weed problem emerged. It took several hours of hand weeding to work around the young plants, but I was able to restore order.

Contributor Eliot Paine, director of the Holden Arboretum in Kirtland, Ohio, usually vacations near the end of summer. He writes, "I start the garden as early as possible in the spring — on the first day the soil is dry enough to work, which is the first week in April here. I plant all the cool-season crops that thrive in early spring, those that will germinate (usually) despite late snow and abundant rain. So many people wait until May to start and miss the cool growing season. On July 1, we have peas, carrots, beets, cauliflower, broccoli, spinach, lettuce — this year, even squash and beans. I cultivate once a week in May. On June 1, I mulch heavily with hay. It is a labor-free garden for summer."

TIMING TO ESCAPE PESTS

If you, like I, have lost some of your first gardens to pests and diseases, you understand the frustration that accompanies what you feel helpless to control. I've seen radishes and carrots riddled by root maggots, head lettuce rotted to a brown core, pea seeds disappear back into the earth. In recent years, I've seldom had a wholesale loss, but I frequently suffer from minor inconveniences from cucumber beetles and the wilt disease they carry, as well as from flea beetles on eggplant and cabbage.

In remote gardens, like Elizabeth Berry's market garden burrowed in the Gallina Canyon in the mountains of New Mexico, pests are rare. Her nearest neighbor is 20 miles away and her garden is troubled only by a few tomato caterpillars.

For most of us, however, pests are a way of life. They may be especially bad in the South where they are not killed by winter cold, and in locations where the same crops grow year after year. Most adult insects emerge at the start of a crop's normal growing season. They may eat your plants outright or lay their eggs in or around the plants. The larvae, in the form of caterpillars, leaf miners, or root maggots, then become the destructive element.

One good way to minimize pest damage is to avoid them all together. Plant earlier or later than usual, while pests are dormant or pupating. This works best with insects that have a limited number of generations or spend a part of each season in hibernation or pupation. Examples are cucumber beetles in the North, squash vine borers, Japanese beetles, root maggots, cutworms, snails, and slugs.

In addition to avoiding pests, you can increase plant strength with timing. I've found that eight times out of ten, planting a couple of weeks earlier than usual lets my plants get big and husky, and thus less vulnerable to wholesale damage. If you plant later than the usual season, pests may pupate or otherwise leave the crops alone.

When the last spring frost came six weeks later than usual one year, the pests didn't appear any earlier. The tomatoes were therefore unbothered by aphids. The cucumbers didn't have a single cucumber beetle, usually one of our worst scourges. The beans had narry a hole from a bean beetle until well into July.

Richard Casagrande, entomologist for the University of Rhode Island, was featured in the April 1989 *National Gardening* magazine for his work with potatoes and the Colorado potato beetle. He noted that these beetles emerge seven to fourteen days after the last spring frost. If you plant early-maturing cultivars of potato three to four weeks before the last frost, you can harvest before the beetles are bad. When you dig the potatoes, you will disrupt any larvae existing in the bed.

Keep your own record of when

WHAT ABOUT ANIMALS? TECHNIQUES TO LESSEN YOUR HARVEST'S APPEAL TO WILDLIFE

One factor that will be hard for you to control is the effects of animals. Birds may swarm your berries. Rabbits, chipmunks, groundhogs, and squirrels may sample your greens or gnaw holes into your tomatoes. The raccoons might gobble your corn. Just about the only things that are safe from freeloading animals are fragrant herbs and hot peppers, both of which can actually repel some creatures with sensitive noses. Here is a battery of techniques to keep such creatures at bay.

Physical deterrents. Setting up guards, barriers, or traps is the most surefire means of eliminating vertebrate pests.

For as long as we had a large hunting cat, we never had problems with small creatures in the garden. He would spend the night out there, daring the little ones to show their faces. In the morning, we would find the garden intact and several "treasures" he had caught left tidily on the doorstep.

Strapping tape around ears of corn may be one of the few options for raccoon control.

We learned, however, that cats are not the way to handle raccoons, which are more aggressive than the toughest cat. They scout gardens regularly to know just when the corn is ready to pick, and then they swoop in, without fail, just before harvest time. The 1991 Southern Exposure Seed Exchange catalogue shares a good idea for raccoon control. Circle each ear of corn with a ¾-inch-wide piece of fiberglass strapping tape. Start it about 1 inch above where the ear attaches to the stalk, and swirl it up to just below the tip of the ear. Wind the tape one turn around the stalk, and finish with a circle of tape about 1 inch below the tip of the ear. Expect to use 20 to 24 inches of tape per ear. Say the folks at Southern Exposure, "The tape keeps the raccoons from pulling the ears off the stalks because they are unable to break or unwrap the tape. We can't help smiling when thinking of the raccoons we've frustrated."

Another good deterrent for raccoons, as well as for other small animals in cat-free homes, is an electric fence, (the same device used around livestock yards), elevated about 1 foot high around the garden. Although it will not harm a creature, most wildlife are quite unaccustomed to shocks and will not soon return, despite the temptations within.

Contributor Hazel Weihe also relies on fences. She surrounds her growing area with a 7-foot-high deer fence and another lower one for rabbits. "We've been so overrun with deer, rabbits, and other wildlife for the past several years, that we've fenced our entire property 2⅓ acres; within that fencing we've also fenced the vegetable garden, so it is double fenced," Weihe says.

For animals that can burrow, submerge mesh fencing about 1 foot or so under the ground. For those that can climb, cover the fencing with slippery plastic sheeting that is hard to grip.

Eliminate brushy or untended areas of the yard that can become home to animals. Or, if you know where rabbits are living, plant crops they like elsewhere. I often can grow lettuces in the front yard foundation planting, even if bunnies eat it in the backyard.

Nebraska gardener Rose Marie Whiteley writes the following: "I must tell you that my current site is just off a creek. It's like a nature habitat — rabbits, 'possums, skunks, and raccoons visit my garden nightly. This year we have a fox with babies. The rabbits I can deal with — a 12-inch chicken-wire fence keeps them from enjoying breakfast, lunch, and dinner 'on me.' Last year, I put up a 3-foot-high black plastic fence around the sweet corn with a 50 percent success rate — they still got half, but I got the other half. Last year, too, a groundhog dug his home right next to my garden. He drove me crazy, as he absolutely ravaged my garden. So, this year, I have put up an electric fence that thus far appears to be keeping all the four-legged critters on the outside, looking in."

When the above tactics are unsuccessful, you can trap and remove animals to another location. There are a number of humane traps on the market. Sometimes commercial trappers will handle the job for you.

The best bet for bird control is to cover nearly ripe berries with fine bird nets, securing all openings carefully so nothing can slip in. Even better are wire-fence bird cages that surround the plants from top to bottom. You can make a similar barrier out of interwoven tape or string strips. Birds also may be frightened for a short period of time by scare eyes, balloon snakes or owls, rock music, taped aviary distress calls, and other startling mechanisms. But most birds learn, once disaster does not occur, that it is safe to venture into the berry patch.

Another option is to plant cultivars that have less appeal to creatures. Birds, for instance, see red best. They hone in on red berries with an eagle eye. If you plant yellow strawberries and raspberries or green gooseberries you will find your problem diminished.

Chemical deterrents. Sometimes if a crop smells unappetizing or dangerous, animals will leave it alone. The success of these methods often depends on how hungry the animal is.

Rachel Snyder has left human hair around the garden to spook off rabbits. "I tie it into mesh bags and scatter it around," she says. She also ties small bars of fragrant soap in fruit trees to deter deer browsing.

You can buy or make a variety of chemical repellents. One homemade option is hot peppers blended with garlic. Some commercial repellents are not labeled to use in edible gardens, so read the label carefully before you buy. For example, the Peaceful Valley catalogue notes that the Magic Circle Deer Repellent, the strongest and longest lasting of the repellents they tested, should not be applied to foliage close to harvest. If this animal-bone tar oil is enough to turn away voracious herbivores like deer, it won't make an appetizing meal for you.

pests became a problem. You can then plant to avoid them or take other preventative measures. Your local Cooperative Extension Service can keep you up to date on which pests are a particular problem during each season.

SEED STARTING

Starting your own plants not only saves you money and gives you more control over your garden and cultivar selection, but it also adds another dimension to garden timing. You can tackle seed sowing in a very simple fashion or take on more complex techniques.

Direct Sowing

Sowing seeds directly outdoors is the least troublesome way to start your harvest garden, but crops take longer to mature than when given a head start indoors.

Broadcast seed by sprinkling it lightly across a wide bed, mixing sand in with small seeds to disperse them more evenly, or place the seeds one by one in a single row. To save wear and tear on your back and knees, purchase a mechanical seed planter. These are relatively inexpensive hollow wheels that you can preset to release seeds at various regular intervals. It rolls on a long handle down a prepared seed bed leaving seeds in its wake. To place the seeds in firmer contact with the soil, you can dibble (drill) or poke individual seeds down into a level area. Judge planting depth and spacing according to instructions on the seed packet. Cover the seeds with fine soil, and use a rake, hoe, or your hands to level the soil to the proper depth. Author Eleanour Sinclair Rhode noted that some old-fashioned British gardeners drilled the seed into the ground, and then twitched each heel alternately to cover the seed evenly.

A long-handled mechanical seed sower.

Direct sowing introduces a larger element of chance into the planting process. If the temperature is not right, or the weather is too wet or dry, the seeds may not germinate quickly or abundantly. When they do germinate, they may not be in the ideal place. You may have a dozen all bunched up together and a couple scattered far from any neighbors. If you have a quick-maturing crop of salad greens you expect to harvest young, or if you want to thin overcrowded babies to fill your salad bowl early, uneven spacing may not matter. If you catch the seedlings young, you may be able to move them. But you have to do something, because overcrowded plantings will not produce well.

You can solve some of these difficulties by planting seeds in seed tapes. Although my best carrot crops have come from these handy strips, I have not been entirely happy to buy them. In the past, I paid top prices for a limited selection of carrot cultivars. However, this need not be the case.

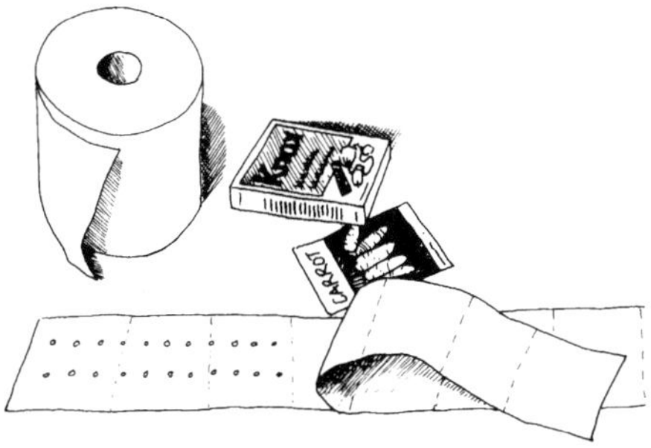

You can create homemade seed tapes by sandwiching seeds between layers of toilet tissue, held together by gelatin.

Contributor Lloyd Evans makes his own seed tapes. He takes unscented toilet tissue and splits the double layer in half. He then mixes up a package of unflavored gelatin, which is about 15 percent nitrogen. The gelatin serves to stick the whole affair together, while releasing nutrients for fast initial growth. He dabs some of the damp gel on the toilet tissue and presses a seed into it, using whatever spacing is ideal for the crop he is planting. In the case of carrots, he makes a double row of seeds on the "tape." When the strip is as long as he wants, he firms on the top layer of tissue. Evans says, "This really works and I don't have to thin."

Presprouting

Direct sowing works best for small crops and those that resent transplanting. To get many plants off to a faster start and ensure good spacing, however, most gardeners prefer already-started plants. Instead of buying all your seedlings, you can plant a tiny, presprouted embryo and get good results.

Presprouting is a simple technique that requires little or no special equipment. You control temperature and moisture, and you can speed germination rates from a month to a couple of days, especially if temperatures outside are not ideal for germination. Bob Thomson writes in *The New Victory Garden* that he presprouts nearly everything he grows, even beans. This avoids delays and lets him control his spacing more tightly.

Temperature. When you, not nature, are in control of the temperature, you can be sure to give the seeds exactly the conditions they need to emerge fast. Find or create a variety of warm or cool locations, something for each cultivar. Use your refrigerator, basement, air conditioner, unheated bedroom, kitchen, the pilot light in your oven, soil heating cables, or a hot attic. See page 79 for optimal germination temperatures.

Moisture. When the temperature is right and seeds are prepared to germinate, they must have a steady source of moisture. To turn dormant seed into swelling plant, water must seep through the seed coat and dissolve chemical barriers that prevent germination. Moisture triggers a series of reactions that allow the seed to grow. It splits out of its shell — usually root first — and rises up to cast off the seed coat and spread fleshy cotyledon (seed) leaves, which are soon followed by the first true foliage.

Some seeds have tough coats, tiny embryos, or other peculiarities that may call for special treatment. For example, soak beet seed for a few hours before planting to wash away chemical inhibitors. Freeze slow-germinating parsley seed for a couple of days before planting. Place lima beans with their dark spot (hilum) down for easier root penetration. Give lettuce and other tiny seeds light to help them germinate; the presence of light tells the seed it is buried at the right depth. When I presprout small seeds, I sprinkle them on the surface of the soil and lightly tap them down rather than actually cover them.

Light. Once the seedlings begin growing, they need bright light. Whenever I leave seeds on top of the refrigerator for warmth, I have to check them every day. Forget once, and they will surely come up, and I will find skinny white shoots that can't survive outdoors.

Media. You can presprout seedlings in a variety of ways, but they must be housed in something sterile that holds moisture. Ordinary soil is rich in disease-causing bacteria and fungi, which will quickly move in to consume the seedlings. *Damping off* (rot of the basal part of the stem), is the most common result of planting in unsterile soil.

Try synthetic planter's mix (a combination of peat moss, vermiculite, and perlite) or straight vermiculite. First wet the medium thoroughly with warm water. Level it and set the seeds in, then cover the seed tray with clear plastic wrap to make a minigreenhouse. Or, you can dampen three pieces of sturdy paper towel or a clean dish towel. Place the seeds inside so they do not touch; roll the seeds up in the towel. To keep the towel from drying out, set it in a clear plastic bag. Check frequently.

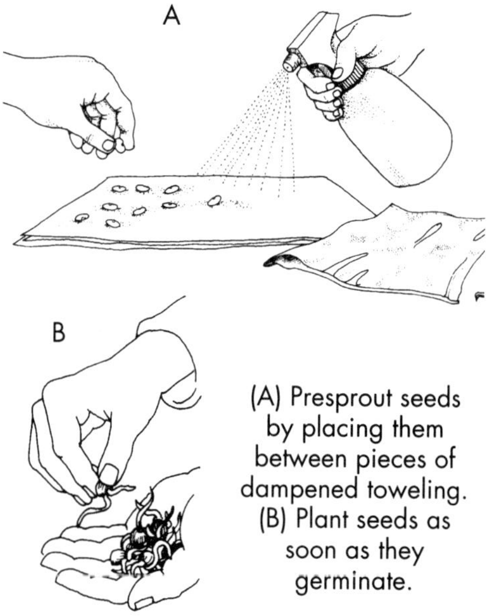

(A) Presprout seeds by placing them between pieces of dampened toweling. (B) Plant seeds as soon as they germinate.

Planting outside. Ideally, you should plant the presprouted youngster outside as soon as the seed coat cracks and the root emerges. Have the garden ready ahead of time, so you can pop the seeds in without

OPTIMAL GERMINATION TEMPERATURES FOR SEEDS

Crop	Ideal Temperature (degrees F)	Minimum Temperature (degrees F)
Asparagus	75	
Basil	70	
Bean	80	
Beet	85	50
Cabbage	85	45
Carrot	80	45
Cauliflower	80	45
Celery*	70	60 (not over 85)
Swiss chard	85	50
Chervil	55	
Chives	70	60
Corn	85	60
Cucumber	95	60**
Dill	70	
Eggplant	85	75**
Fennel	70	
Lettuce	75	40 (not over 85)
Lovage	65	
Muskmelon	90	75
Okra	95	70
Onion	75	50**
Oregano, Greek	60	
Parsley	75	50
Parsnip	65	50 (not over 85)
Pea	75	40 (not over 85)
Pepper	85	65
Pumpkin	95	70
Radish	85	45
Sage	70	
Sorrel	70	
Spinach	70	45 (not over 85)
Squash	95	70
Summer savory	70	
Tomato	85	60
Turnip	85	60**
Watermelon	95	70**

*Best with a 10°F drop at night

**Germinates at over 100°F

delay. If the weather makes this impossible, transfer the seedlings to individual pots and a sunny windowsill for a couple of days until conditions improve. You may be able to move these vegetable infants outside slightly out of season if you protect them from unfavorable elements (see pages 65–69).

Which crops to try. Presprouting smaller seeds is easier and especially worthwhile because they are the ones that come up slowly or end up growing in dense thickets. Lloyd Evans has a great way to prestart troublesome carrots, which will not poke up unless the soil is very fine. To overcome germination difficulties, Evans starts his carrot seeds in the cardboard rolls found inside paper towels. He fills the tubes with moist sterile soil, and then plants the seed. Once the plants emerge, he digs a hole outside and sinks a 9-inch-deep cardboard box into the garden. He fills the box with potting soil and humus. Then he nestles all the tubes in the box, cardboard and all, without disturbing the roots.

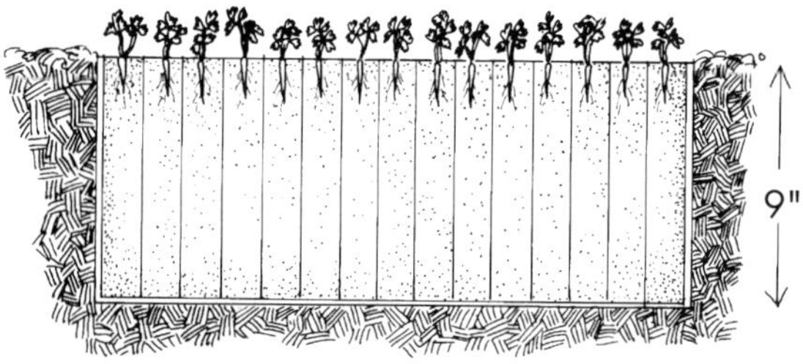

Prestart carrots in soil-filled cardboard tubes that can be planted directly in the garden.

The larger legume seeds, such as peas and beans, require a little special care if you attempt to start them indoors. As soon as the seed swells, it is easily broken. Pea seeds may snap in two with even gentle handling. You should therefore put the seeds in some kind of container that you can simply slip into the garden without jostling the seed.

Likewise, use extra caution with tap-rooted crops, *cucurbita,* and corn so you don't disturb their roots. You can presprout these plants in peat pots or Jiffy-pots. Although these are biodegradable, they are good for

Tear off the top edge of peat pots so that they don't protrude above the surface of the soil.

only one use, become expensive when used in large quantities, and don't always prove ideal once planted. I have noticed that occasionally a pot does not decompose and the roots never break free into the garden soil. Furthermore, if the edge of the peat pot emerges above the soil, the pot may dry out — along with the delicate seedling roots inside. You will know your seedling is safe if the roots are escaping through the pot sides when you plant. If not, tear the bottom off the pot so they can exit that way.

I have tried several other quick-start products as well. One was a system of circular paper pots, consisting of a honeycombed cluster of paper wrappers that surround the planting mix. This did not generally prove successful. Unless the plants were nearly root bound in these containers, the soil tended to slip out of the encircling paper and the seedlings were shuffled, twisted, or broken.

Soil blocks of damp planter's mix pressed out of a grid have been slightly more successful for me. Some time is required to determine how moist to make the soil so it will cling together in a cube, as well as how much to pack into the shaper. The trick is to keep the block moist until the seedling roots hold the structure together. Peat-based growers or seed starting mixes dry out rapidly, and then the whole structure falls to dust. To avoid this, I put them in a seed flat with a few perforations in the bottom and cover it with plastic wrap to keep the moisture in. When the blocks begin to look a little crumbly before planting time, I gently bottom-water by setting the flat in another lined with water. Don't water any way but delicately or the blocks will fall apart!

Commercial soil block tool

Starting Seedlings in a Light Garden

You can go a step beyond presprouting by growing the seedlings larger in a light garden, cold frame, or protected location outside. This can give you a headstart on the growing season, an advantage where fall frosts or summer droughts cut the growing season short.

Spend a few minutes planning the timing so the seedlings will be ready just after the last spring frost date. Seed packets indicate how many weeks before the last frost to start seeds indoors. Call your local Cooperative Extension Service or farm bureau, the reference librarian at the local public library, a top-quality garden center or nursery, or a botanical garden, or use your computer modem to access an electronic bulletin board with weather information to find out your average last frost date and work back from it. I usually begin in February with seeds of onions and perennial herbs, as well as a few eggplants, peppers, tomatoes, and other tender vegetables that I want to fruit extra early. Crops like tomatoes, peppers, eggplants, alpine strawberries, sweet marjoram, and summer savory need six to eight weeks to reach a hale-and-hearty size suitable for transplanting.

Using the windowsill for sprouting will work only in climates with sunny spring weather. In Ohio, we have at least a couple of weeks of continual rain, which limits the bright sunlight seedlings need. Without light, they stretch up long and weak.

I now have some beautifully working alternatives to windowsills — two sets of four fluorescent light fixtures on chains from nails in the basement ceiling, which dangle over a sturdy table, about 5 feet square. A second light garden consists of two tiers of shelves, three flats long, with two sets of fluorescent tubes hung 8 inches above. To maximize the light that shines on the plants below, I lower the bulbs to just inches above the plants and cover the perimeters of the growing areas with shiny aluminum foil, which reflects stray light back on the plants. I rig both sets of lights up to a timer set for fourteen to sixteen hours of light a day. It switches the apparatus on and off as necessary.

Although I often germinate the seeds in the warmth upstairs, the basement has some advantages. The temperature remains about 60°F, slightly higher near the light. Cool-season seeds germinate well there. Once the seedlings are up, growth is a little slower than in warmer locations and plants stay stockier. Tomatoes and peppers grown cool for several weeks after they develop their first true leaves will have an earlier yield. After about four weeks, they need to have more heat — 65°F for tomatoes and 70°F for peppers.

Both light gardens are near the outlet for my well pump. Since our water is quite hard, we soften it for human use. For plants though, I capture the water before it runs through the water softener. I have a hose that reaches to both gardens (and a few drips on the cement floor is not a problem). With the warmth-loving plants, I sometimes let the water warm up for an hour or two before applying it to the tender roots.

A nearby potting table has enough room to lay out the seed packages, make out labels, wet the sterile potting mix, fill the containers, and transplant.

I sow the seeds quite shallowly — up to ¼ inch deep, depending on their size and seed packet instructions. I then cover the container with plastic wrap. I often leave the plastic wrap on until the seedlings push it up, because it saves me from having to water as often. If the humidity becomes too high, the seedlings could suffer fungal diseases, but I have never had this problem. When the seedlings are very small, you are wise to water from the bottom of the flat, if possible. A strong stream of water could uproot them and wash them away.

If I have a lot of seeds to plant, I put them into a flat, lined out in rows and carefully marked. If you can't figure out what you have planted and where you planted it, your efforts at organization are in vain.

I transplant seedlings when they develop two sets of true leaves in addition to the cotyledons. At this point, their roots generally are growing straight down — not yet entangled with their neighbors but large enough to support the leafy growth, even if disturbed slightly. If you try to transplant them any earlier, the seedlings tend to wither; any later, and you are bound to tear the roots and set the plants back. Using flats lets me start hundreds of plants in a limited space, but the trade-off is that I eventually have to separate each individual into its own container, which takes time and much more space.

If I want just a few plants of a certain variety, which is usually the case in the vegetable garden, I sow only one or two seeds (more if I question the germination percentage on older seeds or from less-reputable suppliers). I like to plant in plastic foam coffee cups with holes poked in the bottom. These are larger than the average six-pack-size containers and let the plants do

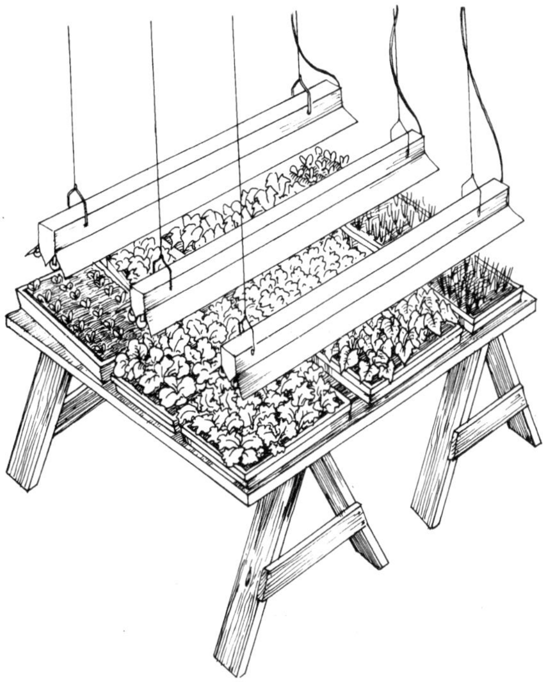

Fluorescent lights hung over a sturdy table create a good indoor growing environment for starting seeds.

a lot of growing before they need more attention. They are prone to tipping, however, and do not pack as closely into a crowded flat as square containers or six-packs.

A plant started six weeks earlier indoors usually has just filled out the cup and is primed for transplanting outdoors. If I have started it earlier than that, I usually have to transplant into successively larger containers. I usually do not fertilize seedlings in the light garden, because extra nutrients seem to make the plants grow scrawnier. I wait until I transplant the seedling outdoors, unless the plant begins to look stunted or off-color.

When the weather begins to warm outside, I move the larger and more cold-hardy plants out to an unheated glass-enclosed breezeway between my kitchen and garage. You can also use a cold frame, enclosed porch, unheated sunroom, or other bright but chilly spot. This opens up more room for you to start new waves of seedlings in the light garden, as well as gives the more mature plants a chance to harden to outdoor life. I cut back on water and fertilizer to toughen the tissues. As long as the weather stays mild, I may begin moving them outdoors in the warmth of the day. After a week or so of this treatment, the crops are ready for the garden.

What If You Buy Seedlings?

In the past few decades, most American gardeners have tended to buy their seedlings from commercial greenhouses, and this practice is certainly a time-saver. You do need to be careful to pick and choose the best possible plants. Check the form and shape of the seedling. Is the plant dark green? Is it sturdy, with relatively short internodes (the length of stem between sets of leaves)? If so, this indicates that the plant has received enough light and fertilizer in the greenhouse. If it is light green and lanky, with a lot of stem between sparse leaves, it has suffered some setbacks and will have some catching up to do to match the performance of a better-grown counterpart. Look under the leaves and shake the plant to see if any insect pests are hiding there. How large is the pot? If it is small, there is a good chance the plant is root bound within. When the roots can no longer spread outwards, they wrap around themselves and can choke off their own moisture supply. Root-bound plants may send roots out the bottom of the pot or, if you slip the plant out of its pot, you may find a solid mass of white roots. If you have no choice but to buy such a plant, tear the outer layer of roots off so the inner ones can grow out into the soil without obstruction.

Check the general quality of the garden center or greenhouse that you frequent. Is there a cultivar name tag given for the plant? Is there a chance someone has mistakenly switched some tags, so that your meaty, red-fruited Big Boy tomato turns out to be a small, yellow plum tomato?

When you buy from a nursery, look for stocky, dark green, insect-free plants in adequate-sized pots.

four

Keeping Crops on Track

TO KEEP PLANTS healthy and thriving, you will need to follow up early planning and planting with some extended care. Think of the garden as if it were a car: Maintenance keeps your car running well, but if you neglect routine servicing, major problems will soon develop. Just as your car needs oil and gas, your garden needs sun, moisture, and nutrients. Beyond that, it performs best with protection against weeds and pests, as well as provisions for adequate pollination. Be aware of all of these needs and you can increase crop yields and improve appearance and flavor.

A word of advice may save you some unnecessary worry and work in the garden: Learn to tell when a problem is really a problem and not a superficial blemish. Although you would not buy a dark-spotted tomato or a slightly torn head of lettuce at the grocery, both may be perfectly safe and delicious to eat, if you simply remove the unsightly portion. More on this later in the chapter.

Equip yourself with all the tools you need to bring those crops along to their ultimate goodness. The basic mechanical tools are commonly known — hoe, rake, shovel, hand trowel, and, for larger gardens, a rototiller. But you also need a ready source of nutrients and organics to tune up the soil, a healthy serving of sunshine, and a headful of techniques at your disposal — trellises, irrigation, pruning, fertilization, and pest and disease control, for example.

SOLAR POWER

In a society so heavily reliant on oil and electricity, you may be inclined to forget that sunshine is the power that fuels the entire natural world. It is captured by green chloroplasts in plant stems and leaves and used to combine carbon dioxide and water into sugars. Other portions of plant cells break down the sugars to release chemical energy that drives growth and development. Given full sun, most plants can perform to their maximum ability. Contributer Alan Cook calls sunshine the most important factor for a flavorful harvest.

The areas of a plant with sunlit foliage produce maximum levels of sugar, most of which are commandeered by nearby fruit. The fruits hidden in the shaded interior of the plant, on the other hand, are smaller, ripen later, or are less sweet. Plants with too many fruits will divide the photosynthate up until it is inadequate. On certain plants, therefore, you may need to thin new growth or fruit to get optimum results for your harvest.

The sun can bring out the best color in fruit. You will see that the sun-warmed side of a peach is the first to blush red and soften. One strawberry fruit peeks out from beneath a cluster of leaves. Its emerging tip warms, softens, and begins to change to a warm ruby red, rich in sugars and flavorings, a delight not commonly encountered in prematurely picked berries. At this point, the fruit is much more visible to birds, who are likely to take their share, too.

Too much hot sun, on the other hand, can discolor or scald tomatoes, peppers, and other fruits. While foliage profits from sun, fruits have their limits. Like a fair-skinned child who has spent the day at the beach, your pampered fruit can burn. This condition is known as *sunscald* in fruits. It usually remains skin-deep, bleaching tomatoes, peppers, and berries to white or brown on the exposed side. You can cut off the damaged area and eat the produce, but the fruit will be more susceptible to disease and will not store well.

A little shade from nearby leaves discourages scalding. Light shade also keeps growing conditions cooler and moister, good for growing lettuce, root crops, or newly planted seedlings. Generally four to six hours of sun a day is enough to keep these crops strong. Their energy needs are not as intense without flowers and fruit to support. In hot, dry climates, you may even want to shade fruiting crops for part of the day.

Crops need both foliage to capture energy to support plant processes and exposure to sunlight to ripen fruit. Thus, you may have to manipulate crops to balance sun effects. Get the best of light and shade by thinning excess branches, canes, or stems or by trellising.

Pruning Excess Growth

You may have noticed how the first tomato to ripen at the end of a branch is plumper than the rest. This is because it has a monopoly on the sugars produced by nearby leaves. Once the energy trickles down to lower fruit clusters, it is diminished, and fruits cannot grow as big. If you thin out (remove) excess fruit, the remainder will swell larger and be more packed with sugar. Here's how to treat different crops:

◆ On raspberries, blackberries, and tomatoes, remove some of the canes or suckers to limit overly thick growth.

Remove some of the suckers on tomato plants.

◆ On mature fruit bushes like blueberries and gooseberries, take off weak, old, or excess growth to limit fruit numbers, increase sunlight penetration into the center of the bush, and improve air circulation.

◆ Remove most or all of the runners on strawberries to beef up the remaining berries.

Remove runners on strawberries.

Trellising

Growing crops upward on trellises not only maximizes sun exposure, it also gives you cleaner fruit and better air circulation, which in turn lessens the chance of disease problems. The bottom side of a vine that would otherwise lie in the shade along the ground has access to full sunshine if lifted on a support, giving it more potential for productivity. On the down side, with more sun and air exposure, foliage transpires more moisture and wilts more easily.

You have a number of trellising options. You can sink permanent wooden or metal poles into the ground and string wire or twine across them for crops to climb. This technique is excellent for raised beds or berry patches. For annual crops that rotate through the garden, I prefer temporary trellises that are simple to use, clean up, and store. Here are some suggestions:

◆ A 3-foot-high metal-grid pea fence that zigzags across a wide bed is one of my favorites for shorter plants, like compact peas, pole beans, and cucumbers. It's easy to pull out the old vines and fold the pea fence flat for winter storage.

◆ Nylon-mesh netting is easy to attach to upright poles, but the old vines are difficult to clean out of it so it can be reused. In my opinion, the netting is too expensive to justify just one use.

◆ Homemade twine grids can be easy and inexpensive to make and use. String them up and down over wires strung between two posts. Toss out or compost both string and vines at the end of the year.

◆ Wire-grid tomato cages that form an inverted cone are handy. These allow shorter tomatoes, or even compact-vined bush squash, to grow through the openings and cascade out into full sun with just enough support to keep them off the ground. And they stack together, with ten taking little more space than one to store.

◆ Homemade tomato cages constructed of concrete reinforcing wire can be designed so they are the perfect height and width for a particular cultivar. Because of their varied sizes, however — and because they warp — they can take a great amount of room to store.

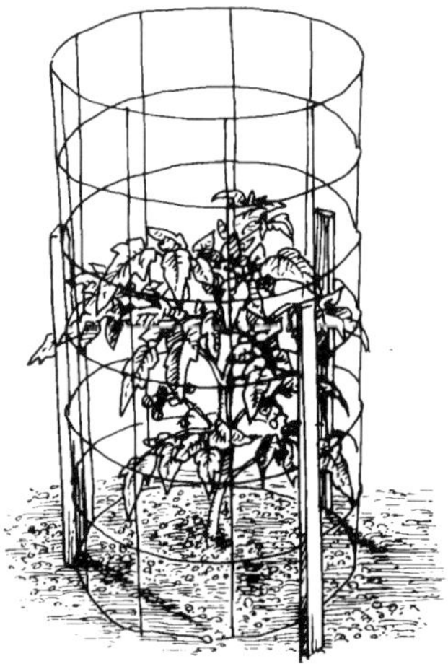

Homemade tomato cage, with wooden stakes for support

◆ A tepee created of six or eight long poles is great for twining legumes, especially pole beans. I make mine of saplings. You can do the same with 2 x 2 boards or even snowfence slats. I plant the beans around the base and let a couple of vines climb each pole. The center is a good place to grow greens in midsummer.

Plant 4 to 6 beans around each pole of a bean tepee.

◆ The A-frame is another great trellis. To construct one, build two rectangular wooden frames and connect them at the top with hinges. Set both legs at an angle in the garden so the trellis becomes self-supporting. Fill the framework with wire mesh or twine, depending on the crop.

Peas, beans, and some cucurbits will climb trellises unassisted. To get them started, however, you may need to loop soft, flexible new growth around the lower one or two rungs, if the plant does not climb for itself. When you grow large fruits, such as winter squash, on a trellis, support

An A-frame trellis filled with wire mesh for cucumbers

them when fist-sized with a sling made of old pantyhose. Otherwise, the fruit may fall when young or tear the vine.

Day Length

Some crops will fruit, flower, or swell as the days change in length. Long-day plants need about sixteen hours of light; short-day plants need about twelve hours; day-neutral plants develop independent of day length. A good example of a plant affected by the amount of daylight is the strawberry. Spring starts with short days, the cue for June-bearing strawberries to flower. Everbearers return to flower again in the short days of fall. Day-neutral strawberries, uninfluenced by day length, continue to fruit and flower the entire season. Most other berries are similarly prompted to flower and fruit at the same time(s) each year.

Other cultivars influenced by day

THE C-4 CLUB

Just as some cars get better gas mileage than others, certain plants use sunlight more efficiently than other varieties. Those that make the most of the sun's energy are all of tropical descent and thus adapted to high levels of light and heat. They include corn, sugar cane, and sorghum. These members of the C-4 "club" (C-4 is a reference to the chemical pathway carbon follows when fixed into sugar) skip a process called *photorespiration,* which wastes as much as half of the sugars other plants manufacture. Consequently, corn has a photosynthetic rate two to three times higher than wheat, rye, oats, and rice. Although plant breeders are working on inserting C-4 effectiveness into more crops, most of them still photosynthesize in the more common, less-efficient way.

length include annual greens and roots, such as lettuce, spinach, Chinese cabbage, and radishes, all of which bolt with increasing day length. You can often get a longer harvest season if you plant these crops in the fall, when days are growing shorter and heat does not add to the pressures to flower.

The day-length phenomenon is complicated by the fact that different parts of the country have different day lengths. In Anchorage, Alaska, days reach over nineteen hours long (in Fairbanks, twenty-two hours) with cool 45°F nights and 70°F days. The combination is great for growing monster-size cabbages and snap peas, says resident Jeff Lowenfels. Spinach, however, a short-day crop, bolts so fast it is seldom worth growing.

Onions will not bulb unless given the proper day length. Thus, you must plant cultivars appropriate for the amount of daylight your climate receives if you want to harvest a fat bulb. Northern gardeners can grow long-day, pungent, storage onions. Gardeners in the South cultivate sweet Spanish types that need only twelve hours of day length.

MOISTURE NEEDS

A harvest garden usually grows well if you keep it evenly moist, neither soggy nor bone dry. Usually an inch of water a week will do. Keep track of how much rain has fallen each week. Use a rain gauge or set out a container in which to measure rainfall. If you need to supplement rainfall, you can irrigate. Water deeply enough to encourage the roots to dig deeper, but do not overwater and drown plant roots.

You can water either overhead with a sprinkler or at ground level with soaker hoses or drip irrigation systems. Bill Bricker gets water to go deeper into the soil by filling up submerged, perforated, or bottomless pipes, pots, or 1-gallon buckets. The water trickles out and filters into the rooting zone.

If you learn what water does in plants, you will better understand what can happen when there is too much or too little moisture. Water is more than a thirst quencher. Plants pipe a steady stream of water from root to leaf. The moisture escapes by evaporating through pores in the leaves. Plants cycle gallons of water through their systems, many times more than similar-size animals. A single corn plant, for example, loses 50 gallons of water during a growing season, or at least 1 gallon a day. A tomato plant may lose 35 gallons and a potato plant, 25 gallons. Moisture loss increases in high winds or with heat and low humidity. Botanist Peter Raven notes in his *Biology of Plants* that evaporation doubles with each 10°C increase in temperature. It can accelerate to the point that plants will wilt on a hot day just because the roots cannot pull in enough

IRRIGATION OPTIONS

Chapter 4 contributors Deb and Paul Doscher, former market gardeners from New Hampshire; Bernard Penczek, from New York; and Virginia and Ed Nix, from North Carolina, use a very different method of irrigating.

The Doschers grow about 80 percent of the vegetables eaten by their family of four on a half-acre garden of intensively planted raised beds. They mulch most of the garden so they don't have to water anything except areas they plant during hot or dry weather. In the main garden, they have a drip-irrigation system, but in smaller gardens, they water overhead with a sprinkler. Deb acknowledges that some of that water is lost to evaporation, saying, "It is a waste of water for what the plants get, but it is not worth setting up a whole drip system for temporary watering."

Bernard Penczek keeps a rain gauge out in the garden, so he can tell when the garden gets below an inch of rain a week. "If you let the soil dry out too much you won't have much of a crop," says Penczek. He lays soaker hoses throughout the garden and lets them slowly trickle water for five or six hours. He does not know exactly how deep the irrigation water goes as it seeps, but expects it to soak below the plant roots, about 6 inches or deeper.

So that he can use warm water on eggplant, tomato, pepper, and squash plants, Penczek fills 5-gallon pails of water in the morning before work, leaves them out all day to warm up, and applies the water in the evening.

The Nixes, who have a large organic garden and sell produce twice a week at a tailgate market, say irrigation is essential during periods of dry North Carolina summers. From their pond, they draw water through 1½-inch plastic pipe laid under the center of the garden and hooked to a series of eight spray heads. They can turn on one or all of the sprinklers, as needed. "There is just too much garden to do to use soaker hoses and this really works well, especially if I water early in the morning or late at night," Ed says.

moisture to support the loss through the leaves.

Contrary to how it may seem, this system is not a wasteful one. The water already inside a plant pulls in even more water and nutrients from the soil and helps to funnel them through the plant. If you have ever seen a water bug scooting on top of a pond, you have seen in its "wake" evidence of how water molecules cling together. In plants, this phenomenon creates a cohesive string of water molecules that rise up through the plant. As water evaporates out of the leaves, it draws moisture from the soil into the roots, stem, and ultimately back to the leaves.

When the roots can no longer bring in enough moisture to keep the system running well, however, the crops begin to decline: Photosynthesis slows. Roots and stems become more fibrous. Without an ample supply of food, fleshy roots, flowers, and fruits are set back. Seeds will not germinate, and newly transplanted seedlings will not survive. Corn pollen may lose viability; leaves may curl. Cucumbers can become bitter. Tomatoes can develop blossom end rot.

If you cannot provide enough water to support most crops, find drought-tolerant plants. These often have narrow, leathery, or waxy leaves, which lose less moisture through evaporation. Many herbs fit in this group. Most are native to dry, sunny Mediterranean climates and are well adapted to low moisture conditions. In sandy soils with relatively low nutrient and water levels and full sun, they grow slowly and develop heavier concentrations of the essential oils that are responsible for their fragrance and flavor. You can grow certain herbs, like parsley, basil, and mints, in moister or shadier conditions, but don't expect them to be as flavorful. Grown indoors, these herbs will be milder still, possibly even bland.

The other soil extreme — soil that is too wet — is equally bad. Oversaturation of the soil, be it from heavy rain, poor drainage, heavy soil structure, or overwatering, drowns plant roots. In such situations, plants usually rot.

To improve drainage, raise rows within the garden or the garden as a whole so extra water will run off to lower areas. Beneath the garden, cobweb drainage tiles that are hooked to the storm sewer.

In addition to supplying enough moisture for plants to grow well but not smother, you can juggle the water supply to provide a better harvest. Potatoes and onions will cure better if you stop irrigating the last week or two before you dig them. Limit water for nearly ripe strawberries, tomatoes, and cabbages to delay splitting, as well as for melons to keep them sweet.

Contributor Judy Lowe writes, "Too much rain the last couple of weeks before a melon is 'dead' ripe just ruins the flavor, washes it out. So, during rainy spells, I cover my melon rows with plastic row covers, which keep most of the excess moisture off. It's important to remove the plastic the minute the sun returns or you'll have baked melons!"

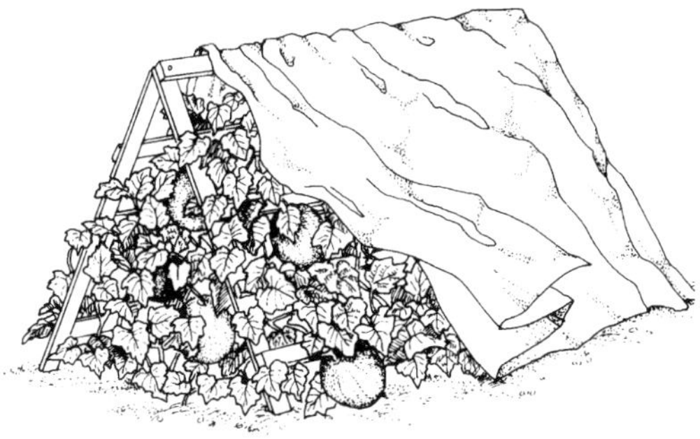

During rainy spells near harvest time, cover melons with plastic.

Another juggling act is keeping container-grown plants moist. When the temperature reaches 85°F in full sun, an eggplant or tomato can consume every drop of water in the soil within hours. You need to have a back-up system in place, unless you are available to water a couple of times a day. Here are a few options:

◆ Custom mix your potting soils so they will hold moisture without compressing excessively. I blend 3 parts planter's mix (a sterile combination of peat, vermiculite, and perlite) with 1 part compost. The compost holds some moisture and nutrients, while the planting mix keeps the soil fluffy. Garden soils pack down when used in containers, especially with repeated watering.

◆ You can put extra moisture reservoirs in a pot by adding wetting agents, which are jell-like substances that store a limited amount of extra moisture. These look like crystals until you wet them, then they assume a more liquid form. Mix the moistened wetting agents into the soil before planting, or sink pockets of the moistened agent into holes in the soil after planting.

◆ Elevate the planter above, but not in, a water reservoir, such as a large tray, pan, or bucket full of water. Extend a wick of thick felt or rope through the lower drainage hole and into the water. The plant can draw extra moisture up the wick and into the container.

◆ If you grow a lot of plants in containers, you may be able to justify buying an irrigation system. Each planter will then have its own water hose connected to a main line. You can set a timer to water automatically.

Run small-diameter tubing from container to container to automate watering.

Mulches

By covering the surface of the soil, you can help hold moisture in and reduce evaporation. We discussed inorganic plastic mulches in chapter 3, but you may want to supplement these with organic mulches; they keep the soil temperature moderate and relatively consistent, reduce weeds, and keep plants cleaner. Unlike plastic, however, organic mulches break down into soil-enriching humus.

Layers of leaves, grass, or wood products are more porous than plastic sheeting, and they allow additional interchange of both air and moisture. This is especially true of coarse-textured mulches like pine boughs and bark chunks, which are ideal for winter use. You can layer these up to 4 inches deep. Finer-textured mulches like grass clippings and peat moss, on the other hand, tend to compact into a dense mat if applied too thickly; use these in shallow layers only or mix them with larger materials.

Spread a thick layer of mulch, but keep it a couple of inches away from the base of plants.

It's a good idea to push mulches back a couple of inches away from the plant crown or base. The soil should be slightly drier at that point to avoid crown rot. Creating an open space also discourages pests from moving in close to the crop.

All organic mulches eventually break down to enrich the soil. The microbes responsible for this decay absorb nitrogen from the soil. Nitrogen loss is greatest with the woodier mulches, especially if they are fine textured and decompose quickly. Shredded bark seems to suck the life out of nearby plants, especially high-nitrogen users like roses and corn, unless you correct for the additional draw it puts on the soil. Give the garden 1 pound of usable nitrogen per 100 pounds of woody mulch, an easy task if you buy your mulch by weight. If not, you can broadcast nitrogen fertilizer lightly under the mulch and then supplement plants with water-soluble fertilizer whenever they begin to yellow or grow slowly.

Once your mulch decomposes, it becomes humus and releases some nutrients back to the soil. Even more important, the organic matter chemically holds small mineral particles together to create more air space and a ready anchor for nutrients floating in soil-borne moisture.

Here is a sampling of the kinds of mulches you may find, with their advantages and disadvantages:

SHALLOW-ROOTED BERRIES AND HERBS

Use several inches of a fluffy organic mulch on perennial berries and herb beds during winter. Wait until after the soil freezes in winter to apply this, as it will help *keep* the earth frozen. Alternate freezing and thawing in unprotected areas causes the soil to shift and push shallow-rooted plants right up out of the ground. Remove the mulch once warm weather arrives in spring.

Straw. This common vegetable garden mulch is lightweight and medium textured. In a 2-inch layer, it lets plenty of air and moisture through to plant roots. Some gardeners apply it even more deeply over potatoes or around strawberries. Potatoes produce tubers in the decomposing straw, and strawberry runners extend through the rich organic layer. Straw can blow away in high winds or burn if sparked by the charcoal grill or a cigarette. Technically, straw should contain no seeds, but in reality, you may soon see wheat or oats sprouting up from beneath the mantle of yellow.

Grass clippings. The price is right on this mulch, especially since it is no longer welcome in most landfills. Grass, fine textured and prone to settling into a dense mat, breaks down quickly to release beneficial nitrogen. It is likely to harbor weed seeds, however, if you do not use an herbicide on your lawn. And, if you do treat your lawn, you may not want to have those chemicals around your edibles. To make the most of your grass clippings as a mulch for your garden, limit the sprays you use on your yard, mow frequently before seed heads form, and mix the clippings with something coarser, like ground corn cobs or shredded leaves.

Newspaper. This is a processed plant product that makes a good mulch if you stick to black-and-white newsprint. Colored inks and glossy papers may contain chemicals you would not want to let flow into the garden soil. Before you begin mulching, wet the newspaper so it doesn't blow away. You can shred newspaper and use it like straw, or lay three to ten sheets in any given spot. The amount to apply varies by how long you want the mulch to remain in that spot and how much air and moisture exchange nearby crops need. Thicker layers last longer and are more effective in blocking elements. Anchor the layers with soil or rocks, or better yet with straw, compost, or some other more-attractive mulch. This looks good and works twice as well.

Shredded leaves. Contributor Bernard Penczek likes to mulch with maple leaves, which he has in abundance in his yard. "In the fall, I rake them up, grind them, and store them in plastic leaf bags all winter. If they are dry, they don't seem to break down. In the spring when the soil has warmed up, I mulch with a 3-inch layer around strawberries, tomatoes, peppers, carrots, and onions, if I have enough. This keeps moisture levels more even and reduces all but the most persistent weeds. I till the mulch under in the fall as a soil amendment."

Ornamental mulches. If you mix your edibles into your ornamental garden or just enjoy the look of attractive mulches, you may want to use shredded bark or bark chunks. You can buy these bagged or by the truckload, or make your own. Recycle pruning scraps with a chipper/shredder, if you have one. The finer products are more likely to carry weed seeds; the coarser products may look out of scale with fine-textured vegetables and herbs.

Other options. As you look around your yard, neighborhood, or local farms or manufacturers, you may find landscape leftovers, pulverized hops, mushroom compost, cocoa and buckwheat hulls, crushed corn cobs, or other organics in need of recycling. Give any of these a try.

MAINTAINING THE SOIL AND CATERING TO ROOTS

Although you can easily judge the health of leafy parts of the plant, what is happening below ground to the roots is more mysterious. As you become more experienced, you can make some assumptions by inspecting the parts of the plant you can see. They often echo the health of what is happening below, as well as indicate how conducive to good growth the fertility and structure of the soil is (for more on soils, see chapter 1).

Occasionally, specific crops need special treatment above and beyond good soil preparation. Corn stalks — and sometimes sunflowers — are less likely to topple if you mound earth up around the bottom of the stem. Bernard Penczek puts a hiller attachment on his rototiller. Early in the season, he makes several passes between the corn rows, rerouting soil on to the planted areas. "The roots grow above ground, right into the hill, so they are better supported," Penczek says. Potatoes produce more prolifically if their stems are well covered with soil. To make celery and leeks more tender, blanch

To provide support for shallow-rooted corn, mound earth around the base of the stems.

by covering them with soil before harvest.

Some crops are easily damaged by careless soil handling, like hoeing too deeply or too near crops, pulling out large weeds that are in the crop's root zone, or trampling the soil too near the plant. Be especially careful when working near young crops that do not have extensive roots or around shallow-rooted crops like onions. A small setback early in the plant's life can influence the entire season. For instance, young corn plants develop surface-clinging fibrous roots that are easily damaged by an over-aggressive hoe. Once corn tassles, however, the roots grow as deep as 3 feet, and you can then hoe with an easy mind.

WEEDS

Try to keep the garden free of weeds that otherwise would steal sun, space, nutrients, and moisture away from your crops. Be certain to pull, cut, or hoe down the weeds before they go to seed. I like to hoe, which limits the amount of kneeling and stooping I have to do. I hoe the way I sweep a floor, by scraping the flat blade along the surface of the garden. The idea is to sweep out the debris and weeds but not to dig so deeply you take the "finish" off the floor. Hoeing lightly loosens the soil surface and lets in more air, but it also increases evaporation a bit.

Hoe by sweeping shallowly along the surface of the soil to rid it of debris and weeds.

Inevitably, you will have to hand weed or clip weeds off with pruning shears, especially in closely planted areas or wide beds. Alternatively, you can rototill between widely spaced single rows to keep paths weed-free.

It is easy to keep weeds between rows under control, since they are easy to identify and hoe. Some, however, look very much like certain crop plants — pigweed in potatoes, lamb's quarters in bush beans, or oxalis among johnny-jump-ups in the flower edging. Look closely to find weeds when young. If a large weed sneaks past you, cut it off with pruning shears. Be sure to handle the plant gently so you don't shake the seeds off.

A weeding system can help. Establish a regular time every week to pull or hoe weeds. Double that time allocation in spring or after rain, when more weed seeds germinate. Don't neglect weeding later in the season. Some weeds go to seed twice as fast then.

The following are some common weeds found in much of the United States and some organic methods for their disposal.

Bindweed

Bindweed. This relative of morning-glories wraps itself around any crop and cuts off its sun and air. Once bindweed flowers, it sets copious seeds, and each seedling develops a shallow, fleshy taproot that can run along for many feet below the soil surface. The root has regular nodes, each of which grows into a separate shoot if given the chance. Rototilling is thus not a good solution, as it will only make one root into many. Loosen the soil, and follow this root as deeply as possible — pull it up before it goes to seed. If you are persistent, you can keep bindweed under control.

Dock. This burr-fruited weed is another with a long root. Unlike bindweed, however, dock roots run deep, like those of dandelion, so it is hard to pull them all out. Moisten the soil first, and use a dandelion digger.

Dock

Chickweed. This creeping annual has small, daisylike flowers that bloom from the first touch of warmth in spring (or even winter) through the fall. In the process, it sets hundreds of seeds and can quickly take over a garden. It is easy to pull up, however. Be sure to get it before it goes to seed. To help deter chickweed, grow a cover crop in empty garden spaces.

Chickweed

Ground ivy. This member of the Mint Family creeps on the soil surface, sending out roots on its new stems. This growth habit makes it impossible to pull the whole plant out at one time. It regenerates from both seed and stem sections and is especially difficult to remove from perennial beds. Pull up as much as you can before it goes to seed.

Purslane. Another creeper and rooter, this succulent colonizes large areas by sprouting from tiny seeds or fleshy stems. It is best to pull the weed quickly and move the uprooted pieces out of the garden. You might put them in your salad bowl — they are a delicacy.

Other common weeds. You will also want to be on the lookout for thistles, which have bristly, piggyback-riding seedpods; lamb's-quarters, identifiable by their triangular leaves that are grayish underneath; mustards, distinguished by their toothed leaves and yellow flowers; pigweed, a coarse plant with bristly flower spikes; smartweed, a succulent with sheathing stems and pink flowers; and oxalis, with foliage like a three-leaved clover and seedpods that catapult their seeds. All of these are prolific seeders.

In addition to these widespread varieties, you will have local weeds to deal with. In the South, it may be kudzu; in the West, tumbleweed can be a problem. I once used a truckload of topsoil from a perennial nursery. For the next three years, I weeded out *Dianthus* and *Viola* seedlings.

You will also have to debate the dilemma of the self-sowers. Are seedling tomatoes, basil, parsley, dill, arugula, and lettuce weeds, or productive members of your garden? In my opinion, that depends on where they emerge and what their ancestry is. I usually let "volunteer" plants grow unless they are crowding a crop I am specifically counting on. I am more ruthless with seedling tomatoes, which are usually not as good as their hybrid parents. I welcome seedlings of open-pollinated plants, especially on the outskirts of the garden. A squash that came up in the compost pile one year proved to be able to evade cucumber beetles and became my most productive plant. Arugula and lettuce come up when conditions are right at the end

CASE STUDIES: NUTRITION AND TOMATOES

When it comes to growing tomatoes, many gardeners develop their own systems, rather like trying to build a better mousetrap. Among the most novel methods are those of Leopold Klein, author of *100 pounds of Tomatoes out of an Inexpensive Foam Box* (see "Suggested Reading"), and Bill Bricker, President of Bricker's Organic Farm, who grows 100 pounds of tomatoes per plant.

Bricker suggests that you make a compost pile in the fall and enclose it in a ring of wire fencing. Layer straw, leaves, and hay with nitrogen-rich fertilizer or blood meal. In the spring, plant tomatoes just outside the ring. Make a hole for each tomato 2 feet square, loosen the soil within, and mix in 1 cup Kricket Krap (which Bricker sells) or 16-4-8 fertilizer. Water well, and let the soil rest for three days. Remove all the side branches except the top two from each tomato plant, and sink the stem deeply enough so that only the top tuft of leaves emerges. If the weather is warm, mulch with a fungal-free mulch, such as straw or pine bark. To prevent fungus diseases, soak the plant with seven-day-old compost tea. If you touch tobacco, wash your hands before handling the tomato plant. As the tomato plant grows, prune off suckers and tie the main vine to the compost cage with old pantyhose.

Bricker plants tomatoes around wire-enclosed compost.

Leopold Klein has been doing tomato-growing experiments for forty years. He advocates making a bottomless 22-inch box of plastic foam sheets held together with wire strands. This insulates against summer heat, is easy to make, and may last as long as seven years. In the spring, you can top the box with a clear plastic greenhouse and start the plants extra early. Place the box in full sun, and fill with topsoil enriched with fertilizer and lime, if necessary. You can plant four tomato plants, one in each corner, if you stake, or five to six plants if you let them hang over the side. Water with 5-10-5 liquid fertilizer weekly and give the plants 1 to 4 gallons water every twenty-four hours.

of the season, becoming automatic season extenders.

NUTRIENTS

Chapter 1 contains information about how to evaluate and improve your soil. As the garden grows, you may now begin to see symptoms of nutrient shortages or overages. Different crops may use more or less of different nutrients — a good reason to rotate crops and vary demands on the soil. Too much of a certain element can burn roots or alter normal growth patterns. Nutrient deficiencies can be hard to distinguish from diseases (see box, pages 102–103).

If a growth problem arises and a nutrient imbalance is not obvious, get help from a soil test, professional horticulturist, or local horticultural society before dumping on additional fertilizer.

Contributing harvest gardeners offered their secrets for success when growing individual crops:

◆ Judy Lowe sprinkles Epsom salts around her pepper plants to keep them dark green and to bring in a larger harvest.

◆ Bernard Penczek finds abundant nitrogen essential for his peppers. "A lot of gardeners have problems growing peppers, but I seem to have pretty good luck with them. I get fifteen to twenty-five peppers per plant on Park's Whopper or Big Bertha. I give them high nitrogen — just the opposite of tomatoes. If I did the same on tomatoes, they would become all vine and no fruit," says Penczek. Penczek also sidedresses his onions three times a season with either 5-10-10 or 10-10-10 fertilizer.

◆ Bill Bricker gets bigger, sweeter onions by using industrial grade urea (which is 46 percent nitrogen) and saturating the 12-inch-deep bed once a week to flush out excess salt. He also sidedresses them once a month with Kricket Krap (which is rated 4-3-2).

> Eleanour Sinclair Rhode wrote, "In the olden days, cottagers' gardens were usually rich in natural manure. In such soil, the stumps [what remains of cabbage plants after the head is harvested] continued to afford a supply of greens for a long period. Unless in very rich ground, cabbage stumps yield a poor crop."
>
> *Eleanor Sinclair Rhode, 1938*

◆ Deb and Paul Doscher fertilize the entire garden with a water-soluble and organic fertilizer in the spring and whenever plants begin to look yellow.

NUTRIENT DEFICIENCY: SIGNS AND SOURCES FOR CORRECTING

Nutrient	Deficiency Symptom	Common Source	Comments
Macronutrients — Necessary in larger quantities for normal plant growth; listed on fertilizer labels as N-P-K:			
Nitrogen (N)	Slow growth, yellow color, especially new leaves	Manure, bloodmeal, fish emulsion	In excess, makes root and fruit crops grow lavishly, but without producing many flowers or fruit. The type of fertilizer makes a difference in how quickly the plant uses it and how long it remains effective in the soil. Organic sources may need some decomposition before they become available to plants.
Phosphorus (P)	Stunting, purple foliage	Rock phosphate, bonemeal, superphosphate	It is important for good root, flower, and seed development; strong stems; and disease resistance. If peppers lack phosphorus, their leaves may narrow and turn gray.
Potassium (K)	Slow growth, older leaves turn bronze colored, weak stems, poor flowering and fruiting	Sulfate of potash, greensand, seaweed, wood ashes	Contributes to vigor and disease-fighting abilities of the plant. Helps plants use nitrogen.
Micronutrients — Needed in limited quantities and may or may not be present in fertilizers; read fertilizer label for specifics:			
Calcium	Poor crop development, stunting, woody stems	Limestone, eggshells, wood ashes, oyster shells	Especially needed by cole crops and to avoid blossom end rot in tomatoes and peppers. In large quantities, makes soil alkaline and can tie up iron and zinc.
Boron	Stunted or brownish cauliflower, rutabagas, beets, and carrots	Borax, manure	

Nutrient	Deficiency Symptom	Common Source	Comments
Copper	Bleached lettuce, thin-skinned onions	Chelated metal, blends of trace elements	Can be tied up in acidic soils.
Iron	Chlorotic foliage (leaves yellow, veins green)	Iron chelate	
Magnesium	Discolored patches on foliage	Epsom salts, dolomitic limestone	
Manganese	Sluggish growth, leaf discoloration	Manganese oxysulfate	Can be tied up in alkaline or over-limed soil.
Sulfur	Poor growth	Sulfur	Makes soil more acidic.
Zinc	Yellow and/or mottled tomato, mustard, and squash leaves	Zinc sulfate	Can be tied up in very acidic or alkaline soils.

Note: Use caution if you amend to correct a trace-mineral deficiency. Too much of a trace element can be as damaging to growth as too little.

◆ G. M. Dunn, from New Hampshire, recommends using plenty of phosphorus under tomatoes. "It is the only major nutrient that won't burn seedlings and that can be safely used in the row."

◆ Hazel Weihe and Virginia and Ed Nix prefer compost and manure over any other kind of fertilizer. These products provide nitrogen as well as most of the essential micronutrients. The Nixes compost leaves, grass, and horse manure for up to two years and then lay the finished compost on the bottom of the row before planting. They may supplement with a blend of fish emulsion and Bt (*Bacillus thuringiensis* — see page 108) when cabbages suffer from caterpillars. All root crops get extra bonemeal.

SUSTAINABLE AGRICULTURE

Contributor Debbie Pleu, supporter of sustainable agriculture and owner of Earthly Goods Farm and Garden Supply in Tulsa, Oklahoma, takes garden additives seriously.

"I think we need to start taking better care of the soil we grow our food and fiber on," says Pleu. To begin with, she advocates using only clean amendments that work naturally with soil processes, as Nature planned. This is the approach of sustainable agriculture, using pure rock minerals and animal by-products instead of synthetic materials to create a healthy soil.

Most of these amendments must degrade before they release their nutrients, and it can take a year or longer to produce results. Applied in fall, minerals like limestone and rock phosphate have the winter to begin to break down; their effects are then revealed in spring. Nitrogen sources like blood meal, feather meal, leather tankage, fish meal and emulsion, and hoof and horn meal, however, are more water soluble; wait until spring to add them. Handle pests and weeds using natural methods, so that soil microbes remain active and continue to decompose amendments.

"It is best to apply just what you need when it is needed, rather than give the total requirement in spring and no more. The soil overdoses," Pleu says.

"I look at feeding a plant the same way I regard feeding people. You need good balanced meals daily. Treat your soil as if it was your dinner table. Put a balanced diet on it every season."

Correcting Deficiencies

To adjust a bed for a certain nutrient-hungry crop, or to revitalize tired soil, dig in nutrients beneath or beside the planting row. Or, add water-soluble nutrients when transplanting seedlings or whenever plants need a fast shot in the arm. When larger-scale corrections are necessary, you may sprinkle fertilizer over an entire bed and rototill or shovel it in to spread it around. At the same time, you can begin long-term correction with organic rocks, minerals, and animal products, as well as additional organic matter.

The following are some nutrient-adding alternatives that will affect plants differently:

Water-soluble fertilizers. Whether synthetic or organic, water-soluble fertilizers work especially quickly on plants. They are absorbed through leaves and roots. Use caution with concentrated fertilizers, which can burn plant tissues. Come the first heavy rain, you can expect most of the water-soluble nutrients to wash off, a problem that has caused concern for watersheds and water tables. Some organic growers also believe that a quick shot of nutrients can upset the natural ecology of the soil, possibly limiting beneficial organisms that would deter disease and release other nutrients.

Granular fertilizers. These release nutrients more slowly when dissolved by rain or irrigation water. In my garden, I use a granular once or twice on long-growing crops, and then hit individual slow-growing plants that need a boost with some water-solubles as needed. In areas of the garden that I have heavily enriched with manure and compost, however, neither may be necessary —a time-, money-, and environment-saver.

Mined mineral elements. Limestone, granite meal, greensand (a potassium-rich underwater deposit), and rock phosphate are some of the mined mineral elements that slowly release nutrients as they break down in the soil. Although they may not help this season's crop, they gently enrich the soil without disrupting natural cycles. They tend to be more expensive than synthetic products but can last for years.

Synthetic fertilizers containing ammonium or nitrate. These fertilizers allow plants to absorb the extra nitrogen immediately. Instead of these, you may wish to use organic fish emulsion or blood meal, which require conversion by soil microbes and thus do not work as fast.

Seaweed fertilizers. These products have gained a solid reputation in recent years. Contributor Debbie Pleu says they increase photosynthesis, root development (and thus tolerance to drought), and root membrane permeability, and they decrease susceptibility to frost, insect, and disease damage. A seaweed spray even chased flea beetles off her tomato seedlings.

Blends of beneficial nitrogen-fixing and humus-making microbes, enzymes, and major and minor nutrients. These blends are a new class of bioactivators that have been praised across the country. In my garden, they seem to be more helpful where compost and manure are minimal and the microscopic soil environment is depleted. One of these is Nitron Industries Formula A-35, a catalyst that helps release and activate nutrients already in the soil. It is said to loosen soil, aid germination, and improve nutrient exchange. "I have tried Nitron Formula A-35 and it really seems to have an almost startling effect on the germination rate of seeds," writes Rose Marie Whiteley.

The Ringer Corporation is another manufacturer that specializes in biological fertilizers. "Our fertilizer is not just organically produced but also a special blend of microbes and enzymes. We take our formulas from biologically active soils and from research that shows which microorgansims reduce disease and break down natural material the best," says Rob Ringer, company president. "We give you a complete system. Even if you were to spread it on cement, you would have everything you needed for plants to grow."

PESTS AND DISEASES

A vigorous plant, grown with enough light, nutrients, moisture, and fresh air — especially a plant endowed with some disease resistance — is less attractive to pests and diseases. The principle is the same as for humans: Those of us who, at the start of the winter cold and flu season, are well rested and fed are less likely to suffer runny noses and watery eyes.

Where disease is a chronic problem, buy cultivars with disease resistance. If there are none available or appropriate, take steps to prevent infection: For instance, to avoid spreading disease spores, don't bustle around in the garden when the plants are wet. "I try to stay out of the garden when it is damp in the early morning or after a heavy rain," says Bernard Penczek. "I am convinced that people do transmit diseases from one end of the row to the other, especially when the row is beans." You may also try a preventative fungicide spray, perhaps a low-toxicity organic product. Before use, read the label carefully and see harvest guidelines in chapter 5.

If you do find a plant that is wilted, blighted, or spotted beyond repair, pull it out and bag or burn it so the disease won't spread. Cut diseased branches off fruiting bushes, and disinfect the pruning shears with bleach between each cut. At the end of the growing cycle, remove all plants and compost the healthy ones. Till the soil and cut back any remaining debris to eliminate winter hiding places for disease spores.

When insect problems arise, try the Integrated Pest Management (IPM) approach. The philosophy behind IPM is simple: Excuse small losses, or plant a little extra for the inevitable scavengers. Limit pest numbers by encouraging insect predators and parasites, installing traps and barricades, or, as a last resort, spraying with the least-toxic product that is effective. Try nearly benign insecticidal soap, Bt, or botanical products first. (For more information on common pesticides, see pages 127-131.) Here are some of a variety of options:

Traps. Using some kind of attractant, these draw pests away from crops and trap them in containers or sticky traps that immobilize them. Be aware, however, that some of the best-known Japanese beetle traps may not be the most effective, since they may be drawing all the beetles in the neighborhood and thus do you a disservice.

What you plant as a garden border can attract or repel pests. Nasturtiums draw aphids, which you can then blast with a spray from the garden hose; marigolds discourage root nematodes.

Let slugs and other lovers of cool, damp places accumulate under boards or rocks, and then step on them. Leave them a bowl of old beer set with the rim at ground level. Once slugs crawl in, they cannot get out. During damp weather, I have caught hundreds this way. Just be sure to clean the bowls out frequently, because they become very smelly.

Use yellow-colored traps coated with sticky Tanglefoot to attract aphids and whitefly. Hazel Weihe coats similar yellow disks with vegetable oil to find out when whiteflies arrive in the tomato garden. She then washes most of the tiny pests off with a hose. "They usually end up stuck to the disks," Weihe writes.

Barriers. You can use barriers to keep some insects away from their preferred foods. Floating row covers are the best way to keep most bugs off plants that do not require pollination, or even off the young plants of varieties that do. Cover the newly planted crops with this new breed of lightweight fabric, leaving enough slack so the fabric can rise up over the growing plants. If secured where it touches the soil, a row cover will deter many insects, including caterpillars, moths and butterflies, beetles, and flies that lay the maggot eggs that riddle root crops. Unfortunately, soil-tunneling grubs can still do their worst, or flying insects may move to unprotected crops. These glitches are uncommon in my garden, however.

Surround the stems of young seedlings with a tight paper collar to prevent cutworms from severing the stem. Sprinkle wood ashes, coarse sand, or granular fertilizer around plants to keep slugs away.

Hand picking. Physically removing pests from plants by hand picking is not my favorite job. It makes a good nature lesson for my boys, however. They revel in discovering the perfectly camouflaged cabbage worms on the cole crops. You may get animals to do your work for you — some people turn chickens loose in their gardens to catch the pests.

Beneficial insects. Just as lions eat gazelles, some insects eat those who munch on your plants. Others lay their eggs in or on garden pests; as the beneficials raise their young, they kill the host. You can buy predators or parasites of insect pests through mail-order catalogues or encourage them to come naturally to your garden by giving them a diversity of crops to hide and feast among. If you choose the beneficial insect route, do not spray with pesticides that will harm them, or you will lose your protection and investment. You also will have to tolerate some insect damage. After all, there must be some plant eaters for the beneficials to prey upon.

If you are ordering a shipment of insects or a timed sequence of repeat releases, order early. I called a company for whitefly killers and spined soldier bugs but got only the whitefly parasites. Most mail-order sources were sold out of spined soldier bugs. The bean beetles, which the soldier bugs would have relished, thus thrived.

Nontoxic sprays. A little soap can go a long way. Blend a teaspoon or two of a mild soap in a quart of water. Avoid soaps with additives that burn plant leaves. You may also try commercially produced insecticidal soaps, which are becoming quite popular. Sometimes a blend of garlic and hot peppers is enough to turn some insects away. "Very hot chilis can be ground fine, mixed with water, strained, and sprayed on plants to ward off soft-bodied insects like aphids," writes contributor Dave DeWitt, who grows about thirty cultivars of chili peppers each year.

For caterpillars, try a little *Bt,* a nontoxic bacteria sold under several different brand names, including Dipel, Bt/berliner-kurstake (for caterpillars), Bt/kurstake Bait (for European corn borers), and Bondide or M-One (for Colorado Potato beetles). I use *Bt* against the cabbage looper on cabbages and other cole crops, but it works on any caterpillar that eats leaves coated with the bacteria. In the day or so it takes to halt them, they contine to eat, though eventually their damage diminishes.

Botanical insecticides. When other options do not work, I turn to botanical insecticides. Pyrethrum is my favorite for most insects. It decomposes rapidly when exposed to light and can kill caterpillars, aphids, beetles, and bugs. For more information on pesticides see pages 127–131.

POLLINATION

Among the beneficial insects you should encourage are the pollinators. If you grow small fruits or melons, cucumbers, pumpkins, or squashes, you will soon realize the value of honeybees, nature's pollinators. Actually, they really don't deserve *all* the credit because bumblebees, hummingbirds, some beetles, and flies also pollinate plants. Bees, however, do most of the work in a garden.

These nectar- and pollen-feed-

KEEPING HONEYBEES

Honeybees are the primary means for pollinating fruit trees, bush fruit (including raspberries, blackberries, gooseberries, and currants), strawberries, and cucurbits (including cucumbers, cantaloupe, pumpkins, watermelons, and squash). "We need bees or we won't get fruit," says Victor Thompson, retired apiarist for Ohio State University. But, you probably don't need to keep your own hive in an average-size home garden, Thompson adds.

Thompson keeps two colonies near his garden in northwest Columbus, Ohio. Since he lives in an urban location, his bees roam for several miles to find enough flowers to support the hive. His own garden is well covered, and the fruit bushes produce quite well, with few misshapen fruit. Exceptions occur when the weather is too cool or wet for bees to be active while the plants are blooming.

Even if your area is short on pollinating insects, Thompson does not recommend casually setting out your own hive, unless you are willing to learn some basics so you can care for the bees. Rather, rent hives from knowledgeable beekeepers who know how to tend the colonies.

Thompson became interested in insects as a teenager, earned two agricultural degrees in beekeeping, and has worked with bees for fifty years.

ing creatures carry pollen from one flower to the next and from one plant to another. Since honeybees visit one species of plant at a time, they are the most efficient workers. Flowers have developed intricate forms, tunnels, and even ultraviolet guides to channel bees and butterflies past the pollen to the nectar reward. Brushing past the stamen, they are smeared with pollen, which they pass on to the female portion of the next blossom they visit.

Some crops do not need insect pollinators. Peas, beans, tomatoes,

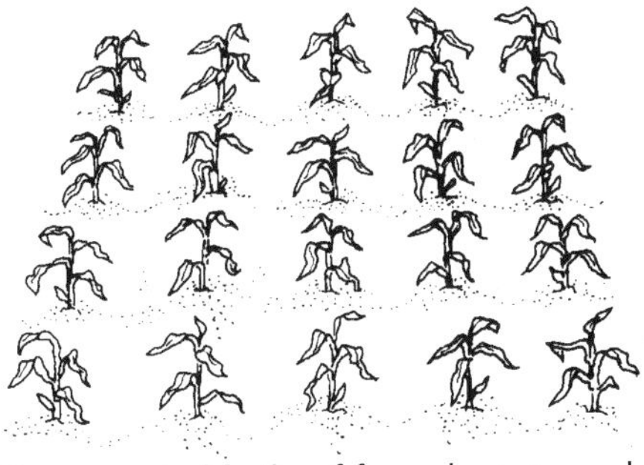

Plant corn in blocks of four plants in each direction to ensure adequate pollination.

and peppers develop fruit with their own pollen. Corn, on the other hand, requires wind to carry its lightweight pollen from one plant to another. Since this method is more random, corn should be planted in blocks of at least four plants in each direction to ensure adequate pollination. If your planting is smaller or if you have found the wind to be inadequate, you may try spreading the pollen by hand.

DAMAGE: COSMETIC OR DESTRUCTIVE?

If you pick a few tomatoes with white scorch marks or a few lettuce leaves with brown margins, evaluate the extent of the damage. If a beetle has chewed a small hole in a lettuce leaf, you can easily trim it off. If the interior of a tomato is blighted, however, it is not safe to eat.

Sometimes it is hard to tell surface from interior damage without cutting into the fruit. You may have a clue if you see small insect tunnels heading into the interior or if the fruit feels unusually soft or mushy. For the acid test, take a knife out into the garden with you and cut into the fruit. I sometimes slice out bad sections right there, so I don't have to bring them into the house. It is probably best to cut away spotted, dotted, or partially blighted portions and eat the remainder right away, because it will not keep well. Do not use such fruits in your dried, canned, or frozen goods.

"I am pretty cautious when it comes to canning," says contributor Deb Doscher. "I won't use anything blemished or even questionable, although I might cut it up and put it in a salad. I had food poisoning years ago and never want to go through that again."

five

Think Before You Pick

YOUR PLANNING and tending of the garden have paid off. Root crops are fat and sweet, tomatoes are juicy and red, peas are bursting at their seams. At my house, we tend to snatch the first of the crop and eat it right out in the garden. Sun-warmed or touched with dew, the flavor and texture — even of fingerling baby snap beans — is delightful. In my opinion, this is the ultimate experience for anyone who savors delicious food, and it certainly would wake up the taste buds of nongardeners, who have to satisfy themselves with much less fresh produce.

Plucking garden goodies and popping them into your mouth is fine for special occasions — or if you just can't help yourself. But the time will come when you want to gather enough for a meal. To do so successfully, you need to know a bit about harvesting, storing, and transporting different crops, even different cultivars. Some crops are best picked and cooked right away. Others taste better if harvested at certain times of the day and stored until mealtime. Some will stay crisp and sweet in the harvest basket for an hour or more; others need special treatment while you comb the garden for other harvestables. Furthermore, not everything is a candidate for popping into the refrigerator. Tomatoes, for instance, lose aroma and flavor when chilled.

The goal of this chapter is to get you organized before you harvest anything. It's important to know when to harvest what, and what to do with the harvest once you get it indoors. Once you are prepared, picking is easy and every vegetable or berry you eat later will taste as good as those nibbled in the garden. The key to preserving fresh flavor is to head off delays. Imagine these scenarios:

You are out harvesting on a beautiful sunny Sunday. A friend drops by and you gab for an hour. You return to the garden — oops, you left the beans and lettuce out in the sun. They've gone flabby. Too bad you weren't better organized. If you had put them in plastic bags in the shade or in a cooler, they would have stayed firm longer.

Another time, you are ready to bring a big bunch of carrots in. You wash the roots off well in the sink. Oops — clogged with soil, the sink backs up. If you had been organized, you could have rinsed them off outside and saved this mess from happening.

On another day you dash out into the garden before work to grab a few things for dinner. The vegetables are stubborn and will not yield without a fight. Carrots snap off in the soil; cucumbers and zucchini stab you with their spines; eggplant cling tenaciously to the plant with their fibrous stalks. You now realize you should have brought your gloves, clippers, and a shovel. Instead of picking quickly, you find yourself running back to the house, shed, garage, and basement searching for the right tool. You may actually find you don't have what you need and have to go borrow from the neighbor or, worse yet, buy the tool.

Just before you are ready to give up, you finally discover the flat-nosed spade buried under the sandpaper in the basement. You may be a little late for work, but you think you can run out there and get those carrots. You dash out, kneel down beside the raised bed, and run your pantyhose or get a big blotch of mud on your linen suit. You forgot the kneeling pad, too. You now have to change clothes and you are really late, grumpy, and still don't have anything picked for dinner.

These scenarios may seem ideal for a Three Stooges comedy routine, but believe me, I can relate them to you from personal experience. If you want to do justice to yourself, your schedule, and your crops, plan ahead.

WHEN DO YOU NEED TOOLS?

Plucking something you grew from a vine in your backyard is a down-to-earth feeling, much like digging bare toes into warm sand, and having crops that snap or slip off easily in your bare hands can have certain advantages. You can use your sense of touch to evaluate when a fruit is "done." For instance, squeeze the swellings of peas and beans to see if the contents are mature. Gently press tomatoes and strawberries to see if they are soft and ripe. Press your thumb lightly on the skin of an eggplant; if it leaves a temporary depression, the vegetable is ready for kitchen duty. With your finger, probe the shoulders of root crops to get an inkling of how their below-ground portions are faring. Check whether the cantaloupe is ready to slip free from its vine by lifting it or shifting the stem. It will slide free if ready. Work your hands through block plantings of lettuce or herbs and select by feel tender inner and mature outer leaves; weed out any look-alike weeds or renegade crops that otherwise could spoil the salad. Twist off Brussels sprouts rather than wielding a cumbersome kitchen knife.

On the other hand, you will not always be able to manhandle the harvest with bare hands alone. Unless fruit and vegetables pop easily off their stems, you can damage both the harvest and the mother vine by twisting, turning, and tearing the whole structure to remove it. There is no reason harvesting cannot be a quiet, gentle experience.

Likewise, for your own sake, you may not want to finger everything. If you pick a sprig of herbs, you will wear the essence for the whole day. If you prune your tomatoes while plucking, your fingers can be stained black. (Hazel Weihe soaks her hands in household chlorine bleach to remove the black stain.) Stick your hand into a zucchini or eggplant bush, and you may be rewarded with a spine under the fingernail. You may want to use a tool in many conditions.

Cutting tools. Use a cutting tool, such as a knife or pruning shears, to sever the heads from cabbage, broccoli, cauliflower, and Chinese cabbage plants. Cut head lettuce, celery, radicchio, and corn salad at the base, preserving their handsome heads or rosettes. Alternatively, you can pull up the entire plant, roots and all, for a longer storage life. Or, shear off cut-and-come-again greens like leaf lettuce, chives, and mesclun and let them resprout.

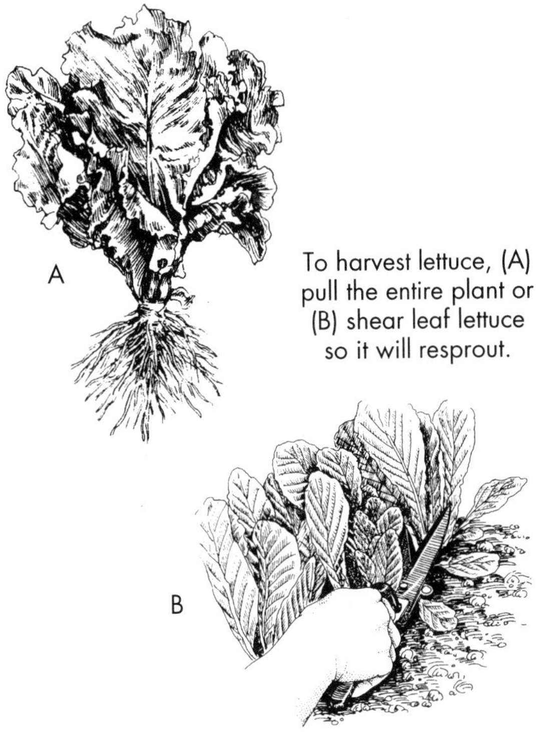

To harvest lettuce, (A) pull the entire plant or (B) shear leaf lettuce so it will resprout.

Cut off sprigs of woody-stemmed herbs, like thyme, sage, rosemary, and winter savory. Shear or shape the herb with pruning shears while you harvest the tender young stems. With soft-stemmed herbs, like basil, parsley, dill, chervil, and the mints, pick individual leaves by hand, or for faster progress, use a pair of sharp scissors. To shear off a large quantity of softer-fleshed chives or parsley, try a Stanley utility knife, which has replaceable blades.

Shear bunches of chives with a utility knife.

To avoid breaking the brittle stems of ripe peppers, snip peppers off. Cut through the fibrous stalks of eggplant and some cucumbers. Slice winter squash free at the juncture of stem and vine; be sure to include a long, undamaged stem. Snip off the stem of a strawberry you intend to dip in chocolate.

When you cut or pluck, escape the prickly spines of zucchini, cucumber, cardoon, and okra by growing thornless Park's Burpless bush cucumber and Spineless Zucchini Hybrid, Shepherd's Arlesa low-spine cucumber, or Okra Clemson Spineless. You will find fewer spines on Thai Green, Vigerba, and Bianca Ovale eggplant.

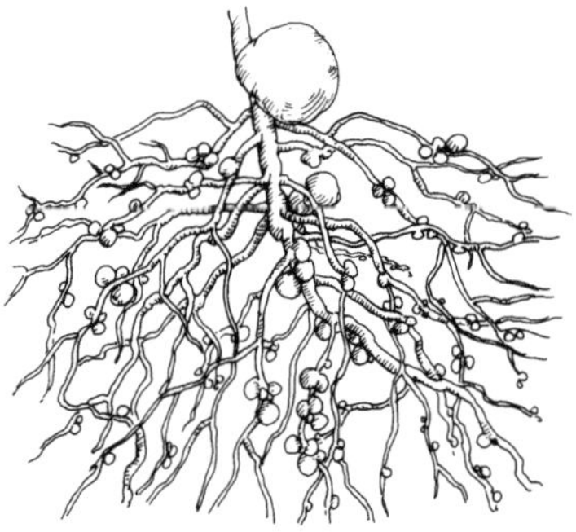

The root system of peas and beans contains nitrogen-fixing nodules that enrich the soil.

Cut off the old stems of peas and beans, and leave the nitrogen-fixing nodules on the roots to enrich the soil.

Digging tools. Use a digging or soil-loosening tool for unearthing potatoes. Contributor Tom Eltzroth uses a straight spade or garden fork to dig potatoes and works slowly in from the outside of the bed. "I've pierced only about a dozen potatoes over a lifetime of gardening," Eltzroth says, "It's the approach you take, not the tool." Alternatively, you can grow potatoes on the surface of the soil by covering the seed potatoes with a thick layer of compost and mulch. "A friend of mine grew potatoes in wood shavings and straw, and they really developed well. All he has to do to harvest now is to push the mulch back," Eltzroth says.

Dig beside deep-rooted parsnips, salsify, black salsify, carrots, parsley root, Daikon radish, and burdock. Use Eltzroth's potato approach, starting beside the bed and loosening the soil so the roots pull up more easily.

Use tools to free long-rooted carrots or cylindrical-rooted beets grown in heavy soil. Eleanour Sinclair Rhode wrote in 1938 that gardeners should spade beet roots out, never fork or pull them, or they will bleed and be worthless.

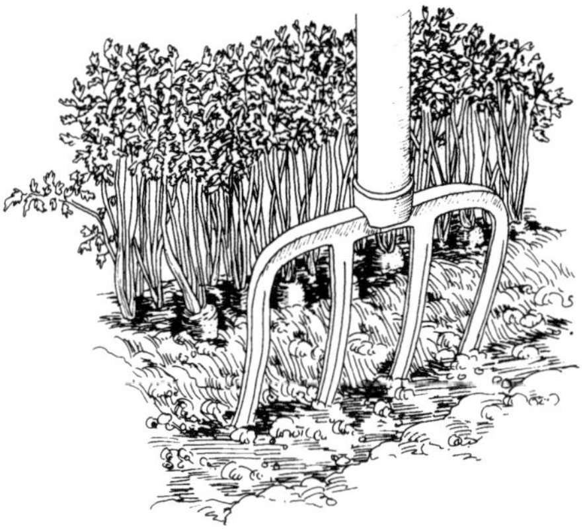

Dig alongside a row of carrots to loosen the soil without cutting into the carrots.

Contributor Chris Werronen finds shoveling large quantities of roots very time consuming. "But if we pull them by hand, they'll just snap off unless the soil is very wet." He is working to raise beds so the soil stays looser and the work is easier. Another alternative is to grow baby carrots or especially strong-topped cultivars, such as Napoli and Rumba or grow globe-shaped beets.

Dig to unearth garlic. Contributor David Stern writes, "For small areas, digging by spade or fork is the harvest technique of choice. Dig straight down several inches away from the plant, lever the handle back away from the row until the plant moves up. Once it's loose, pull out by hand."

Bring a shovel to find all the Jerusalem artichoke tubers before they escape and colonize neighboring areas. Dig systematically and carefully through the area to find them all.

"In taking up the crop, be careful to remove the soil to sufficient depth so as not to injure the roots. The thrust of the spade that easily lifts a carrot without essential injury, will, if applied to the parsnip, break the root of 9 in 10 at scarcely half their length from the surface of the ground. As the roots keep much fresher, and retain their flavor much better, when taken up entire, the best method is to throw out a trench beside the rows, to the depth of the roots, when they can easily, as well as perfectly, be removed."

Fearing Burr, Jr., 1863

SHOPPING FOR TOOLS

More and more seed and nursery companies are adding supplies to their lists to supplement off-season sales. Prices and quality vary from supplier to supplier, so make some comparisons. When you tally prices, be sure to add handling and shipping costs, usually indicated on the order form. You may be able to save by ordering several items from the same supplier for one handling fee, rather than paying repeatedly at separate merchants.

Price is not the only factor to consider. Evaluate the strength and durability of the product. Is there a warranty for the higher-cost merchandise? Will metal pieces rust or bend? Are knives and shears suitable for large as well as small jobs, or do you need a separate tool for each? Will they be comfortable for you to use? Is the grip soft? Are the handles long enough? Are the wheels wide enough not to get stuck in soft soil? Is the company credible, and will they stand behind their merchandise if something is faulty?

Ask your neighbors and friends, local market gardeners, or botanical gardens what kind of tools they are happy with. Tools that stand the test of time are the real bargains.

If you are a do-it-yourselfer, you may be able to create homemade substitutes for simple things like knee pads or harvest aprons at a fraction of the ready-made price. Study catalogue photos and descriptions, or check the construction of accessories at local garden centers.

Evaluating Tools

Imagine that you have decided to buy an inexpensive garden fork for $37, hand shears for $85, a knife for $9, a set of knee pads for $15, a $27 Chesapeake Bay basket, and a garden cart for $198. Buying these from several different companies might add another $25 for shipping and handling. Your total for this order would be $396, enough to buy $3 of vegetables a day for 132 days. On the other hand, should the equipment last ten years, you would amortize their cost over that time and spend the equivalent of 12.4 days' worth of vegetables per year. If you are going to invest in tools, choose products that will last, and in the long run you will save.

When you choose a cutting tool, find one with a sharp blade, and then keep it sharp so it will slice, not crush.

With digging tools, look for one that you can easily handle and that will reach deeply enough to do the job you want. Remember, however, that the deeper it digs, the more soil weight you must lift.

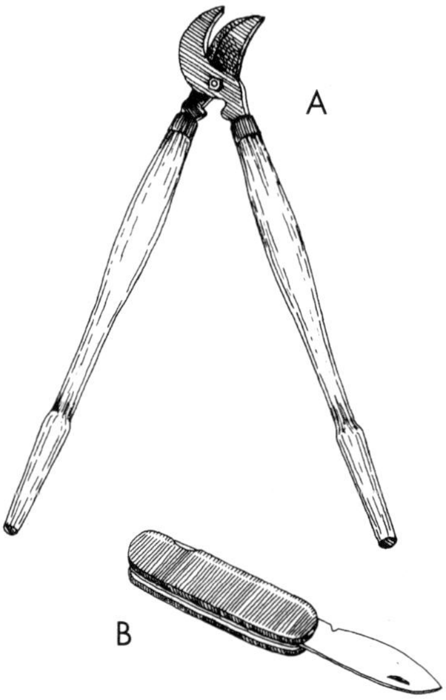

Choose good-quality cutting tools that suit your needs: (A) loppers to clip off hard-to-reach fruits; (B) an easy-to-carry pocket knife.

CLEAN-CUT HARVEST

Be careful not to spread disease while you harvest. If you suspect you are cutting plants with wilts, spots, rots, blights, or other contagious diseases, sanitize the cutting blades by wiping or dipping the tool in Lysol, methanol, or household chlorine bleach diluted 1:1 with water between every cut, or at least before you move on to harvest another plant. Dry the blades well after use so they do not rust.

With these criteria in mind you may find that many household tools will serve as ideal garden harvesters. Chris Werronen is just as happy using a linoleum knife to cut cabbage heads as he would be with a $50 clipper. Eltzroth prefers his pocket knife; he says, "Any time I go to the garden, I automatically carry a knife. It has a fold-up blade and fits in my pocket. It is especially good for cutting zucchini and squash, because I can reach down in the plant with it." I often employ a kitchen knife to sever squash or eggplant, though I do not put it in my pocket. My experience has been that if a knife does a good job paring and slicing in the kitchen, it will work well out in the garden, too. If a knife is dull or too long to handle easily, however, it will be a flop for either use.

I also like my pruning loppers — long-handled pruning shears that are useful for all kinds of garden chores. They let me reach into a tangle of vines, cut the fruit, and grab it by the stem to pull it out without straining my back.

Contributor Hazel Weihe harvests exclusively with her hands or small hand tools. "I crawl around with a trowel because I don't like to lean over or dig. My husband does all that. Usually, by the time harvest comes, all I have to do is pluck crops out. I grow carrots in the cold frame for late fall. I fill the frame with sifted soil, so that it has no stones. They pop right out, nice and straight," Weihe says.

More specialized harvesting tools may or may not be helpful. If you are on the mailing list for mail-order gardening equipment companies, you may be led to believe that you cannot make do without lots of automatic, stainless, natural, penetrating products, all at premium prices.

Were you to buy everything you could possibly use, plus many things you might not need but *could* use if you had them, you could spend several hundred dollars on harvesting equipment. (Make that several thousand if you dabble in automatic harvesting machinery.) Add that to the cost of seeds and supplies, and your garden will be considerably less cost efficient. If you consider the garden to be an artform or a type of entertainment, however, some tools may provide their own enjoyment and that alone may justify their expense.

WHEN DO YOU NEED CONTAINERS?

Once you have the fruit, shoot, or root safely removed, you need to put it in something that will protect it and keep it cool for the trip between garden and house. What kind of container you use depends on how much you are picking and how long you will take to get to the house.

Use containers that are appropriate for the crops you are harvesting.

When I pass the garden and snatch some crops that are ready to be eaten, I sometimes haphazardly stuff them inside my jeans or jacket pocket and rush in to the house, trying not to leave a small trail of escaped vegetables behind me. It is not an ideal system, but it can work. Don't dare duplicate this with soft cherry tomatoes or ripe berries, however, as they will turn into pocket purée.

Save yourself stained pockets and bruised and lost produce by keeping an array of plastic berry baskets, peach crates, and plastic bags within easy reach of the garden like Wendy Krupnick does. Add a few 5-gallon buckets and sturdy laundry baskets for larger things. When my cold frame is out of use in midsummer, I sometimes store containers there where they are within an arm's reach whenever I need them.

I try to have enough containers so I can separate different cultivars, rather than jumbling them in together and losing sight of individual identities. Whenever possible, I try to label crops so I will know just which cultivar I am eating and can compare flavors and keeping qualities. I write the cultivar name and harvest date in waterproof pen on a piece of masking or freezer tape and stick it on a bag or box — or right on squash. If I transfer the produce to the freezer or to a jar, I then just peel off the tape and if it is still sticky, affix it to the new container. (If the glue is low, it is better to replace it with a fresh label.)

Collect soft and succulent items in shallow containers with flat bottoms, and carry the containers levelly to eliminate pile-ups. To keep berries, ripe tomatoes, and the like from being squished, arrange them in a single layer, if at all possible — certainly not more than two layers. Pack large, fat berries in the individual nests in an egg carton.

Use plastic bags to move slightly sturdier things, like greens, which don't need the same physical support as soft items but do need protection from drying out. Put some damp paper towels in the bottom of the bag to raise the humidity. When the bag is about half full, set it in the shade until you can refrigerate the produce. On hot days, it's worth storing perishables in a small cooler containing a refreezable block of ice. You can recycle the cooler to picnic duty when you are not harvesting.

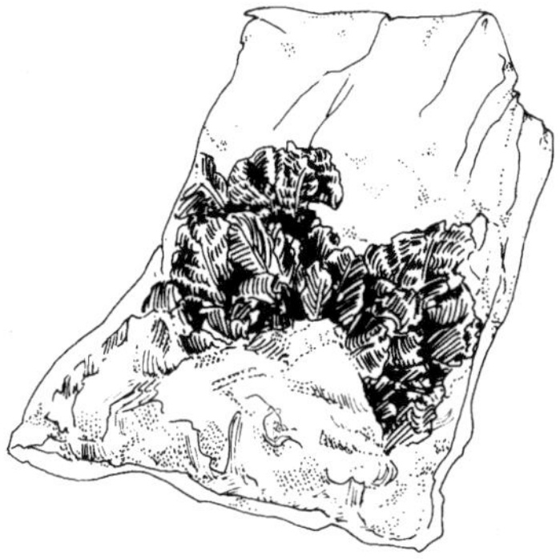

To keep greens moist and crisp, place some damp paper towel in the bottom of the plastic storage bag.

If you reuse plastic containers, wash them well with warm soapy water, and then dry them. If you suspect the last crop held disease spores, throw the container away or disinfect it with a slightly diluted bleach solution. When a bag comes directly from the grocery store, it can have any number of other contaminants on it, such as the juice from raw chicken or pork. Even seemingly harmless bread bags may be coated with hazardous chemicals, the by-products of mechanical packaging.

A brown paper bag will hold produce such as dill, fennel, or mature bean pods for drying without letting the seeds escape. I usually encourage a few to find freedom as volunteers that will bring me a new crop for next year, but I leave the rest to dry in the bag on top of the dehumidifier.

For large volumes of firmer crops, like peppers, snap beans, summer squash, and cucumbers, a 5-gallon plastic bucket is a perfect container. You can buy new ones or rescue used buckets. My husband, Ted, buys ours from his office at wholesale prices. Chris Werronen gets jelly and jam buckets at a discount from a bakery.

I like to collect roots in a laundry basket with a fine weave on the sides. I place a layer or two of harvested roots on the bottom and pull the hose over to get the extra soil off then and there, without messing

For potatoes, a well-sealed dark box or cooler is essential. As you pull the tubers out of the ground, stock them away immediately. Fearing Burr wrote. "In the preservation of potatoes, it is of first importance that they be excluded from the light. If this is neglected, they become not only injurious, but actually poisonous. This is especially true when they are allowed to become a green color, which they readily will do on exposure to light."

Fearing Burr, Jr., 1863

up the kitchen. Remember, though, that some crops keep longer if you wait to wash them until just before you are ready to use them. (For more on washing, see pages 123–126.)

When it comes to the big stuff — the pumpkins and winter squash — a large container on wheels is in order. I use my wheelbarrow, taking care to load it lightly. If I get too ambitious and pile on too many pumpkins, the wheelbarrow may tip. The contents, as well as my shins, then become bruised. If you grow super-sized pumpkins or don't like to try your luck balancing squash in wheelbarrows, you may benefit from a more stable two-wheeled garden cart. Or, make harvesting really easy for yourself and get a cart to hook on behind your riding lawn mower.

You will need a large, wheeled container to move heavy garden produce like pumpkins.

Think about any way you can do two operations with one set of equipment. Can you store the produce in the same container you picked it in? If so, you will save yourself from transfering all the harvest from one container to another and washing out the former for reuse. Any move to minimize dishwashing is a good move! For instance, put cured onions in low, open flats or crates so

GARDEN GROOMING

Many people wait until they get indoors to free their harvest of unnecessary stalks or roots, but I prefer to cut, pull, and pare outdoors whenever possible. I have enough trouble keeping my kitchen clean with two juice-spilling little boys around. Why bother hauling in a big harvest only to haul the remains back outside to the compost pile?

My outdoor grooming method is quite simple. If I am picking a few things for dinner, I just make a sidetrack over to the compost area and twist or cut off what I don't want. If it is time to freeze a bushel of lima beans, I set up a card table under a tree near the compost bin so I can work comfortably. When a head of lettuce or some carrots are especially heavily covered with soil, I rinse them off under the hose before doing a final rinse inside. Garden grooming works with only some crops, however. In general, anything you are going to cook or eat immediately is a candidate for outside cleaning.

Crops You Can Peel Outdoors

Corn. When you have the water boiling inside, pick, shuck, and pull all the silks off the ears outside — a perfect system. If you want to refrigerate sugar-enhanced or supersweet cultivars, however, leave them in the husk so they don't dry out. Let popcorn dry right on the plant inside the husks. When you are ready to rub off the kernels, bring the ears back outside to peel and process.

Eggplant. You can peel eggplant outside, if you are ready to pop it into whatever you plan to cook it in immediately. If you leave it sitting naked too long, however, the flesh will oxidize and brown, rather like an apple.

Peas. Pop green peas out of the pod, if you have a cool place to work. If it is too hot, they will deteriorate faster. You may be better off in the house.

Dried peas and beans. Outdoors is a great location for shelling dried beans and peas; if done inside, they send bits of chaff all over the house.

Green beans and summer squash. Pull off the faded blossoms and bean strings outside.

Asparagus. Peel tough outer fibers on thick stalks outside just before cooking.

When Can You Cut off the Roots?

Leeks. Cut off the roots when you are ready to wash the stems.

Lettuce. If you will be making salad soon, cut off the roots and any yellow leaves outdoors. When you want to keep the foliage perky in the refrigerator for a couple days, however, leave the roots on and let them dangle into a container of water.

Beets. Leave the fibrous roots on while you cook or they will bleed a staining red sap.

Winter storage. You may leave the roots on long storers (for information about root cellaring, see pages 192–199).

When Can You Cut off the Tops?

Peas and beans. I snap off the tops and bottoms of edible-podded peas and beans just before cooking them.

Cole crops. Cut off a head, trim off the side leaves and fibrous stems from cole crops, and fire up the microwave.

Herbs. Trim off the long, tough stems on parsley, thyme, and other herbs outdoors. Compost the remains, or dry and save them to burn in winter fires.

Root crops. Remove the foliage from carrots, radishes, and beets, leaving as little greenery at the top as possible. Moisture is lost through leafy tops, making the roots dry out and become flabby, and eventually decay into a rotten mess. The exception is beets. If you have trouble with them bleeding, twist off the foliage and leave a longer stem stub.

you can move them right out of the garden into the root cellar or basement. Pick edible-podded peas and beans, string them then and there, and plop them into a colander. You can then rinse them and plunk the entire contraption over boiling water to steam. Cucumbers and lettuce will stay crisp in their plastic bags in a cool location; tomatoes will continue to ripen in an open basket at room temperature.

THE WHYS AND HOWS BEHIND WASHING AND DRYING

Although you may wash produce automatically after harvesting, it is not always your best option. In fact, you may be able to extend produce storage life if you delay washing. Furthermore, when you do wash, the method you choose can make a difference. Different techniques can save water *and* flavors, as well as ensure the removal of pesticides and debris. Beyond washing, drying methods can also be vital for some crops.

Tom Eltzroth writes, "In the last 7 or 8 years, I have sprayed with chemicals very little. Beyond using a little mild soap, there is no need to wash things off too much, but berries always seem to have dust or insects on them, so I wash and lightly dry them with a towel before I freeze them."

When can you skip washing? Certain crops do not need washing, because they are kept safely clean beneath a wrapper of leaves, pods, or husks. Assuming insects have not been at work, you can husk ears of corn, shell peas, or peel cucumbers and find a pristine product below. Sometimes, produce grown on mulches or trellises or under floating row covers stays clean enough to escape washing.

The skin of many vegetables has a protective coating that helps prevent decay or dehydration. In fact, washing often removes this barrier and makes the harvest more vulnerable to problems. This is especially true of asparagus, green and dried beans, beets, broccoli, Brussels sprouts, cabbage, cauliflower, chicory, corn, fennel, leeks, okra, parsnips, peas, peppers, radishes, salsify, and summer squash. Likewise, wait to wash long-term storage items like melons, onions, potatoes, rutabagas, winter carrots, and winter squash.

"I wash only stuff that is dirty, such as roots and crops like squash or cucumbers with fuzzy stuff on the skin," says Wendy Krupnick. "I also don't wash anything I blanch and peel, like tomatoes."

Try to minimize washing of culinary herbs, edible flowers, and berries. These can harbor grit or bugs, so they may need some rinsing, but their foliage and flavorings are delicate and cannot take soaking or scrubbing.

On the other hand, it seldom hurts — and often helps — to wash freshly picked greens. They are not long keepers, and they are prone to drying out unless sealed in plastic and/or supplemented with extra moisture.

For other crops, washing is vital.

A FEAST FOR THE EYES

When the garden is in full gear, it is as lovely as any flower garden. Cool blue cabbages, red hot mustards and tomatoes, sunny yellow squash blossoms, orange pumpkins, and the mosaic of green in every hue, shape, and texture make a striking picture. You can absorb the scene as a whole or close in on individual elements. Or, when you are gathering things in containers, you can combine fruit, flowers, and even roots to make an edible bouquet.

Looking down the lens of a camera gives a different perspective on the beauty of the harvest to Tom Eltzroth, a horticulture teacher who spends his summers photographing his garden. In the past, his vegetable gardens have been more than nourishment for his family — they have been the models that you may have seen in *National Gardening, Organic Gardening,* and many other gardening publications. Eltzroth has captured miniature strawberry corn on a blue background; glossy, bursting ears of white-and-cream corn; twining pole bean shoots; miniature white eggplant topped by purple flowers; and the perfect ruby seedless watermelon.

To create a well-rounded picture, the container can be as important as the produce. Eltzroth says he chooses his containers for their appearance. "I like baskets woven with natural materials or shallow wooden boxes. They have to be interesting looking and fit the mood," Eltzroth said. "I occasionally wash the vegetables, too, to give them a little extra sparkle for the photograph." You, too, may want to splurge on some handsome harvest baskets or bowls. After all, you have worked hard to bring in this bounty, and you should be able to savor its beauty as well as its taste.

Create edible art with a bouquet of dill in an antique pitcher.

SOME LOCATIONS FOR CURING AND STORING LONG-LASTING CROPS

While you are getting organized, be sure you have containers and locations for curing and storing long keepers.

Some crops will cure in the sun, as long as they are not damaged by insects or critters. Lay onions on their side and let them dry for a week; cover them with plastic, if it rains. Hazel Weihe cures her onions on a wooden flat in her greenhouse. "The flat lets some air circulate below the onions," she says.

Popcorn and sunflowers dry easily indoors or out, but outside they may need to be covered by nylon-mesh netting to protect the seeds from birds.

Cure winter squash and pumpkins with about ten days of sun. If frost threatens, cover with a tarp at night, or move them indoors. Keep them very warm — 80°–90°F — for three to five days. Cultivars such as Sweet Dumpling and Ebony Acorn don't need curing.

Potatoes need a warm, dry, dark spot to let their skins dry and cure for storage. They may get what they need outside in the hill after the vines die back, but if the weather turns cold or wet, or if mice might find the tubers, you should bring them in.

Low-growers like spinach and thyme that collect grit in their foliage, plants blanched in soil like dirt-trapping leeks, crops sprayed with pesticides, and those grown where air pollution is a problem need thorough cleaning. But washing may be able to wait until you are ready to cook or eat the item.

Washing Methods

Wendy Krupnick lives in California, where water is scarce. She gardens organically and thus does not have to deal with chemical residues. Thus, she advises washing with water conservation in mind. "If you are dealing with produce of unknown origin or have a lot of dirt to deal with, wash in basins of water. Bugs and soil will float away, and you will use less water than if you were to run a faucet. Also, flowing water can miss spots. Never soak produce for over a minute, however, or it will leach out vitamins," she says.

The most thorough job on hard-to-clean greens may come from a hardy swish. Sam Forbes, organic market gardener in Oklahoma City, says, "I wash lettuce in a big trough, sloshing it around between four different tubs. In each tub, it gets a little cleaner. You can do the same thing in the kitchen sink."

For heavy-duty cleaning, you may decide to soak broccoli, cauliflower, or Brussels sprouts in cold salt water for a half hour to eliminate bugs. For leeks, you may need to split each stalk in half and peel off each piece to wash it individually.

City gardeners and pesticide users who harvest crops coated with inedibles may want to supplement clean water with mild soap or a vinegar solution to remove inedible coatings. Furthermore, the National Pesticide Hotline recommends removing pesticide residues under running water. If you dunk them in a tub of water, you may simply recoat the produce with the floating chemicals every time it emerges from the water. (See pages 127–131 for Pesticide Breakdown.)

Drying Methods

How you dry produce is sometimes as important as how you wash it. Wipe or blot delicate items on paper towels or cloth towels washed in a soap that is free of fragrances and additives. Remove any water droplets before fungus spores can germinate in them. Be sure the produce does not sit in a puddle of runoff, which is certain to make them rot. If I am pressed for time, I sometimes blow-dry herbs in front of the air conditioner. Where thorough quick-drying is essential, I roll herbs up in a thick towel and run them through the spin cycle in the washer. A salad spinner removes most of the wash water from greens, leaving enough to keep them fresh and moist, but not so wet they will dilute the salad dressing.

STORAGE

If you are not ready to use your harvest immediately or if you want to store it for future months, you will have to have a suitable place to keep the crop. In some cases, that place will be the refrigerator. Refer to chapter 7 for details on storage needs for individual cultivars.

You should scout out possible storage sites *before* the produce comes rolling in. You may need to use a little creativity to satisfy varying temperature needs. Think about temperature and moisture and how much they will fluctuate in locations like a cold frame, garden shed, storage pit, or window well. Indoors, you may have an unheated room, enclosed porch, attic, or basement with potential.

PREPARE SO THE HARVEST STAYS FRESH

From the moment you pluck a fat root or soft tomato, the clock is ticking. Your harvest is free of its lifeline, the vascular system of the plant. No longer are sugars, enzymes, and hormones pumping through its body to nurture it. At the moment you pick the fruit, it will never be better. You want to capture that perfection on your dinner table or in the freezer or canner for future use. Don't dally trying to find, buy, and assemble assorted kitchen equipment. In the intervening seconds, minutes, and hours, the harvest begins to age.

Get organized before you harvest by collecting all the equipment you need in order to dry, can, or freeze. Preview chapters 7 and 8 for more details.

WHAT TO DO ABOUT PESTICIDE RESIDUES

If you must spray your homegrown produce to control insects or fungi, use a product that is safe for yourself, the environment, and the crop. Safety extends beyond merely choosing the right product and applying it properly. Oily pesticide residues can render a crop inedible for several weeks, especially if you have coated the plant heavily in the first place or if it has the kind of surface that holds residues. For instance, leaf lettuce and curly leaved spinach are notorious for trapping reservoirs of pesticides. Head lettuce will be affected only on the outer leaf layers.

I think of pesticides as similar to human medicine: It's best to avoid using them if at all possible, but if I must take an aspirin or antibiotic, I try to use the lowest dose possible. Tim Closs of the National Pesticide Telecommunications Network at Texas Tech University Health Sciences Center, cautions that even the milder organic pesticides are not entirely trouble-free. They still need to be treated with care.

Before you buy any pesticide or fungicide, read the label carefully. It will list ingredients, directions for use, warnings, and the number of days you should wait between application and harvest. Label information is supplied by the product manufacturer after an extensive period of federally mandated testing. Testing can take from ten to fifteen years and cost the manufacturer as much as sixty million dollars. Tests analyze toxicity to animals, effects on wildlife, how long a product takes to degrade (and what it becomes when it degrades), where it goes in the soil, and how much residue remains on a crop after a certain period of time. With this data, the manufacturer proposes the product label, which is then reviewed and approved by the Office of Pesticide Programs in the Environmental Protection Agency.

When you review these labels, you will see that there is a big difference among products in how long you have to wait to harvest after spraying or dusting. The reasons are not always clear. Seemingly similar products made by different manufacturers may list different waiting times. Closs says the specific formulation as well as the physical and physiological individualities of each crop add many variables. One of the most important variables that Closs looks at is the LD-50, the measure of toxicity of the pesticide. The lower the LD-50 number the more poisonous the chemical is. He then considers short-term symptoms, long-term complications, and other factors. "The more we know about these factors, the better we can start minimizing the risk," he says.

If you have questions about any product, you can call the Pesticide Telecommuncation Hotline twenty-four hours a day at 1-800-858-PEST.

Here is a summary of label information on the more common vegetable garden pesticides. The information comes from the Ortho, Ringer, and Safer Label Guides, the National Pesticide Telecommunication Network, and other sources as noted. The harvest intervals for these specific products are not applicable to other brands.

Malathion. Ortho Malathion has the following recommendations: a one-day delay for asparagus, beans, and okra; three days for broccoli, leeks, and peas; and seven days for Swiss chard, cauliflower, and Brussels sprouts.

According to Sally Lee in *Pesticides,* malathion is a biodegradable organophosphate that kills only certain targeted pests. It can be dangerous if inhaled or touched. Lee notes that organophosphates usually transform into harmless compounds during cooking. One exception is Alar, once used for apples, which was found to cause cancer in lab mice. Likewise, malathion has been found to degrade into a compound that increases the incidence of tumors in lab rats. (Cristine Russell, *American Health Magazine,* 1990).

Sevin. The label of Ortho's Liquid Sevin lists the following waits between application and harvest: one day for asparagus, beans, carrots, corn, cucumbers, melons, squash, peas, peppers, potatoes, tomatoes, eggplant, and strawberries; three days for cabbage, broccoli, cauliflower, radish, roots, and head lettuce; seven days for raspberries; fourteen days for turnip greens, kale, leaf lettuce, spinach, and Swiss chard. The active ingredient in Sevin is carbaryl, a type of carbamate. A newer group of insecticides, carbamates are less persistent in the environment than organophosphates, but they are particularly toxic to bees, says Lee. In addition, carbamates can be converted to carcinogenic nitroso compounds in mammal stomachs (Cristine Russell, *American Health Magazine,* 1990).

Rotenone. Ortho's formulation recommends a one-day wait on vegetables.

Rotenone, originally derived from a tropical tree and found in similar forms in at least sixty-eight species of legumes, is the most potent of the organics. It is moderately toxic on the LD-50 scale. Small doses of rotenone and other ingredients that may be present in natural mixtures can stimulate respiration. Contact with the powder or ointment can cause eye and skin irritation. If eaten, rotenone is about equal in toxicity to DDT, but it is more toxic than DDT when injected. "The toxicity of rotenone and related compounds varies greatly, depending on particle size and manner of dispersion," says Wayland Hayes in *Pesticides Studied in Man.*

Rotenone and Methoxychlor. Ortho Vegetable Garden Insect Dust combines rotenone with methoxychlor and lists a three-day wait for beans; fourteen days for raspberries; one day for potatoes; and seven days for eggplant, melon, and tomato. Methoxychlor is one of the last pesticides in the organochlorine class to remain in use. Others include DDT and chlordane. Methoxychlor is of low toxicity to mammals and birds, but highly toxic to fish.

Pyrethrum. Ortho Tomato and Vegetable Insect Killer, a mixture of pyrethrins and piperonyl butoxide, can be applied up to the day of harvest.

Ringer Yard and Garden Insect Attack with pyrethrin and piperonyl butoxide may also be used up to day of harvest. The label cautions: "Harmful if swallowed. Avoid breathing vapors. Avoid contact with eyes, skin, or clothing. Remove pets from area being treated."

Pyrethrum, a derivative of an African daisy *Chrysanthemum cinerariifolium,* which contains pyrethin as an active ingredient, is considered an organic of low toxicity on the oral LD-50 scale. The United States Department of Health and Human Services and Labor Occupational Health Guidelines notes pyrethrum can cause a rash or hay-fever-like symptoms if inhaled or if it comes in contact with eyes or skin. The Guidelines recommend washing hands thoroughly after use.

Pyrethrins decompose and deactivate with exposure to light, so they do not remain long as residues. Their stability can be increased, however, with additives like piperonyl butoxide. Piperonyl butoxide itself can be slightly poisonous, writes Hayes, since it is feared to encourage liver damage at high levels of exposure. However, one study showed that a dose fifty times greater than what would build up from spraying an aerosol heavily in a small room did not produce a toxic effect in lab animals.

Synthetic pyrethroids, which are laboratory improvements of pyrethrins, can be more effective and less toxic toward mammals than native pyrethrins. The synthetics may remain effective up to ten days after application, however, according to Taunton Press's *Common-Sense Pest Control*. Pyrethroids are sold for tick, termite, and flea control, the book notes, and may not have been formulated into garden products yet.

Insecticidal soaps. Safer's insecticidal soaps break down into harmless substances within two days of application. Although the labels read that these products may be used up to the day of harvest, they still caution, "Harmful if swallowed and avoid contamination of feed and food stuffs."

Insecticidal soap products use potassium salts of soaps to kill a broad range of insects. They damage the outer waxy layer of the insect skin, which makes the pest dehydrate. They are quite useful on soft-bodied insects, but they have little effect on bees. The Pesticide Telecommunication Network calls them quite low in toxicity. *Common-Sense Pest Control* indicates that eating high doses may cause stomach upset, but otherwise no serious effects. Rob Ringer, owner of Safer's and Ringer, which is a supplier of natural fertilizers and pesticides, does advise washing off soap residues. "It doesn't taste very good," he said.

The soaps are sometimes combined with essential oils or other chemicals of botanical origin as with Ringer Aphid-Mite Attack for Fruits and Vegetables, which combines insecticidal soaps and citrus aromatics and which is most effective on newly hatched insects. It is labeled for use up to the day of harvest but cautions, "Contact causes moderate eye irritation. Avoid contact with eyes or clothing. Wash thoroughly with soap and water after handling. Keep out of lakes, streams, and ponds."

Insect diseases. Safer's Bt Caterpillar Killer for cabbage loopers, tomato hornworm, and other leaf-eating caterpillars may be used until the day of harvest.

The Ringer Tomato Worm Attack label reads: "Can be used up to day of harvest and during storage, since there appear to be no harmful residues."

The Ringer Colorado Potato Beetle Attack is 5.6 percent *Bacillus thuringiensis* var. *San diego* (a variety of *Bt*). Label cautions: "Avoid inhalation and contact with eyes, skin, and especially cuts or wounds. When handling this product, wear gloves, dust mask, or equivalent pulmonary tract covering and goggles. Keep out of lakes, ponds, or streams. Do not contaminate water when disposing of equipment washwater."

Bt, a bacteria available in different strains to handle different caterpillar and beetle problems, is one of the best very low-toxicity cures for caterpillars. Proteins in the bacterial spore damage the insect's stomach so it cannot eat; the insect thus starves or has stomach failure. There is some delay between time of ingestion and when the insect is actually incapacitated.

Fungicides. Ortho Multipurpose Fungicide with Daconil 2787 is used for botrytis on beans, celery, bulb onions, leeks, shallots; it requires a seven-day wait. For alternaria on Brussels sprouts, broccoli, cabbage, cauliflower, potatoes, carrots, cucumbers, melons, and squash there is no delay, but there is a fourteen-day wait for corn, green onions, and garlic.

Orthocide (Captan Fungicide) may be used up to the day of harvest on strawberries, but the label warns, "Danger: Causes irreversible eye damage. Harmful if swallowed or inhaled. May cause allergic skin reactions. This product is toxic to fish."

Safer Garden Fungicide is 12 percent sulfur. The label suggests applying to grapes within twenty-one days of harvest and that it may be used up to the day before harvest on beans. Do not use on strawberries that will be used for canning.

Safer's 4 percent sulfur formulation may be used on almost all vegetables and fruit up to the day before harvest; strawberry fruit for canning is the exception.

Fertilizers. Vegetable builder fertilizers do not list a waiting period. John Marshall of O. M. Scott's consumer services explains: "Fertilization is like taking vitamins yourself. Straight nitrogen, potassium, and phosphorus are the basic building blocks of a plant. There is nothing there that isn't there naturally. These nutrients are not harmful for humans once taken up by plants. However, if you spread fertilizer around and find some stuck on lettuce leaves, that could be a concern. You will need to wash edible plant parts off well."

Likewise, Ortho Consumer Products Label Guide makes no note of a delay time on their fertilizers. They do caution, however, to keep their natural Fish Fertilizer and Liquid Plant Food out of the reach of children, to wash hands after each use, and to avoid contact with eyes, open cuts, and sores.

Rob Ringer notes that all of his fertilizers are food-grade substances and fine to eat. In fact, the raccoons once snatched my package of Ringer Vegetable Garden Restore fertilizer, ate the whole thing, and even licked the wrapper. Ringer says dogs will do the same thing.

A representative of Stern's Miracle-Gro said it is safe to apply this water-soluble the day you harvest.

six

When Is It Ready?

WHEN YOU BAKE a cake, you know the batter is done when it firms, rises, and turns golden brown. If in doubt, you can stick a toothpick into the center — if it comes out clean, the cake is ready to remove from the oven, cool, top with icing, and eat. Identifying when garden produce is ripe may be more intimidating to the newcomer, however. There are more variables. The moment of perfect ripeness depends on the cultivar, temperature, stage of growth, your preferences, possible uses, and other factors. Still, with a little experience, picking delicious produce can be simple. "You just taste it," says Rachel Snyder.

Experiment by picking your crops at different sizes. As the season goes on, you will recognize just how "done" you like them best. Develop a checklist of criteria to judge how a crop is progressing. (For specific details, see pages 136-141.)

Rose Marie Whiteley from Omaha, Nebraska, writes, "I'm sure most experienced gardeners know all the standard signs. We certainly develop a schedule that we feel is right for our particular taste and needs. I also suspect there is a 'sixth sense,' as I seem to develop almost a kinship with those vegetables and simply know when they are ready to harvest — with one exception, watermelons. I guess I need to talk to them about working on this kinship; I kind of do that one by guess. And, yes, I have to admit there are times I get so busy that a veggie's prime stage sneaks past me."

I put vegetables to the acid test — the kids. If they eat a vegetable right up, I know I've picked it at the right time. My family likes certain crops "well done" and others "a little gooey inside," like a warm, sticky chocolate chip cookie. My toddler will not touch green beans unless there is a substantial "shelly" bean inside. Although I agree with him when it comes to Romano beans, for most other green beans I prefer the opposite — tender, 2-inch-long baby beans, captured before the bean beetles

WHEN IS A VEGETABLE A FRUIT?

Both edible and inedible seed coverings qualify botanically as fruit, even when they are more commonly called vegetables. Realizing where the seed coverings came from and understanding their role on wild plants will help you determine when to harvest.

Harold William Ricketts, in his *Botany for Gardeners* (1957), described this subject aptly: "In short, in our use of words, we classify things — very properly — by their appearance or taste or by other qualities of direct concern to us rather than botanical facts. It is perhaps a little foolish of the scientist to insist upon his own definitions when they run counter to everyday speech. However, the alternative would be for him to adopt an entire new vocabulary for these familiar things, these seeds and fruits; and we should have to learn it also if we want to understand the botanist. So we must humor him to some extent."

According to the scientific definition, not all fruits are fleshy and succulent. You need to know the difference in fruit types to understand why you harvest some immature and wait for others until they are completely ripe.

When early seed-bearing plants developed, fruit coated the growing seeds in order to protect them. For some plants, the fruit became a way to transport offspring away from the parent. If all seed fell at the foot of the mother plant, the resulting thicket would overwhelm water and sun supplies. To get the "kids" out on their own, plants use wind, water, and animal transportation. Sweet, fleshy fruits or nutritious nuts appeal to animal appetites. Not only people, but mammals, lizards, and occasionally even fish pocket or eat the fruit and carry it elsewhere. Although producing a sweet, colorful fruit takes energy away from the plant, the commitment is justified. The seed may be deposited less randomly than wind-carried fruit, perhaps in nutrient-rich manure or in a cultivated garden.

Plants bearing dry fruit that is unappealing to animals call on other means of dispersal. Prickly burr fruits hitchhike on passing legs and coats. *Oxalis* and *Impatiens* catapult their seeds into neighboring areas. Maple and elm trees wing their seeds so they swirl away. Dandelions and milkweed employ feathery parachutes.

When you eat fleshy fruit, such as tomatoes, eggplant, ground cherries, grapes, and berries, it can be said, in botanical terms, that you are eating a simple berry with a thin skin surrounding pulp. Strawberries, blackberries, and other bramble berries, on the other hand, are actually aggregates — clusters of small fruit on a single receptacle. Other berries, called *pepos*, develop a hard rind; these include pumpkins, squash, and cucumbers. (Summer squash and cucumbers are harvested young while the fruit and skin are still tender.)

In some cases (dry-fruited crops, for instance), we use the seeds, instead of the fruits. We treasure the seeds of many herbs that are rich in essential oils, including dill, parsley, anise, caraway, and coriander, all of which bear a *schizocarp* — a dry fruit with two halves hanging from a central axis. Another favorite seed is corn, which is actually a collection of fleshy seeds held on a cob and wrapped in leaf husks. In other cases (green beans, for example) we eat the pods, when they are still fleshy and immature.

or bunnies discover them. We all agree that we prefer larger cucumbers. They take longer on the vine and limit the growth of new cucumbers, but they are juicier than less-mature fruit.

I try to pick summer squash when they are young. Overgrown, they take a lot of jazzing up in the kitchen — too much bother for an old fruit. When one or two escape me and reach whale proportions, they become Nerf-ball bats for the kids, saving me the obligation of cooking with them.

You can either pick to order in your garden, taking whatever produce is in the right condition for the recipe you have chosen, or you can find out what is done to perfection and look up the right use for it. For green tomato pie, of course, you need immature tomatoes. For tomato sauce, the tomatoes should be soft and ripe. For slicing on sandwiches, a firmer but well-colored tomato is best. If you are canning, you may need extra-firm pickling cucumbers, summer squash, or beans. Sweet young carrots freeze better than older ones. (For more ideas, see pages 154–167.)

If you save seed for another year, you may have to let the fruit pass the good-eating stage to get fully developed seeds. Nancy Pippart at Landis Valley Museum writes, "In almost all cases, our fruits and vegetables are harvested for seed, so they stay on the vine longer. Tomatoes are dead ripe; beans and peas are usually allowed to dry on the vine."

SIGNS OF RIPENESS

You can identify ripeness relatively easily in fleshy vegetables and vine fruits. Ripe fruit usually changes from green to some brighter color, more distinguishable from the plant's foliage, as the flavorings develop. In the apple, for example, starches are converted into sugars. These sugars react in sunlight to form red anthocyanins, pigments common to red flowers. Fruits lose any sour, bitter, or astringent qualities and beef up sugar levels. They also grow softer. In a tomato, what was whitish placenta degrades to a gel-like center enriched with the colorful vitamin beta-carotene and other yellow-orange pigments. Bean seeds swell and develop a "beanier" taste.

Don't wait for maturity before you harvest crops that do not mature to a fleshy fruit. When pods prepare to split and release mature dried beans, they lose their succulence and grow fibrous and inedible. Cucumbers develop an open, airy cavity and dry flesh. Roots and greens grow tough and sometimes bitter. In these crops, instead of waiting for color or softening to prompt picking, let size be your guide.

The following are some other clues that can help you determine when to harvest.

Changes in Color

It is no quirk of fate that fleshy fruits often turn red. Pure red, unadulterated by blue or yellow, is invisible to insects but a neon beacon for birds and some animals. It is not fate alone that brings deer to your apple trees and birds to your strawberry and raspberry beds.

Red, of course, is not the only color that indicates ripeness. Some peppers and tomatoes, for instance, mature to yellow, orange, pink, or purple. Winter squash and pumpkins turn varying shades of red and orange just before, during, or after the seeds are set and the rind hardens. Blackberries change from red to black, and red raspberries from green to red. Blueberries turn from red to blue, and gooseberries remain green or blush red.

Less glaring color changes signal harvest time for other crops. The background color of muskmelons changes from green to tan. Spaghetti squash skin changes from light yellow to gold. Cucumbers, peas, and beans bleach to a lighter or yellow color when they are past ripe. Most eggplant cultivars begin life the same dark purple color as when they near maturity; learn to depend on skin gloss and fruit firmness to evaluate them.

For crops such as cauliflower, celery, endive, escarole, and leeks, you can initiate a color change by blanching. This develops a milder flavor and more tender texture.

Gloss

A high gloss on a fruit indicates that that fruit is healthy and growing. The parent plant is still sending energy to maintain the fruit epidermis, which, in the case of some beans and edible-podded peas, is part of what we harvest. By the time the seeds are set or the flesh inside the fruit begins to overripen, the skin becomes dull. This is particularly apparent on eggplant fruit but also noticeable on peas, summer squash, peppers, and tomatoes. The exceptions are watermelon and blackberries,

WHAT TO DO ABOUT CAMOUFLAGED CROPS

Certain green vegetables are hard to find amid green foliage. Even when you look closely, you can pass right by an ideal bean, pea, cucumber, or summer squash. To get the most out of these crops, you need a harvesting system.

Wendy Krupnick suggests, "Always start at one end of the row and use the same routine motion to go through. Go back and forth between rows or up and down, whatever method works best for you, as long as you cover all the area. Follow a schedule. Either pick daily or every other day, as necessary, but go out at the same time routinely."

As she recommends, I sweep through the bean patch in early evening just before dinner every day, moving up one row and back on the other side to reinspect the plants. I have found that looking at a bean plant from a different angle often reveals pods that were hidden the first time through.

You can save yourself inspection time if you grow cultivars that fruit in colors other than green. Purple beans stand out particularly well, and the purple brightens to a more-normal green during cooking. Yellow and striped pods, although less obvious, are different enough to stand out in a crowd. Grow yellow summer squash, Golden Crown watermelon, or Burgundy, a purple-podded okra. Some cultivars, like E-Z Pick bean or Novella pea, which produce easy-to-see pods on the top of plants, are adaptions for commercial growers; they can be worth trying. Or, grow vining crops on a trellis. The dangling fruits stand out more when free from the tangle of vine.

BLANCHING: THE FINAL PHASE

Some vegetables are naturally strong flavored or tough. You can make them more tender and mild by treating them to a short period of darkness, a technique called *blanching*. During this time, chlorophylls and related pigments break down or never form at all, or new shoots arise that are soft and etiolated. For a change of flavor, try blanching the following crops:

Asparagus. Extend your asparagus harvest by hilling up soil over asparagus beds so the shoot grows long and white. This is a favorite delicacy in Europe. Blanched stalks emerge later than green stalks because they have further to travel.

Cardoon. Grow cardoon in a trench. When it reaches about 3 feet high, mound soil up around the base. In about six weeks, dig out and harvest the tender white inner hearts.

Cauliflower. Cauliflower heads turn a cabbage-tasting green if exposed to sunlight. Tie outer wrapper leaves around the head, or cover the head with a paper bag as it begins to expand. Self-blanching types have leaves that naturally curl around the head and reduce sunlight exposure.

Blanch cauliflower by tying the leaves up over the developing head.

Celery. As stalks grow during late summer and fall, hill soil up around them and leave the foliage exposed at the top. To keep the plant cleaner, wrap black plastic or newspaper around it before you bury it in soil. Self-blanchers, which stay a lighter green color naturally, have a milder flavor and tend to mature earlier than plants that require blanching assistance. They, too, can become even milder with additional hand-manipulated blanching. Commercial growers may blanch celery with ethylene gas. (See page 170 for more on ethylene and its effects.)

Blanch celery by enclosing developing stalks in black plastic, newspaper, or even boards.

Endive and escarole. The heads on these bitter-tasting chicories will become milder if you enclose the head in long wrapper leaves, a paper bag, or clay pot for seven to ten days before harvesting.

Florence fennel. When this licorice-tasting bulb reaches the size of a tennis ball, cover the bulb with a clay pot or mound soil up around it to blanch it for two weeks before harvesting.

Leek. Blanch older leek bases so they develop a mild, creamy white flesh. In late summer and fall, cover the base with paper or plastic and a mound of soil. Or, plant the seedlings in a trench and mound soil up around the plants as they grow.

Salsify. Mound soil up over the dormant plant; it will send up mild-tasting, white shoots in spring.

which look dull when they are ripe.

Firmness and Plumpness

Your sense of feel will serve you well when you evaluate ripeness of fruiting crops. With fleshier fruit, softening accompanies ripening, as enzymes gradually degrade pectins, the connective substance in cell walls that helps hold them upright. In melting flesh peaches, the cells actually disorganize or wash out of their original locations. An apple becomes mealy because the cells separate and let air fill the gaps. Any fruit let go too long will continue to progress until the seeds are released.

With tender-podded bean cultivars, you can feel the seeds beginning to swell. However, cultivars with thick pods or slender seeds may fool you. Break a few "guinea pigs" open and see if seeds are there.

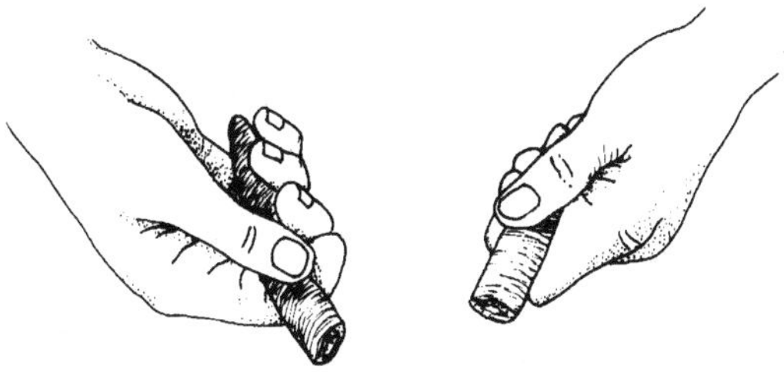

Break open a bean pod to note the stage of the developing seeds.

Abscission

The natural separation of fruits from plants is known as *abscission*. In muskmelons and berries, the connection between fruit and mother

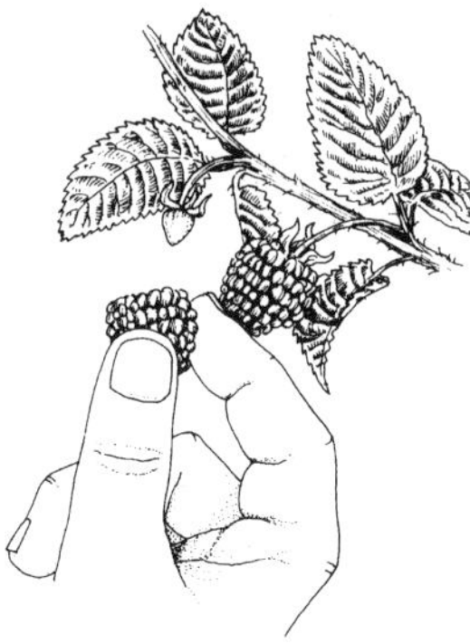
Raspberries are ready to eat when the fruit easily separates at the abscission point.

plant begins to degrade as the fruit ripens. Where the fruit connects to the stem or the stem connects to the mother branch, two layers of cells form. One is protective and seals off the parent stem; the other is a row of weak cells that easily break to release the fruit. You know these fruits are ready to eat when they pop easily off the plant. A cherry tree actually develops three abscission zones. The first is at the top of the fruit; the second, at the base of the stalk; the third, at the base of the short spur branch that bears the fruit cluster.

Bolting

When you harvest crops for their leaves or roots, fruit signs are of little help. You can judge when to pick them by the size of the foliage or the amount of time they have grown. It's important to catch annual crops like lettuce and radishes before they bolt to flower upon reaching a certain size or day length. Some carrots, beets, or the *Brassicas* may flower if fairly large plants are exposed to spring temperatures below 45°F. Once that flower stalk starts to emerge, plant priorities change from growth to reproduction. Plants channel most of their energy reserves into blooming, and swollen roots and fleshy or tender leaves stay scrawny or become tough or bitter.

Lettuce *bolts* (grows quickly upward to flower) when it reaches a certain size.

Preflowering Essential Oils

Fragrant herbs also change priorities when they near flowering. Instead of becoming unpalatable, they develop higher concentrations of essential oils, the flavoring and fragrance that has made them part of gardens for centuries. Annual herbs such as basil, summer savory, and sweet marjoram slow or stop growth after flowering and produce few quality leaves. Keep the flowers picked off if you want to continue harvesting.

With perennial herbs like thyme, rosemary, Greek oregano, sage, winter savory, and others, harvest when

Pick the flowers off basil so that the leaves will continue to develop.

you see the first flower buds form. With some herbs, like thyme, you may want to cut and dry herbs in full flower to use in herb wreaths. French tarragon never flowers and thus does not experience the rise in oils before blooming.

Root Signs

These can be tricky. Above-ground growth does not always parallel below-ground spread. Watch the calendar and the weather to get some idea how hidden roots should be progressing. Some cultivars show their size in the girth of the root shoulders or stem base. If in doubt, pull an apparently large one and see. You will be able to base future decisions upon what you find.

GETTING THE EDGE ON FLAVOR

Like human biorhythms, a plant has its own ups and downs during the day and the season. It may build up sugars or vitamins at a certain time of the day, release them later, and stockpile bitter elements. Some fruits are more succulent in the morning; others have more flavor in the afternoon. Finding the right time to harvest, even if you have to reshuffle your own schedule, can make a difference. Whenever possible, take advantage of natural rhythms when you harvest.

Changes Based on Time of Day

Just as you get up, eat, and sleep on a fairly regular schedule, plants also follow routine daily changes. These can vary according to the plant's maturity, or they may fluctuate with changes in the weather or the season.

The biggest variation in flavor depends on weather, particularly sun and water levels. Most plants photosynthesize most actively in the morning, increasing their sugar and protein production as sunlight intensifies. The production begins to decline in the heat of the afternoon as the plant becomes water stressed. In the evening, evaporation decreases and internal moisture levels rise. Plants become more succulent. Toward morning, they can flush out unnecessary salts and wastes.

Internal cues follow a circadian (twenty-four-hour) clock. Over the season, this clock records changing

PLANETARY INFLUENCES ON HARVESTING

Gardeners who follow Rudolf Steiner's biodynamic methods of gardening may plant, fertilize, prune, and harvest according to the alignment of the moon and planets. When harvested during the right astronomical period, crops are believed to taste better and store longer. The idea is echoed in many almanacs and mentioned by the Amish gardener Emma Byler.

The biodynamic community Kimberton Hills annually publishes an *Agricultural Calendar,* which includes a "Guide to Cosmic Rhythms." Calendar editor Sherry Wildfeuer writes in the 1991 issue that astrological tables are meant not to replace the gardener's common sense but to help them plan their own agricultural activities. "Much as we might choose favorable weather conditions for planting or avoid working in a thunderstorm, we may wish to be aware of more subtle influences active in our field of work," Wildfeuer writes.

Wildfeuer explains the theory that assigns each of the four parts of the plant (root, leaf/stem, flower, fruit/seed) to four elements of nature (earth, water, air, and fire), respectively represented by three constellations each. For example, the earth relates to plant roots and Taurus, Virgo, and Capricorn; water is leaf/stem and Cancer, Scorpio, and Pisces; air equates with flowers and Gemini, Libra, and Aquarius; fire with fruit/seed and Aries, Leo, and Sagittarius. When the moon passes the actual position of these constellations in the sky, their influence is strong on crops.

Since some crops are not easy to separate into greens or flowers, Wildfeuer explains that trials have shown that cabbage and leeks don't store well if harvested on a "leaf" day, but broccoli and cauliflower do. Treating them like a flower may encourage bolting.

Simpler programs are documented in Blüm's *Farmer's and Planter's Almanac* (1991), which calls for harvesting during the dark of the moon, which lasts from the time you can see the last quarter illuminated in the sky to when it fades and the new moon arises. Within this period, the moon will pass certain constellations. The best harvest comes during Sagittarius, Aquarius, and Aries.

Ed Hume, a West Coast seedsman, also advocates gardening by the moon in his 1991 *Garden Almanac*. "Just as the moon's gravitational pull influences the ocean's tide, it is theorized that it also influences the movement of fluids contained in plants. Moon gardening is based on this belief. It has not been scientifically proven or disproved but subscribers report continued success from this method," Hume writes. He lists dates that are best for canning or drying and includes a weather-permitting caution.

If you want to add another dimension to your harvest garden, astrological gardening may be one to try. "Following the Kimberton Hills calendar keeps things moving along. You keep changing to different plants or harvesting new things according to the planets. It makes gardening more interesting," says Chris Werronen. (For more information, see the addresses of the above publications in the Appendix.)

day length to trigger flowering or dormancy. It is easy to see it in action on daylilies, which open their flowers at the same time every day. Watch a sunflower follow the sun across the sky or an orchid blossom release its fragrance every morning. Scientists have also documented the rhythms of increasing and decreasing amounts of photosynthesis, hormone production, and cell division. Circadian cycles vary little with changing temperatures. Instead, they are controlled genetically, with each cultivar being different from another. Try harvesting lettuce or corn or beans at different times of the day to see if you can tell a difference.

Harvest Gardener contributors have done their own experimenting and found certain timings work best for them. Wendy Krupnick likes to clip greens in the morning. Elizabeth Berry harvests delicate squash blossoms then, too. Amish gardener Emma Byler equates morning with gardening. "Grandmother would do her hoeing early in the morning and her canning by noon. Afternoons were spent in the front porch rocker, mending or reading or doing handwork that was not too strenuous," Byler writes in her *Recipes and Remedies for Plain and Happy Living*. Krupnick waits to pick tomatoes and beans until later in the morning. "If it is warm, a tomato plant will continue to grow even if you brush against it or disturb it," Krupnick said. To avoid spreading disease through a patch of beans, she waits until later in the morning, so that the

HARVESTING FOR HIGH VITAMIN C LEVELS

Still-growing plant tips and buds and the sunlit side of fruits are where most vitamin C accumulates. Plants tend to manufacture more vitamin C in the spring than in late summer or fall. Individual plants, however, have their own quirks. To get the most vitamin C, harvest large lima beans and the potato tubers from larger plants; cabbages and onions when small; asparagus, peppers, rhubarb, tomatoes, and gooseberries when mature.

dew is completely gone.

A morning-time picking schedule has an added advantage. The temperature is cool and comfortable. Then you have the afternoon to put the food by and do not have to leave it sitting overnight, losing quality for twelve idle hours.

Other Weather Factors

Moisture. When fruits are swelling, heavy rainfall or irrigation may dilute the flavorings inside or actually pump up a soft fruit or cabbage head with moisture until it cracks or bursts. Too little moisture plays havoc with root and shoot crops, which need to grow fast to stay sweet and tender. Cucumbers become bitter from both too wet and too dry conditions. Herbs, however, can thrive in dry soils, actually producing more fragrant and flavorful foliage.

Heat. When the weather becomes too hot, many plants stop growing, reduce photosynthesis levels, and limit flower or fruit development. The result can be bolting, barren plants, or bitter, tough, or stringy plant parts.

Cold. When cold-hardy vegetables such as Brussels sprouts and parsnips are exposed to several periods of frost, they tend to become sweeter. They fill their cells with sugar, an antifreeze that prevents frost damage.

Cool. Warm-season fruits need enough heat to ripen well. If it is too cool, tomatoes and corn will not be as sweet when they mature, and peppers will stay green.

Wind. Hard, drying winds generally do a garden no good. They increase evaporation of moisture through leaves and force stomata to close and photosynthesis to shut down temporarily. Without a steady flow of nutrients, crops will not grow fat and tasty.

Cloudy weather or short days. With less solar radiation during cloudy or short winter, fall, or spring days, plants do not photosynthesize as actively. Expect growth to proceed proportionately slowly and delay harvest.

SOME CLUES THAT INDICATE IT IS TIME TO HARVEST

Certain telltale signs let the observant gardener know when crops are prime for picking. Expect some variation according to cultivar, however. If you don't know what to expect, dig out the seed packet or nursery catalogue to get harvest recommendations. Once you are familiar with the plant, you may devise your own harvest criteria.

Artichokes, Jerusalem. These underground tubers continue to develop even after the flower stalks brown. Harvest them in late fall for the best flavor and size. Give yourself plenty of time to dig out all the tubers, or they could escape and colonize neighboring areas.

Asparagus. These shoots taste best cut or snapped off short, fat, and tender.

Beans. Be certain to double check your cultivar when harvesting beans. Some varieties must be picked young and tender. Others are just as good or, in my opinion, better, if allowed to mature to full-size "shelly" beans.

Asparagus is in the best condition for cutting when the shoots are 4 or 5 inches above the ground and while the head or bud remains closed and firm.

Fearing Burr, Jr., 1863

Cut asparagus when it is 4 or 5 inches high.

French slicing beans or filet beans need to be picked pencil-thin or they become tough. The diameter and tenderness of the pod is of primary importance. The beans are overripe when they snap as you twist them around your finger, according to the William Dam seed catalog.

Standard green beans, on the other hand, are ready if they snap when you bend them. Most cultivars are crisp when they are as small as 2 inches long. Park's Baby Bean matures to only 4 inches. Unless you grow a cultivar with extra-tender pods, the larger the bean gets, the tougher the pod and string, if present, may become.

Shell or flageolet beans are those you harvest when the seeds reach full size but before they dry. You may have to pull a few pods open to evaluate if they are done yet. You can use a tasty-seeded snap bean like Jumbo or Roma for this purpose or a special green shell cultivar such as Taylor Horticultural, Dwarf Horticultural, or Flambeau.

Dry beans can be shell types or special storage types like Jacob's Cattle, Black Turtle, Pinto, and Vermont Cranberry. Let the pods yellow around the seeds before you harvest but don't wait until they split. To store well, the seeds need to be so dry they will not dent under your fingernail.

Lima beans are full of seeds when they are ready to pick. Both ends of the pod feel spongy when the seeds are tender and juicy, say Chicago Botanic Garden horticulturists. For mature dry beans, let the pods mature longer.

Beets. There are several parts of the beet you can eat. All beet greens are edible. Some people grow cultivars like Lutz Green Leaf and Early Wonder especially for their rosette of heat-tolerant foliage. To harvest roots, expect early cultivars to grow and pass their prime quickly, often when they exceed 2 inches in diameter. Harvest them promptly. Detroit Dark Red and Burpee's Golden Beet are good up to 3 inches across. Others, especially long keepers like heirloom Long Season or Bolthardy can grow quite big and still taste good. Longer-rooted Cylindra and Formanova dig deeply like a carrot. Cylindra can get as long as 8 inches with a 1¾-inch diameter without losing quality.

Berries. Pick soft bush fruit and strawberries when fully ripe; they will not get any sweeter once off the vine. The time is right when they change color and turn soft. They may pop off the vine with a gentle touch. Tom Eltzroth notes that the sepals on blackberries, boysenberries, and loganberries turn from green to tan when the fruit is ready. Betty Hofstetter recommends tasting berries of the right color before a wholesale picking. With larger fruit, such as apples and pears, she keeps records of which cultivars ripened when. "Even though actual harvest dates vary from year to year, the sequence is always the same. For example, Prima apples are ripe 1 to 2 weeks before McIntosh each year," Hofstetter says.

Broccoli. Harvest broccoli heads when they are fully expanded but before the buds open into yellow flowers. If you are growing a cultivar that will

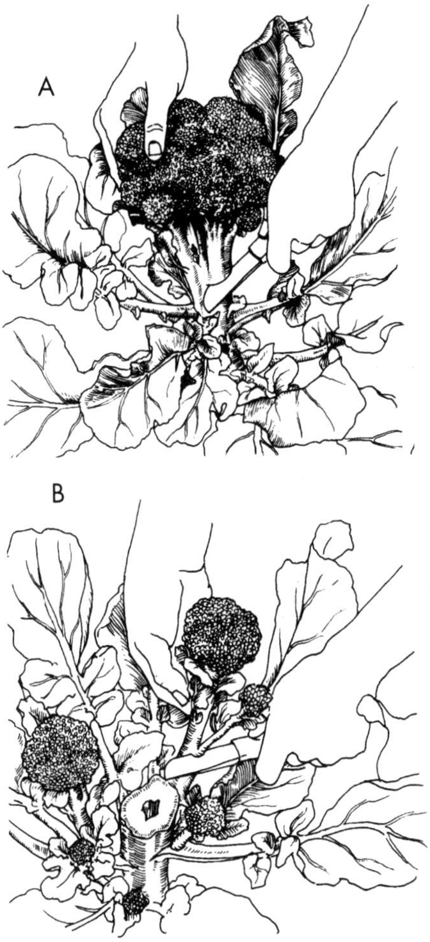

For the first broccoli harvest, (A) cut just below the head; (B) new side shoots will continue to appear.

resprout into smaller side shoots, leave a good bit of the stalk behind to harvest a second or even a third time.

Sprouting broccoli does not produce large heads, but puts out a larger number of small, flowering shoots. Cut off the young tender portion of the stalk about 4 inches from the tip. New shoots should keep coming.

Broccoli should not be allowed to remain till the compactness of the head is broken, but it should always be cut while the *curd,* as the flowering mass is termed, is entire, before bristly, leafy points make their appearance through it. In trimming a head, leave a portion of the stalk and a few leaves immediately surrounding the head; cut the extremities a little below the top of the latter.

Fearing Burr Jr., 1863

Broccoli raab, a short-season, bitter version of sprouting broccoli, can reach 12 inches in height before it buttons into florets. Cut the entire stem the moment you see the flower buds form.

Brussels sprouts. Pick the mini-heads that emerge in leaf axils (the junction between leaf and stem) along the stem when they are big enough to grasp easily, but before they get large and floppy. They can be anywhere from ½ to 1½ inches in width, depending on cultivar, weather, and position on the stem.

Cabbage. Let the head swell to full size and fill out until firm and solid. How big it gets is dependent upon cultivar and growing season. If the head begins to bulge upward, it may burst and should be harvested immediately.

Cabbage, Chinese. There are several types of Chinese cabbage, none of which forms the same tight heads as standard cabbage. Let the head or rosette fill in as long as possible, but harvest before it bolts to seed, especially if grown in the lengthening days of spring or if exposed to temperatures above 80°F.

Cantaloupe/Muskmelon. This is one of the tricky crops, because you need to catch it fully ripe to enjoy maximum sweetness. Muskmelon, the orange-fleshed melon often called cantaloupe, slips easily off the vine when ripe. It smells ripe and aromatic, and the background color beneath the skin netting turns from green to tan.

True cantaloupes, such as honeydew, casaba, and crenshaw, do none of the above. Instead, the rind may turn white or cream colored, begin to crack around the stem, and feel soft if you press the blossom end.

Carrot. The size of the root you harvest will vary widely with carrot cultivar and class. Baby carrots are good to eat as soon as they develop an orange color. Some, such as supersweet A+ Hybrids, need to mature entirely before they develop full flavor. When ready, the tip will become more blunt.

Cauliflower. Harvest these heads when you believe they have reached full size, but before they begin to separate and look rice like.

Chard, Swiss. For salads, break off the tender young leaves before they get taller than about 8 inches. You can cook older, larger, and tougher leaves, but you may want to remove any fibrous parts of the stem first.

Corn. If you are growing standard sweet corn, you will want to harvest promptly at the milk stage — when the kernels are juicy and plump — which is the time of maximum sweetness. The silks turn dark brown and the tip of the ear changes from pointed to more rounded as the final kernels mature. A sugary white sap squirts out when you press a kernel with your fingernail. When overmature, the kernels become large, hard, and darker in color.

If you are growing a supersweet or sugar-enhanced cultivar, you can delay a few days past prime and still have a sweet ear.

For dry corn, let the ears stay on the stalk until the outer husks dry and you cannot pierce the kernels with your fingernail. For baby corn, you can find tiny, undeveloped ears inside husks as soon as silks poke out.

Cucumbers. The proper size for harvesting cucumbers depends on what kind they are. Gourmet Japanese or English types can grow a foot long, and slicers can be 8 inches long. Picklers may be best 2 inches long; the smaller fruits stay firm despite pickling processing. Pick slicers when fully elongated but before the seeds mature to a yellowish color. You may need to slice a few open to see how far you can push size without reducing quality. My favorite cultivar for slicing is County Fair 87, a pickling cucumber that stays sweet, mild, and good tasting up to 6 inches long. Harvest heirloom Lemon cucumbers while lemon sized before the skin turns tough and ripens to gold.

Eggplant. Harvest eggplant when adequately large but still immature; the skin should be glossy. When seeds form, the flesh becomes more spongy and may be bitter. Just how large you can safely let the fruit grow varies with cultivar and type. Many eggplants grow into large, rounded fruit. Oriental types may be smaller and shaped like a teardrop; others are long and slender, like baseball bats. Heirloom eggplants may be as small as grapes.

Garlic. Harvest before the foliage dies, or the cloves will outgrow the paper sheath that keeps them clean and contained. David Stern recommends digging when the leaves begin to yellow and the tips and margins brown. The leaf base should look papery, but not get so dry that the foliage flops.

Greens. The secret with greens is to get foliage that is large enough for your purposes without being so big or old that it becomes bitter or tough.

You can cut young seedlings, especially of mesclun, back to the ground when they are only 4 or 5 inches tall. Or, thin out overcrowded seedlings before neighboring plants touch. For larger leaves, pluck a few outer leaves from strong-growing plants; the inner leaves will continue to grow. Let head types approach their catalogue description, and then harvest the entire head or rosette when full. If the weather turns hot, harvest everything that is prone to bolting.

Let endive and escarole reach a substantial size, and then blanch them for several weeks before harvesting. In the case of Belgian endive, let the plants grow all season and dig the root in the fall. Plant it in a cool, dark place and harvest the blanched shoot when it is about 4 inches long. (For more information on blanching, see pages 138–139.)

Herbs. Many herbs are prime just before flowering, and all have the highest levels of essential oils if harvested early in the morning, just after the dew dries off the leaves.

Kohlrabi. These generally are most tender when harvested small, about the size of ping-pong balls. You may be able to find cultivars that can get bigger and still stay tender, especially if the weather is cool and moist but sunny.

Onions. You can harvest onion leaves, stalks, and bulbs, the size and character of which varies according to cultivar.

For *bulbing onions* and *shallots,* wait until the leafy tops brown and fall before harvesting and curing for storage. If a bulb flowers or splits, however, pull it for immediate use.

Scallions or *green onions* should be picked young as thinnings; eat the foliage and slender leaf base.

Some *leeks* should be harvested young and tender early in the summer. Let others grow into fall or even winter, and blanch them to make them more tender. If overgrown, the inner stem will become woody.

Parsnip. Let these roots mature fully and get snapped by a few frosts before harvesting. They will be bigger and sweeter. In some parts of the country, you can leave parsnips in the ground all winter for an early spring harvest.

> If even a few of the [pea] pods begin to ripen, young pods will not only cease to form but those partly advanced will cease to enlarge . . . It is inexcusable that a gentleman, having a garden of his own, should be served with peas otherwise than in the very highest state of perfection, which they are not, if allowed to become too old or even too large.
>
> *Fearing Burr, Jr., 1863*

Peas. Depending on cultivar, harvest before or after the seeds swell inside the pods. Snow peas, grown for the edible pod, are best picked when they reach full length but before the seeds and strings develop. Sugar Snap peas, on the other hand, are sweeter once the seeds swell but before the pod begins to shrivel. Shelling or English peas, grown for the peas only, not the pods, are sweetest if picked when swollen but before they reach full maturity and the pods become dull. Since this crop suffers in the heat, harvest a little early if the weather turns hot. If you wait too long, the seeds become starchy; they are still suitable for drying, however.

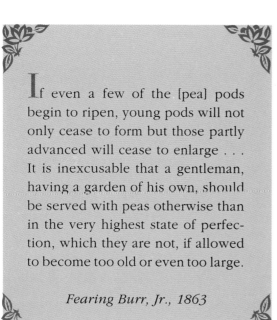

Peppers. You can pick peppers from the moment the fruit appears. Most people wait until the seeds form, however, and the fruits develop a strong vegetable flavor and thick walls. If you let them go until they ripen fully, they develop a sweet, fruity flavor.

Peppers, hot. The heat in hot peppers does not develop until the seeds and placenta grow. Thus, peppers get hotter as the fruit matures. Once the seeds have formed, most peppers achieve their full quota of fiery flavor in hot, sunny locations.

Potato. You can unearth a few tender new potatoes as the vines flower near the end of their growth cycle. The traditional harvest comes after the vines die back and the tubers cure in the soil to toughen their skins for storage.

Radish. Harvest small globe types from the merest swelling until they reach ½ to 1 inch in diameter. It doesn't take long! If the weather is hot, the larger roots are likely to be spicy and tough or pithy and hollow. French Breakfast and Daikon cultivars grow bigger and take longer to mature.

Rhubarb. Stalks of medium thickness are more likely to be tender. The color can vary from green to pink to red, according to cultivar.

Squash. Refer to the information about the cultivar you are growing to identify the proper size for harvesting. Summer squash should have a tender skin and immature seeds. In *The New Victory Garden,* Bob Thomson says that summer squash is at its peak of flavor when the blossoms

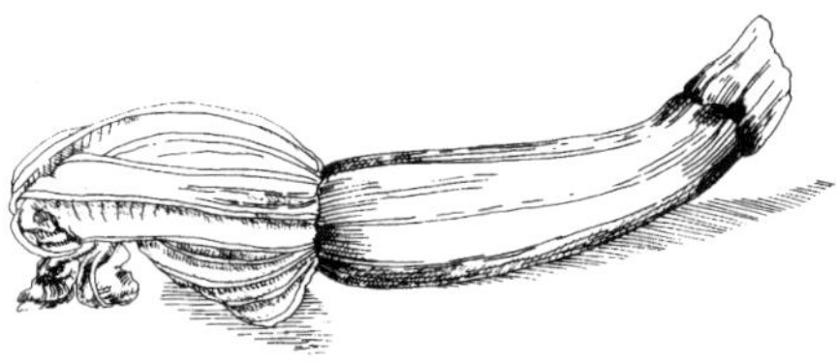

Marigold flowers were once used as a dye. Fearing Burr, Jr., recommended gathering the flowers when fully expanded and then divesting them of their calyxes. The flowers were spread in a light, airy, shaded situation until dried.

He also recommended gathering sage leaves before the development of the flower shoots and cutting the flower shoots off as they appear to increase the harvest. "When thus treated, the product is largely increased, as the leaves are put forth in much greater numbers and attain a larger size."

Fearing Burr, Jr., 1863

turn brown and dry, even if the fruit is just thumb size. I like to pick Green Magic zucchini 3 to 4 inches long, Gourmet Globe squash about 5 inches in diameter, and Kuta squash around 7 inches long. Kuta is sweeter when larger, yet still firm and relatively tender.

Winter squash should have a woody stem and a rind so tough you cannot puncture it with your fingernail. The skin should remain glossy, possibly coloring or changing to cream where it rests on the ground. You can pick some winter squash — though not spaghetti squash — young

HARVESTING UNUSUAL VEGETABLES

Determining just when less-common gourmet crops need to be brought into the kitchen can be puzzling the first time around. To get you started, here are some pointers from Wendy Krupnick at Shepherd's Garden Seed.

French filet beans. Let texture be your guide. If the pods get tough and strings develop, you are too late. "You literally begin to get the feel for them," Krupnick said. "Use your eyes to evaluate the bulge of the seeds in the pod and your hands to feel if the pods are smooth and young still or if they are too small."

The mature length of any cultivar will vary depending on how well the plants are growing and if you are harvesting early, in the middle, or late in the season. For example, La Belle, a mini-filet bean, matures at 4½ inches long. Vernandon, a standard-sized alternative, reaches 7 inches.

Fresh-shelling Borlotto beans. This rich, nutty-tasting Italian heirloom is ready when the first rosy-red stripes show up on the pods. The pods will still be green but getting leathery. You can eat the seeds inside as is or leave them on the plant to mature and dry completely. In between these two stages the bean is less desirable.

Edible flowers. Edible flowers are one of Wendy's favorite harvests. She picks lavender-colored, onion-flavored chive blossoms before they mature. To use the flowers, Wendy pinches off the base of the flower head and sprinkles the individual florets, like confetti, over a dish just before serving. "Nobody will pick up the entire flower head. It just is not appealing," she said. I harvest chive blossoms by necessity. If I don't pick the flowers off, I will have self-sown chive plants everywhere. I sometimes drop chive blossoms into white wine vinegar to use as salad dressing.

Krupnick also harvests the sky-blue flowers of borage. She picks them newly opened, pinches off the hairy sepals, and leaves just the petals to decorate a plate or float in iced tea. Use immediately, she cautions; the flowers won't last long.

Florence fennel. Krupnick sows this licorice-flavored bulb in mid July for fall harvest. With a summer start, it gets larger and has less chance of bolting, than a spring-sown crop. If the bulb begins to elongate, harvest quickly, as a flower stalk is on the way. Otherwise, you can let it continue to grow — but be sure to harvest before the first killing frost.

Herbs. Wendy divides herbs into annual, biennial, and perennial categories when making harvest recommendations. Among perennials, she prefers oregano in full bloom and thyme just as it is coming out of bloom. "They need to be cut back then anyway and you can save the flower heads," she says. For annual dill, she plucks just the outside leaves. With basil, she pinches off the young tips to use in cooking and to make the plant bushier.

Peppers, chili. If you are tempted to pick a chili pepper green, wait at least until it is dark green and pretty hot, Krupnick says. She loves Anaheim peppers when they are half red and half green. If allowed to mature to a full red, they give you a flavorful hot-and-sweet combination.

Radicchio. Radicchio performs reliably in the fall, producing a loose head like butter lettuce. It is not as firm as a cabbage. Peel back the green leaves, just as you would husk an ear of corn, to find the red part on the inside. Where winters are mild, cut the head and leave some of the stalk below the base to resprout.

Tatsoi. Although you can harvest the outer leaves of this type of pak choi (bok choi), Wendy prefers to use the entire head. She recommends planting seedlings close together, so you can thin every other head when the leaves touch. Use the young ones for salad or stir-fries. By the time the thick-stalked rosettes reach full size, harvest the entire plant. If it is too much for a single serving, split it down the center for two servings. Mei Quing Choi, an hourglass-shaped baby pak choi, is particularly lovely presented this way.

like summer squash.

Tomatoes. The best flavor comes from tomatoes that ripen completely on the vine. If possible, wait until a tomato has turned to its mature color but remains firm. If you must pick early and let a tomato ripen indoors, do so after the tomato has begun changing colors naturally, or it will not develop much flavor.

Turnip. If unharvested, turnips grow to a large size, but they are milder and more tender when picked smaller; a 2-inch diameter is plenty. If the weather turns hot, above 80°F, the flavor can get "hot."

Watermelon. When watermelons are sweet and ripe, the tendril on the vine opposite the melon stem shrivels, says contributor Alan Cook. In addition, the underside turns from greenish to cream, and the skin dulls. You'll hear a thump if you flick it with your finger. The fruit should feel heavy for its size.

HARVEST YOUNG OR HARVEST OLD

At any one time you may find yourself harvesting "baby," mature, and slightly past-prime produce. Perhaps a crop escapes your notice until it becomes a little overgrown, or a heat wave strikes and you need to harvest extra early. The following are some alternatives to make the most of vegetables in different stages of development. All of these suggestions are fairly simple and do not require shopping for a lot of extra ingredients — or else I never would have tried them! Contributors Lori Zaim and Millie Adams, both of whom are gardeners and superb cooks, feature some of their favorite recipes here, along with mine.

Beans

Baby. Perhaps the season has come to an end prematurely and you find yourself picking a bagful of baby beans. These tender and highly perishable pods need to be cooked as soon as possible. Steam lightly and serve with a little butter, so you do not mask the extra-mild flavor.

Large pods. Savory Green Beans is a good dish for overly large beans with slightly tough pods.

Savory Green Beans

Serves 4

1/3 stick of butter
1 tablespoon summer or winter savory, minced
1 clove garlic, halved
1 pound green beans, cut into 1/2-inch pieces

Place the butter, savory, and garlic in a microwaveable dish and microwave on High for 1½ minutes. Let the mixture sit for 2 minutes. Drain the beans, and sauté them in the herb butter for 5 minutes.

Shelly seeds. This is the stage where beans produce mature green seeds and the pods begin to shrivel. Remove the seeds from the pods and sauté them in butter with short slices of smoked low-fat turkey bacon for 10 minutes. Add a bit of savory or thyme, if desired.

Dried beans. You can use these pantry standards for soups, baked beans, and other recipes.

Lori Zaim's Black Bean Salad

Serves 6 to 8

1 pound dried black beans, soaked overnight
corn from 4 ears, cooked and cut off cob
3 medium tomatoes, chopped
⅔ cup red onion, diced
½ cup fresh cilantro, minced
½ cup extra-virgin olive oil
juice of 2 lemons
salt and pepper to taste

In a large saucepan, cover the beans with water. Bring them to a boil, and simmer for about 45 minutes until they are tender. Drain the beans, and combine them with the corn, tomatoes, onion, and cilantro in a bowl. Whisk the olive oil and lemon juice in a small bowl, and then toss with the salad. Add salt and pepper to taste.

Berries

Vine-ripened berries are delicious to eat fresh when picked at or just beyond prime. When not fully ripe, most berries will be higher in acid and may make good jellies and jams. If slightly overripe, purée to serve as sauce on a scoop of ice cream with a little blackberry brandy. Or, strain the purée and use to flavor punches or spritzers.

Broccoli

Main head. The main stalk is fine to steam when in its prime. Try this adaptation of a Shepherd's Garden Seeds recipe.

Baked Lemon Broccoli with Cheese

Serves 6

2 young broccoli heads
1 teaspoon grated lemon zest
2 tablespoons lemon juice
2 tablespoons finely chopped fresh parsley
¼ cup chopped basil
⅓ cup tomato sauce
grated mozzarella cheese

Preheat the oven to 350°F. Boil the broccoli heads whole. When they are tender, arrange them in a baking dish and sprinkle them with the lemon zest and juice, parsley, basil, and tomato sauce. Top with the cheese, and bake in the preheated oven for 10 minutes.

Sideshoots. You probably will not be harvesting large quantities of these at any one time. On a good day, you may gather a couple per plant, possibly enough to spice up a stir-fry, salad, or casserole. You can freeze any extras and save up enough for this interesting dish.

Broccoli-Bleu Cheese Casserole

Serves 6

¼ cup butter or margarine
¼ cup all-purpose flour
½ teaspoon salt
1½ cups milk
5 ounces cream cheese
1½ ounces bleu cheese
2 pounds broccoli, cut in bite-size pieces
⅓ cup butter-cracker crumbs (Ritz, for example)

Preheat the oven to 350°F. In a large saucepan, melt the butter or margarine over medium heat. Stir in the flour and salt. Bring the mixture to a boil, stirring constantly. Cook 1 minute. Slowly stir in the milk. Beat until smooth. Bring the sauce to a boil. Cook, stirring constantly for 1 to 2 minutes. Stir in the cheeses until they melt. Stir in the broccoli. Pour the mixture into a buttered 1½-quart casserole dish. Top with the cracker crumbs. Bake in the preheated oven for 30 minutes or until the sauce bubbles.

Millie Adams

Past Prime. The florets are overdue for harvesting when yellow flowers appear. The stem often becomes tough, although you can still use the yellow flowers in a salad or stir-fry.

Corn

Pick baby corn for pickling, in the milk stage for boiling, or dried for grinding.

Milk stage. Eat this the second you shuck it — it's tender enough. Or, boil it until the color darkens, just a couple minutes, and cover with butter.

Just past milk stage. You still will get the corn flavor but not the sweetness. This kind of corn is not unlike what you might buy in the grocery and can be quite good combined with other flavorings.

Louisiana Corn

4 ears of corn
⅔ cup diced onion
2 tablespoons butter
⅓ cup heavy cream
¼ teaspoon cayenne pepper (or to taste)
½ teaspoon salt
freshly ground black pepper, to taste

Cut the corn kernels from the cobs. Scrape the remaining corn from the cobs with the back of a knife. Sauté the onion in the butter over medium-high heat until lightly browned. Add the cream and corn. Cover the pan, and cook for 20 minutes over low heat. Season with the cayenne and salt and pepper to taste.

Lori Zaim

Dried. Once corn is mature, the contents have turned from sweet to starch. You can let the kernels dry on the cob and grind them in a grain or coffee mill to make cornmeal or flour.

Cucumber

Pick cucumbers small for salads or pickles, or let them get large and use them as "boats."

Small. See recipe for pickles, page 237.

Large.

Cucumber Boats

Serves 4

2 large cucumbers
½ cup fresh peas,uncooked
⅓ cup mayonnaise
¼ cup sour cream
1 tablespoon each, chopped dill and chives
paprika

Halve, hollow, and peel the cucumbers, leaving a shell about a ½ inch thick. Discard the seeds, but chop and reserve the center of the cucumbers. Boil the shells for 2 minutes, and then chill in iced water. Mix the reserved cucumber, peas, mayonnaise, and sour cream. Add the chopped dill and chives. Use this mixture to fill the shells. Top with a sprinkling of paprika.

Eggplant

Young eggplant is every bit as good as its full-size counterpart but less likely to be bitter. However, there is something to be said for the appearance of a full-size violet eggplant. It is more versatile for an assortment of recipes.

Baby. Tiny, firm, and mild, these fruits make a statement with their vivid skin, which doesn't need to be mature to be colorful.

Fried Baby Eggplants

Serves 4

6 baby eggplants
olive oil for frying (enough to be ½ inch deep in a 10-inch skillet)
pita bread
6 cloves of garlic, minced
salt , to taste
¼ cup minced flat-leaf parsley

Peel the eggplants, and slice them lengthwise ¼ inch thick. Heat the olive oil to 350°F in the skillet. Fry the eggplants until golden brown, turning once. Drain on paper towels. To serve, wrap in warmed pita bread with garlic, salt, and parsley.

Lori Zaim

Mature but without mature seeds. I like to peel, then slice these eggplants. Dip the slices in beaten egg, and cover with fine bread crumbs.

You can fry them in oil, but they absorb a lot, so I bake them until tender and brown. From this point on, you can use them to make Eggplant Parmesan or Eggplant Pizza.

Eggplant Parmesan

Preheat the oven to 425°F. Layer the breaded eggplant slices on the bottom of a greased casserole dish. Cover with a layer of tomato sauce and a sprinkling of minced thyme, Greek oregano, basil, and sweet marjoram. Cover with plenty of shredded mozzarella cheese. Bake in the preheated oven until the cheese is bubbly.

Eggplant Pizza

Place large individual breaded eggplant slices on a baking sheet and top each with 1 tablespoon herbed tomato sauce and a slice of mozzarella cheese. (If you make your own sauce, boil it down until quite thick, or it will run off.) Microwave or broil in the oven until the cheese is melted.

You can also make pizza by topping the breaded eggplant with a slice of firm tomato, cheese, ham, pepperoni, roasted pepper, mushroom, or any other ingredients you like on pizza. If you add extras, bake in the oven at 400°F for 7 minutes, or until the cheese melts.

Garlic

If you grow the type of garlic that puts up an edible flower stalk in midsummer, you can harvest the bulbils that develop instead of seeds and use them just like the underground cloves. David Stern, director of the New York State Garlic Seed Foundation, recommends making Green Garlic Goo: Blend 4 cups of green garlic in a food processor with 2 tablespoons olive oil to moisten the garlic. Add some freshly ground black pepper and 2 or 3 anchovies. Use thick as a vegetable dip or add more oil for a pasta sauce.

Greens

Young greens are great for tossing in salad, but larger ones can be tough and may need cooking. Some greens are also bitter. Peter Gail says you can reduce bitterness by harvesting greens young or blanching them in a couple of changes of boiling water. Add a bit of baking soda to the first change. Or, serve with lemon juice or vinegar or with meat, beans, tomato, and egg, flavors that disguise the bitterness.

The dandelion, although much milder before flowering, is still a thoroughly bitter green. It is so nutritious, however, that many recipes have been devised to use it. Peter Gail shared this recipe for Amish sweet-and-sour dandelion gravy from his book *On the Trail of the Yellow-*

Flowered Earth Nail. "Cut up a few strips of bacon into a pan and fry. Use part of the drippings to make pan gravy with 1 tablespoon flour. When brown, stir in 1 cup of water. Let boil, then add 1 tablespoon sugar, and salt and vinegar to taste. A bit of sour cream or buttermilk may be added. Fold in 2 hard-boiled eggs, diced. Add the dandelions just before serving." You can serve the gravy as is or over potatoes, rice, or pasta.

Melons

Once fully sweet, melons are great eating all by themselves or mixed in a fruit salad. Nothing is more frustrating, however, than picking a melon slightly too early before the sweetness can develop.

Slightly immature. Even if a melon is not sweet, you can let it continue to ripen indoors; supplement with additional flavorings.

Melon Salsa for Grilled Fish Steaks

Serves 4

2 cups diced honeydew or cantaloupe
1 tablespoon lime juice
1 teaspoon sugar
½ clove garlic, minced
1 jalapeño pepper (seeds removed), minced
¼ cup soy sauce
¼ cup lemon juice
¼ cup vegetable oil
1 pound fillet of red snapper, ¾ inch thick

Combine the melon with the lime juice, sugar, garlic, and pepper. Refrigerate for several hours. Mix together the soy sauce, lemon juice, and vegetable oil, and marinate the fish in it for 2 hours. Grill about 10 minutes until done. Top with the melon salsa and serve.

Fully mature but unripe. This is the ideal stage to freeze or pickle melon.

Slightly overmature. When overripe, melons tend to become too soft to enjoy fresh. They are wonderful, however, as beverages.

Watermelon Punch

Forty-five 4-ounce servings

1 large ripe watermelon
1¼ cups sugar
1 cup water
three 12-ounce cans of chilled ginger ale or lemon-lime soda

Slice a thin section from one end of the melon. Take about one third off the top. Cut off the piece that will leave the best-looking rind so that you can use the larger part for a punch bowl.

Scoop the pulp from the melon; save the rind for a punch bowl. Mash the pulp, and strain out seeds.

Reserve 1 gallon of the juice. If you have any extra, you can freeze it in ice cube trays to serve with the punch. In a small saucepan, bring the sugar and water to a boil. Reduce heat, and simmer uncovered for 5 minutes. Stir the sugar solution into the watermelon juice. Chill at least 4 hours. Just before serving, pour the watermelon juice into the melon punch bowl until it is about half full. Carefully add the soda until the punch bowl is about two-thirds full. Stir gently. Add ice if desired.

Millie Adams

Peas

You will find your definition of under-, just-, and overripe relative to the cultivar of pea you are growing. For fresh eating, pick young, when most sweet. For soups or casseroles, you can use a pea that is a little starchy.

Sugar Snap pea. Eat this oh-so-easy-to-grow delicacy pod and all. It is very sweet until the pods begin to yellow and shrivel.

Snap Peas and Pearl Onions

Serves 4 to 6

1 pound Sugar Snap peas
18 pearl onions, peeled
2 tablespoons butter or margarine, melted
1 tablespoon fresh spearmint, minced
½ cup water
½ cup slivered toasted almonds

Wash pea pods; remove strings and ends. In a large saucepan, sauté onions in butter or margarine. Add peas, mint, and water. Bring to a boil. Cover, reduce heat, and simmer 5 to 8 minutes or until peas are tender crisp. Remove from heat, drain, and add almonds. Serve immediately.

Millie Adams

Slightly overmature. The following recipe works well with slightly overmature peas.

Curried Pea Soup

Serves 8

1 quart chicken stock, divided
4 cups fresh peas, shelled
2 small carrots, sliced
2 medium onions, sliced
2 medium potatoes, sliced
2 cloves garlic, peeled and whole
2 celery stalks, with leaves, sliced
2 teaspoons salt
freshly ground black pepper
2 teaspoons curry powder
2 cups light cream or milk

In a large saucepan, place 2 cups of the chicken stock and all of the remaining ingredients, except the rest of the stock and the cream. Bring to a boil, reduce heat, cover, and simmer 20 minutes. In small amounts, purée the cooked vegetable mixture in a blender or food processor. Return the puréed vegetables to the saucepan through a strainer. Add the remaining broth and cream or milk. Reheat, but do not boil. Serve hot, garnished with croutons or a light dusting of pepper or curry powder.

Millie Adams

Peppers

These are great green or red but each stage of maturity may require different treatment in the kitchen.

Green. Stuff briefly boiled green peppers with precooked rice, hamburger, and onion, and top with tomato sauce mixed with parsley, basil, and Greek oregano. Bake until thoroughly heated.

Ripe red, orange, or yellow. These peppers are sweet and mild, almost fruity, and great for eating fresh or for an assortment of cooking options.

Bell Pepper-Cilantro Salsa

Serves 6

2 cups diced orange-and-red bell pepper
1 teaspoon chopped fresh cilantro
¼–½ cup fresh pineapple, cut into small slivers for contrasting texture
⅛–¼ cup olive oil (enough to give the mixture some body and hold)
a squeeze of fresh lemon juice
a pinch of regular sugar

Combine all ingredients and chill in the refrigerator for several hours to let the flavors mingle. Serve over any fresh fish. It is especially good on grilled salmon or tuna (about 1½ pounds).

Eric Schmiedl,
Chag-Town Cafe

Hot. Around this house, Chili Salsa is a standard item and is so easy to make. Use fewer peppers if you live in an area where peppers grow hotter or more if you like a salsa that makes you sweat.

Chili Salsa

Serves 4

2 jalapeño or 3 Anaheim chili peppers, roasted and skinned
½ clove garlic
2 tablespoons chopped onion
pinch of parsley
2 fully ripe tomatoes (preferably Italian), peeled

Place all ingredients except tomatoes in a blender or food processor, and chop briefly until mixed and chunky. Remove the pepper mixture, and briefly chop the tomatoes. Combine the two mixtures. Serve with corn chips or tacos.

Potatoes

Baked potatoes usually have been cured for storage. When you grow your own, you should also cook up a few tender new potatoes.

Butter-Steamed Peewees

Serves 4

2 cups large marble-size new potatoes
3 tablespoons unsalted butter
salt and freshly ground black pepper, to taste (optional)
fresh dill or chives, chopped (optional)

Wash the potatoes gently to avoid rubbing off their skins. Melt the butter over medium-low heat in a small saucepan. Add the potatoes, and stir to coat with butter. Cover and cook until tender (about 7 minutes), shaking the pan occasionally. If desired, toss with salt and pepper to taste and chopped fresh dill or chives.

Lori Zaim

Sour Cream-Caviar New Potatoes

Serves 4 to 6

1½ pounds new potatoes
3 tablespoons butter
⅓ cup sour cream
1 tablespoon fresh-snipped dill
2 tablespoons salmon caviar
freshly ground black pepper

Wash the potatoes gently to avoid rubbing off their skins. In a medium saucepan, melt the butter in ⅓ cup water over medium-low heat. Add the potatoes, and stir to coat with the butter mixture. Cover and cook until tender, about 15 minutes, shaking the pan occasionally. Stir in the sour cream, dill, caviar, and pepper to taste.

Lori Zaim

Cured storage potato. This is the one to bake or boil or, better yet, microwave and fill with peas and mayonnaise, sour cream and dill, or broccoli and cheese.

Roots

Baby. Tiny baby roots are the most tender and are less-inclined to have strong flavors. Steam them lightly, and serve with dip or drench in butter.

Baby Root Salad

Serves 8

1½ pounds baby carrots
1½ pounds baby turnips
1 teaspoon sugar
1 teaspoon salt
2 tablespoons whole-grain prepared mustard
¼ cup balsamic vinegar
¾ cup extra-virgin olive oil

salt and freshly ground black pepper, to taste
2 tablespoons chives, finely minced

Peel the carrots and turnips. Place them in a large pan with the sugar and salt. Cover the vegetables with cold water. Bring to a boil, and then reduce heat to simmer until tender, about 10 minutes. Drain well.

Whisk the mustard and vinegar until blended. Slowly add the oil while whisking. Season with salt and pepper to taste. Toss the warm vegetables with the dressing. Cool, and then refrigerate. Sprinkle with 2 tablespoons fresh-snipped chives before serving.

Lori Zaim

Small roots can even be used for dessert. Slice baby carrots, coat them with flour, and sauté in butter until lightly browned. Add a little water and 1 tablespoon brandy to the bottom of the pan. Cover and steam until tender. Add a healthy portion of raisins (about ¼ cup per cup of carrots), recover, and gently heat for 15 minutes.

Mature. When full size, some roots become tough. At this stage, you may want to use them shredded. If they have good flavor and are not too woody to shred easily, make a layered salad. Pile up layers of shredded carrots, radishes, and peeled turnips, sliced onion rings, peas, and grated Swiss cheese. Top with a mixture of ¾ cup mayonnaise, ¼ cup sour cream, and a dash of garlic powder and dill.

Cook large carrots in cream. Slice the roots in quarters lengthwise, and remove the tough central core. Boil until they become slightly soft; drain. Cover the carrots with light cream, and simmer without boiling until the liquid is reduced by half. Serve hot.

Rhubarb

Young. When rhubarb is young and tender, you can bake instead of boil with a recipe such as the following.

Rhubarb Custard Pie

One 9-inch pie

Pie crust for 2-crust 9-inch pie
3 eggs, beaten
¼ teaspoon ground nutmeg
¼ cup all-purpose flour
1½ cups sugar
1 pound rhubarb, sliced ¾ inch thick (at least 4 cups)
2 tablespoons butter
1 teaspoon sugar

Preheat the oven to 400°F. Line the bottom of the 9-inch pie pan with pie crust. In a large bowl, mix the beaten eggs, nutmeg, flour, and sugar until smooth. Stir in the rhubarb, and mix until it is coated. Pour the rhubarb mixture into the pie crust. Dot the top of the pie with the butter. Arrange the pie crust on top, and seal and vent. Sprinkle the sugar on top of crust. Bake pie in the preheated oven for 50 minutes, or until the pie bubbles and the rhubarb is tender.

Millie Adams

Slightly tough. Slicing rhubarb small and stewing it will help soften tough fibers.

Stewed Rhubarb Dessert

Serves 4

1 pound rhubarb, cut into ¾-inch pieces (about 4 cups)
½ cup strawberry jam
½ teaspoon almond extract
whipped cream, vanilla ice cream, or vanilla frozen yogurt

In a 2-quart saucepan over medium heat, heat the rhubarb and 2 tablespoons of water to boiling. Reduce heat, cover, and simmer 3 minutes, stirring occasionally. Stir in the jam; return heat to medium. Cook 4 to 5 minutes, uncovered, until rhubarb is tender and mixture thickens; stir occasionally to prevent scorching. Stir in almond extract; cool. Serve warm or chilled. Garnish with whipped cream or a small scoop of ice cream or frozen yogurt.

Millie Adams

Squash

From the first burgeoning of blossoms to the final hardening of the skin, squash is edible. Some people even eat the tendrils.

Blossom.

Ricotta-Stuffed Squash Blossoms

Serves 4

1 pound ricotta cheese
1 medium onion, finely chopped
½ cup toasted almonds, finely chopped
½ cup freshly grated Parmesan cheese
½ teaspoon freshly ground black pepper
1 teaspoon seasoning salt
2 tablespoons fresh minced basil (or 2 tablespoons dried)
2 tablespoons minced parsley
12–15 squash blossoms
2 tablespoons melted butter

Preheat the oven to 350°F. Mix together all ingredients except squash blossoms and melted butter. Carefully stuff squash blossoms with filling mixture, but don't overfill. Drizzle the melted butter over the blossoms, and bake in preheated oven for 15 minutes.

Shepherd's Garden Seeds
Recipes from a Kitchen Garden

Young. Enjoy young squash with the tender, colorful skin attached. Keep it simple to enjoy the delicate flavor.

Yellow Squash with Fresh Thyme

Serves 4

1 tablespoon butter
1 teaspoon fresh thyme leaves
4 young yellow squash, sliced
salt and freshly ground black pepper, to taste

Melt the butter with the thyme in a large skillet over medium-low heat. Add the squash, stirring to mix well. Cook covered, stirring occasionally, for 5 minutes. Season with salt and pepper to taste.

Lori Zaim

Zucchini-Artichoke Casserole

Serves 4 to 6

4 to 5 small (1½ to 2 inches in diameter) yellow zucchini
one 14-ounce or two 8-ounce cans of artichokes, drained and quartered
2 cloves garlic, peeled and minced
oregano, salt, and freshly ground black pepper, to taste
½ cup freshly grated Parmesan cheese
1 tablespoon butter or margarine

Preheat the oven to 350°F. Slice zucchini ¼ inch thick on a slight diagonal. Arrange in buttered 1½-quart casserole dish. Sprinkle artichokes and garlic over zucchini. Season to taste with oregano, salt, and pepper. Top with grated Parmesan cheese. Cut butter or margarine into small bits and arrange on top of casserole. Bake in preheated oven for 30 minutes or until zucchini is tender-crisp.

Millie Adams

Overmature. As with root crops, grating is the best remedy for overmature squash. Use larger squash as a bowl for flavorful fillings; peel off the tough skin or scoop the inner flesh out as you eat. Or, cut out the seeds and make the flesh into bread or cake.

Zucchini Cake

Serves 12

2 cups all-purpose flour
½ cup whole wheat flour
2 teaspoons baking powder
½ teaspoon salt
2¼ teaspoons cinnamon
½ teaspoon ground cloves
3 eggs
½ cup vegetable oil
1⅓ cups sugar
½ cup orange juice
1 teaspoon vanilla extract
1½ cups shredded zucchini, packed

ORANGE ICING

2 teaspoons soft butter
3 cups powdered sugar
¼ cup orange juice
2 teaspoons lemon juice

Preheat oven to 350°F. Grease and flour 13" x 9" x 2" pan.

In a large mixing bowl, mix together flours, baking powder, salt, cinnamon, and cloves. In a smaller bowl, beat eggs well. Stir oil, sugar, orange juice, vanilla extract, and zucchini into eggs. Mix well. Add zucchini mixture to flour mixture, and stir just until flour is moistened. Pour batter into prepared pan, and bake in preheated oven for 35 to 40 minutes. Cool cake on rack.

Mix all icing ingredients together. Beat until smooth. Drizzle icing over cooled cake.

Millie Adams

Italian Gourmet Globe Squash

Choose two Gourmet Globe squashes that are nearing maturity, cut them in half, and scoop out the seeds. Set them, cut-side down, in a dish with a bit of water on the bottom, cover with plastic wrap, and microwave on High for 6 minutes. Let sit for 5 minutes. Cut thin slices off the bottom so the shells will stand upright in a baking dish and flip them over. Fill with a mixture of spaghetti sauce, thickened with crumbled sausage patties, ½ clove minced garlic, and to taste basil and parsley. Simmer the sauce for 10 minutes. Top with grated Parmesan cheese, and broil until slightly browned.

Tomatoes

Surely one of the most versatile of vegetable fruits, tomatoes are delicious prepared green, red but firm, and even overripe.

Green. You can cook these as you would apples. Thick-slice a large tomato and fry it in butter until it is tender and slightly browned. Sprinkle with 1 teaspoon of sugar combined with a dash of cinnamon.

Firm and red. These prime tomatoes are the best for slicing on sandwiches. I love them with mustard or cream cheese and dill. They are also great in salads.

Mom's Garden Salad

Serves 4

4 garden tomatoes, peeled and diced
1 large green pepper, diced
1 sweet onion, diced
¼ teaspoon salt
⅛ teaspoon freshly ground pepper
2 tablespoons vinegar
dash of sugar

Combine all ingredients and toss.

Lori Zaim

Ripe. Sweet ripe tomatoes are good candidates for a variety of dishes. For easier slicing, use partially frozen chicken in the following recipe.

Sue's Chicken Stir-Fry

Serves 4

2 whole boneless chicken breasts
2 tablespoons corn oil
½ onion, sliced and separated into rings
1 ripe full-size tomato, cut into wedges
1 avocado, peeled and wedged
one 8-ounce can whole water chestnuts
¼ cup Oriental stir-fry sauce, such as bottled Kikkoman brand (contains soy sauce, sherry, corn syrup)
pinch of salt
chow mein noodles

Cut the chicken into strips and cook the strips in the oil with the onion. When the chicken is thoroughly cooked, drain off the excess oil, and stir in the tomato, avocado, and water chestnuts. Add Oriental stir-fry sauce to the chicken mixture, and heat until warm. Serve over chow mein noodles.

Tomato-Onion Pie

Serves 8 to 10

8 medium onions, peeled and sliced
5 cups soft bread cubes
8 medium-size tomatoes, peeled and sliced
1 tablespoon sugar
½ teaspoon salt
⅛ teaspoon freshly ground black pepper
2 tablespoons butter or margarine

Preheat oven to 350°F. Boil onions in ½ cup salted water until they are almost tender. Drain. Heavily butter a 2-quart casserole dish. Line the bottom of the dish with 4 cups of the bread cubes, reserving 1 cup for topping. Layer onions and tomatoes over bread cubes. Sprinkle sugar, salt, and pepper over tomatoes. Top with reserved bread cubes. Dot with butter. Bake in the preheated oven for about 30 minutes.

Millie Adams

seven

How the Crop Changes After Harvest

WHAT YOU DO with your harvest after you pick it makes a big difference in its quality when it reaches your table. Produce is alive, not inanimate. It breathes and transpires. Its systems continue to function even after harvesting, though sometimes to the detriment of its storage lifetime.

When plants are ripening, you can see, feel, smell, and taste the changes they are undergoing. During the hours that follow harvesting, however, only taste indicates the chemical changes that are occurring. Sweet, aromatic, starchy, acidic, and bitter components fluctuate, increasing or decreasing according to the weather, elapsed time, and internal characteristics unique to each crop. Some vitamins decompose. Moisture evaporates, and now no lifeline replaces it. Consequently, produce may wilt. Spoiler microorganisms move in, searching for a weak spot to attack.

Commercial produce weathers some of these changes with the help of synthetic waxy coatings, antioxidants, emulsifiers, and stabilizers — chemicals you may wish to avoid on your home-growns. You can achieve similar results, chemical-free, by quick refrigeration or processing.

CHANGES INSPIRED BY THE CROP ITSELF

Enzymes and Hormones

Enzymes and hormones, manufactured by the plant, have encouraged ripening of the crop. They are still on the job after harvest, changing flavor, nutritional value, and texture. If a fruit is immature, the changes can be beneficial. If a fruit is picked ripe, however, hormones and enzymes only inspire deterioration. To slow their action, chill produce promptly. To stop it altogether, blanch, cook, or pressure cook. You'll find more on these methods in chapter 8.

One of the most influential hormones is ethylene gas, released by ripe fruit such as melons, tomatoes, and apples. Ethylene management is critical if you want to ripen something fast or store fruits and vegetables for extended periods.

Ethylene is involved in different phases of growth, but its leading role comes when a fruit reaches full size and begins to ripen. Botanists call this change the *climacteric* — the point of transition between growth and the release of the fruit. At the climacteric, a fruit absorbs many times more oxygen than usual and releases an equal blast of carbon dioxide along with ethylene gas. The ethylene encourages cells to soften and chemical components to mingle, both on the climacteric fruit itself and any neighbors. It can make carrots bitter and leafy vegetables, cucumbers, and peppers pale.

You can use ethylene to your advantage. To quickly ripen a green tomato or melon, enclose it in a plastic bag with a ripe apple. The released ethylene from the ripe apple will act upon the unripe fruit to hasten the maturity of both.

On the other hand, keep a tight rein on ethylene if you are storing fruit with greens, tubers, or roots. An apt old saying states: "Never store green with red." Keep ripe fruit away from potatoes, lettuce, and cabbages, as they may rot more quickly if exposed to ethylene gas. Ventilate a root cellar well to flush ethylene out. Keep fruit cold to slow ethylene release, and seal it in an airtight plastic bag. Once the fruit uses up all the oxygen in the bag, it will stop producing ethylene and ripen more slowly.

Enzymes kick in to turn sugars into starches or vice versa, or to degrade nutrients, especially vitamin C. They work on vitamin C faster if exposed to air, such as through being peeled, cut, broken, or chopped, or kept warm instead of cold. Even with refrigeration, you can expect vitamin C-rich green leaves to lose the vitamin C within two or three days. Other kinds of vegetables can lose 50 percent within a week. Parsley, one of the best sources of vitamin C, scarcely retains any vitamin C when dried.

Vitamin C and the more stable B vitamins are also water soluble. They leach or leak out of a vegetable that has been cooked or soaked in water.

The fat-soluble vitamins, like vitamin A, stay in place much longer. Even though dried parsley has little vitamin C left, for instance, it is still rich in vitamin A. Carrots and sweet potatoes hold near harvest levels even after months of storage.

Flavorings

Sugars can change into starches and back into sugars. The direction and speed of the changes depend on the crop and the temperature.

Peas and sweet corn lose their sugar content within hours. If you cannot eat these immediately, can or freeze them right after harvest to trap those sugars in their present state. In wrinkle-seeded peas, the type most commonly grown commercially for canning, the sweetest moment comes four days before the optimum harvest time, when the peas are slightly immature. At this time, they average 7 percent sugar content. At harvest, sugar levels drop to 6 percent. By ten days after the optimum harvest time, sugar levels have plummeted, and the peas have a mealy texture.

In carrots, sugar content is tied to vitamin A levels, which helps them stay sweet for months. Chestnut winter squash becomes increasingly sweet for several weeks after harvest.

Sweet Sandwich onions are naturally high in sugar but taste hot until the pungent mustard oils decompose after a few months in storage.

Cold-hardy vegetables like parsnips and Brussels sprouts convert starches into sugars if exposed to several frosts.

Potatoes change starch into sugar if stored in the refrigerator below 35° to 40°F. The now slightly sweet tuber tastes odd and cooks into undesirable black potato chips and French fries. Consequently, commercial processors store Irish potato tubers above 40°F and spray them with a growth retardant to prevent sprouting. The alternative is to keep them colder but bring them back to a warm room for several days before cooking or processing.

Moisture Content

Just as plants lose water through stomatal pores when growing, harvested crops continue to lose moisture — though it is now irreplaceable. Moisture loss is especially fast in crops not protected by a waxy or thick skin or rind. If you wash produce before storing it, you may remove this vital covering (see chapter 5). Many commercial crops are washed and then coated with a sticky wax that is difficult to remove without peeling the skin. At home, limit transpiration by enclosing produce in plastic bags or wrap or setting greens, roots and all, in water, as you would an arrangement of flowers. Wrap perishable foliage in moist paper towels and enclose in a plastic bag. Pack thin-skinned crops like carrot, parsnip, and Jerusalem artichoke roots in moist sand.

DAMAGES CAUSED BY SPOILERS

Now that the produce is off the vine, the decomposers move in. Bacteria, molds, rots, and other fungi invade through cracks and crevices, old blossom ends, frost-bitten spots, small cuts, and bruises. They can spread through fresh produce or improperly processed canned, frozen, or dried

VOLATILE FLAVORINGS: HANDLE WITH CARE

To preserve the delightful flavorings and scents of pungent or spicy crops for the future, keep them away from heat and as whole as possible.

◆ Onions and some of the more pungent mustard and cole crops contain an eye-watering sulfurous oil, *plus* a longer-lasting component that remains in plant tissues. When you cut or peel an onion, you release some of the volatile components into the air. They also wash out in water. This is why cutting an onion under running water or boiling it reduces pungent vapors and some of the taste, although it does not eliminate the flavor entirely. Volatile mustard oils, a different class of flavorings, can invade nearby crops in a root cellar or penetrate throughout the house if you store cabbages in the basement.

◆ Herbs contain a number of volatile terpenes that help prevent attack by insects and animals. Parsley and celery leaves contain a similar volatile compound, *apiol,* which is responsible for their characteristic flavor and odor. If you dry these herbs, their flavoring becomes concentrated in the leaf tissues. Keep flavor compounds from evaporating by storing fairly large flakes of the greenery instead of grinding it into powder.

goods and make them inedible. (For more on processing, see chapter 8.)

How you store and handle newly harvested produce makes a big difference in how quickly the spoilers gain a foothold. Treat produce gently. Process or store quickly and appropriately for that crop. Some of your alternatives follow.

STORAGE OPTIONS

When you can't eat everything within a few minutes of harvest, you will have to use one of a variety of storage methods. The refrigerator is ideal for storing many but not all types of produce. (You may keep pickles or jams in there for months.) But, to keep produce through the winter or the entire year, you will have to turn to freezing, canning, or drying. This chapter contains an introduction to each of these long-term methods. For the nitty-gritty information to use them for specific foods, turn to chapter 8.

Using the Refrigerator Wisely

If on Sunday, you tagged a particular summer squash for chicken stir-fry on Tuesday night, you probably will find short-term cold storage is the best and easiest way to maintain top quality. Cold temperatures can limit vitamin, flavor, and texture losses by slowing hormone, enzyme, and spoiler activity. On the other hand, if you will be heading out of town for the weekend, or you already have a bushel of fresh vegetables waiting to be eaten, you should consider long-term storage.

Let's imagine you have harvested only what you want to eat for today and tomorrow. Stop and think for a minute before you stuff everything into the refrigerator. If you stick to a packing system, you may not have as much waste. You can say goodbye to those forgotten cauliflowers or beans that you find furry, slimy, and smelly, hiding in the depths of the refrigerator. This system will let you know when you have harvested more than you can eat in the next week and when you need to get out the freezer bags: If you keep loading new produce in the front of the refrigerator and pushing back

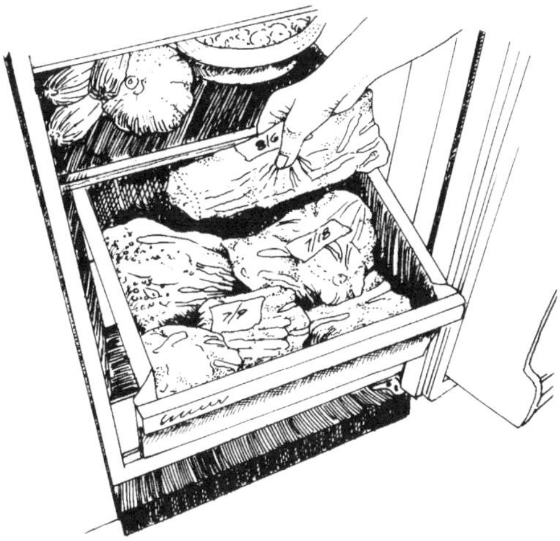

Date all packages, and put newly harvested produce in the rear.

WHEN YOU SHOULD NOT REFRIGERATE

A few foods cannot take the intense cold of a refrigerator. Most refrigerators hover at about 37°F. They are, after all, geared to preserving meat, eggs, and dairy products. At this temperature, tomatoes and berries lose flavor; eggplant and cucumbers develop sunken spots; basil darkens. When refrigeration is essential, keep such crops away from the cold center of the refrigerator. Instead, put them in the door or in the vegetable crisper, which may be warmer, especially if you have an older model.

STORAGE OPTIONS

Crop	Storage Method	Washing Method[1]	Temperature/ Humidity[2]
Artichoke	R,C	A	cold/moist
Artichoke, Jerusalem	R,RC	A	cold/moist
Asparagus	R,F,C	A	—
Basil	R,F,D	A	—
Beans, dry	R,F,C,D	A	—
Beans, green	D	A	cold/dry
Beets	R,F,C,RC	A	cold/moist
Berries	R,F,C,D	B (gently)	—
Broccoli	R,F,RC (briefly)	A	cold/moist
Brussels sprouts	R,F,RC (briefly)	A	cold/moist
Cabbage	R,F (as kraut),C,RC (briefly)	A	cold/moist
Cantaloupe	R	A	—
Carrot	R,F,C,RC,D	A	cold/moist
Cauliflower	R,F,C (pickled),RC	A	cold/moist
Celery	R,F,C,RC,D	A	cold/moist
Chard, Swiss	R,F,C	B	—
Chicory	R,RC (before forcing for Belgian endive)	A	cold/moist
Collard/Kale	R,F,C	B	cold/moist
Corn	R,F,C,D	A	cold/dry if dried
Cucumber	R,C (as pickles)	B	—
Currants	F,C (as jelly),D	B	—
Dill	R,F,D	A	—
Eggplant	R (50°F best),F,C (pickled)	A	cold/moist (55°F)
Endive/Escarole	R,RC (briefly)	B	cold/moist
Fennel	R,F,D	A	—
Flowers, edible	R,D	A	—
Garlic	F,R (in olive oil),RC	A	cold/dry
Horseradish	R (briefly),F,C (pickled),RC	B	cold/moist
Kohlrabi	R,RC (briefly)	B	cold/moist
Leeks	R,F,D,RC	A	cold/moist
Lettuce	R,RC (if winter keeper)	B	cold/moist
Marjoram	R,F,D	A	—
Mustard greens	R,F	B	—
Okra	R,F,C	A	—
Onions	R (if cut),F,C (pickled),RC	A	cold/dry
Parsnips	R,F,RC	A	cold/moist
Peas			
Edible pod	R,F	A	—
Shelling	R,F,C,D	A	—

Crop	Storage Method	Washing Method[1]	Temperature/ Humidity[2]
Peppers (hot and sweet)	R,F,C,D	A	cold/moist
Potatoes	F (if shredded or precooked),RC	A	cold/moist
Radishes	R,RC (if winter-keeping cultivar)	A	cold/moist
Rhubarb	R,F,C	B	–
Sage	R,F,D	A	–
Salsify	R,F,RC	A	cold/moist
Shungiku	R,F (chopped)	B	–
Sorrel	R,F (as purée)	B	–
Soybeans	R,F (green stage),D	A	–
Spinach	R,F,RC	B	–
Squash			
Summer	R,F (shredded, cubed),C (pickled)	A	–
Winter	R (once cut),F (cooked),C (cooked),RC	A	cold/dry
Sweet potatoes	F (cooked),C,RC	A	cold/moist
Thyme	R,F,D	A	–
Tomatoes	R (only if dead-ripe,F,C,D,RC (if green or long keeper)	A	cold/moist
Turnips			
Greens	R,F,C	B	–
Roots	R,RC,F (briefly)	A	cold/moist
Watermelon	R,F (if overripe)	A	–

[1]For more on washing, see chapter 5.
[2]Requirement for Root Cellar Storage

Key:

Storage Method
R=refrigerate
F=freeze
C=can
RC=root cellar
D=dry

Washing Method
B=wash before storing fresh
A=wash after storage but before eating, cooking, or processing

Temperature/Humidity Requirement (listed only for root cellaring)
cold/moist = 32° to 34°F and 90 to 95 percent humidity
cool/moist = 45° to 50°F for melons and peppers, 38° to 40°F for potatoes, 55° to 65°F for sweet potatoes and tomatoes, all with 85 to 90 percent humidity
cold/dry = 32° to 34°F with about 65 percent humidity
cool/dry = 35° to 50°F with about 65 percent humidity (with the exception of winter squash and pumpkins, which need about 55°F and 70 percent humidity)

yesterday's goodies, you probably will eat only the most recent produce and leave the rest to age. To avoid this trap, I load short-term storage items in the back of the vegetable crisper drawer and pull the previous residents forward. When I see vegetables in front, I am reminded to eat them. Once the drawer is full, I freeze or can all new produce until I have more space. I do give myself the option to overflow on special occasions, and then the extras go to the vertical rack on the inside of the refrigerator door. Here, I load from the left, moving older produce closer to the side of the door I open and look at first.

Despite all my organization, sometimes we do not eat everything as fast as I had thought we would. When produce has been sitting for a couple of days, I check its freshness before eating it. If it is discolored, limp, spoiled, or otherwise unpleasant, it goes out to the compost pile, opening up room in the refrigerator for great new stuff.

Signs of Freshness

If you take a little extra care to store produce in the right place and in the right manner, you will be more satisfied with the results, whether a day or a week from harvest. Here are some guidelines for how long different kinds of produce lasts, advice on determining freshness, and suggestions for long-term storage if the produce is not needed for a time. For further information about root cellaring (marked by an "*") see pages 192–199.

Artichokes. Store in the refrigerator in plastic bag for a week. Fresh artichokes should be squeaky crisp. For long-term storage, can or freeze.

Artichokes, Jerusalem. You can store these, wrapped in plastic in the refrigerator, for two weeks; they will last slightly longer if you store them in the root cellar, under the same conditions as potatoes. In warmer climates, you may be able to dig the roots all winter. Jerusalem artichokes that grow moldy, soft, or discolored are no longer good.

Asparagus. Set in a glass of water like a cut flower and cover with plastic wrap. Fresh asparagus should last about three days. It is overdue for eating or processing when it begins to droop, gets wet tips, or loses sweetness. For long-term storage, freeze or can.

Store asparagus, covered, in a glass of water in the refrigerator.

Beans. Snap beans, if stored dry in a plastic bag, last up to a week in the refrigerator. They are past their prime if they lose their velvety fur and "snapability." For long-term storage, can or freeze.

Beets. These will last one to three weeks in the refrigerator, although cultivars noted for long-storage qualities may be good even longer. If you must refrigerate them for over a week, twist off the foliage, leaving about an inch of stem. Beet roots are not fresh if spongy or scaly. For long-term storage, freeze, root cellar,* can, or pickle.

Twist foliage off beets, leaving about 1 inch of stem.

Blueberries. Refrigerate unwashed berries in plastic wrap for up to two weeks. They are past prime when mushy, discolored, or moldy. You also can freeze, can, or dry blueberries.

Bramble berries. For best quality, eat, process, dry, or freeze berries upon picking. You can refrigerate them for a couple of days, although there may be some flavor loss. Lay them in a single layer on a tray lined with a paper towel. Cover with plastic. Remove bad berries daily. If no longer fresh, bramble berries fall apart, discolor, rot, leak, or mold.

Broccoli. This will stay good about a week if wrapped in plastic and kept in the refrigerator. It is overdue for using when it loses its good green color and firmness. For the long term, freeze.

Brussels sprouts. These will last for about a week in the refrigerator if wrapped in plastic or about a month on the leafless stalk in a root cellar.* They are past prime when they yellow or wilt. For long-term storage, freeze or leave out in the garden until the temperature drops below freezing.

Cabbage. A fresh head should last in the refrigerator for up to two weeks. Savoys are more perishable than other cabbages. All yellow and get flabby leaves when no longer fresh. For long-term storage, freeze, can as sauerkraut, or root cellar.

Cantaloupe and muskmelon. You can let these ripen for a couple of days at room temperature until they are slightly soft. Refrigerate for another couple of days. Cut into pieces, wrap in plastic, and refrigerate. Melons are past prime if the husk develops sunken or discolored spots or if the flesh dissolves.

Carrots. In a plastic bag, carrots can last from three weeks to several months in the refrigerator if you twist off the greens. They are no longer fresh if limp or discolored. You may be able to reinvigorate slightly droopy roots in an iced-water bath. For long-term storage, root cellar in damp sand, can, freeze, or dry.

Cauliflower. A head can last a week in the refrigerator if wrapped in plastic. Or, leave it on the stalk in a bucket of soil in a root cellar* for up to a month. The head is overdue for use if it is wilted or it has brown spots. You may be able to perk it up with a soak in cold salt or vinegar water. For long-term storage, freeze or pickle.

Celery. If plastic-wrapped in the refrigerator, celery leaves last about a week and the stems about two weeks. You can root cellar* the entire plant in damp sand for a couple of months. The stems should snap easily and the leaves should remain bright green and fresh. For long-term storage, can, freeze, or dry.

Chard, Swiss. These greens last up to two weeks when wrapped in plastic in the refrigerator. If gone by, they wilt or have dark spots. For long-term storage, can or freeze.

Collards and kale. The last fall crops of your garden, collards and kale withstand temperatures well below freezing. They keep in the refrigerator one week, if plastic wrapped. If overdue for use, they discolor and wilt. For long-term storage, freeze or can.

Corn. Refrigerate supersweet types in the husk for four to eight days. The husks should still look fresh and the kernels should be plump, not dimpled. For long-term storage or more perishable types of sweet corn, freeze or can.

Cucumbers. These may last a week in the warmer parts of the refrigerator. If no longer fresh, the skin develops sunken brown spots and the fruit softens and shrivels at the ends. For longer storage, pickle.

Eggplant. This can last at room temperature for a couple of days or up to a week in the warmer parts of the refrigerator. If past prime, the cap fades from green and the fruit becomes spongy and sometimes develops brown spots. For longer storage, pickle eggplant or slice, bread, and fry it and then freeze it.

Flowers, edible. Brush off dirt and debris, and refrigerate totally dry flowers, loosely wrapped in plastic. Some flowers last one or two days this way. For longer storage, dry or candy.

Herbs. Keep leafy herbs in a glass of water on a cool, dark counter up to a couple of days, or refrigerate them wrapped in lightly moist paper towels and enclosed in a plastic bag. Herbs lose quality quickly. The aroma fades, and they wilt or discolor. For long-term storage, freeze or dry.

Horseradish. Roots last several days if wrapped in plastic and kept in the refrigerator (the flavor quickly disappears) or stored in moist sand in the root cellar.* For longer storage or to preserve the pungency, can.

Kohlrabi. This swollen stem will

HERBAL VINEGARS

One of the easiest and most satisfying ways to preserve culinary herbs is by putting them in vinegar. When their essential oils permeate the acidic fluid, the captured flavor is nearly as aromatic as when fresh. Herb vinegar is excellent for salad dressing or marinade. You will find steep prices on such herbal vinegars in gourmet stores — rather a surprise when you see how easy the process is.

Thoroughly wash a small handful of prime herb sprigs and dry them on paper towels. Drop a sprig or two in a small bottle of white wine vinegar, the light flavor of which does not mask the herbal essence. You can also use red, distilled white, cider, or balsamic vinegars, but they are not as complementary to most herbs. Use a cork or lid to seal the container so it is airtight. Avoid metal lids, however, which corrode or discolor vinegars. Label by herb and date.

Let the herb steep for several weeks. You can strain out the vinegar or leave the herb in, depending on how you like the final result to look. Store the vinegar in a decorative glass jar or utilitarian container.

To speed the process, you can heat the vinegar to near boiling, and then pour it over the herb. Return to a sterilized jar.

last a week in the refrigerator or up to two months in the root cellar. When deteriorated, the leaves yellow or wilt.

Lettuce. More delicate leaf lettuces wilt or rot sooner than firmer types, making refrigerator storage times variable. For the longest life, harvest with roots attached, and set in a glass of water like a cut flower. Enclose the entire container and head in a large plastic bag with lots of headroom. Or, wrap the head in moist paper towels before enclosing it in a paper bag. If allowed to sit too long, lettuce wilts and yellows. You may be able to recrisp older leaves slightly by placing them in the freezer for a minute or soaking them in cold water.

Okra. Okra pods keep in the refrigerator for up to ten days. If damaged or no longer fresh, they blacken and lose the velvety interior texture. For long-term storage, freeze or can.

Onions. Refrigerate scallions but not onion bulbs, unless they are cut and plastic wrapped; in the latter case, they may last a couple of days. Keep cured, whole bulbs in a cool, dry, well-ventilated location. They last from several weeks to many months, depending on the cultivar. If past their prime, the bulbs develop spongy necks, green sprouts, soggy spots, or lose weight. For longer-term storage, chop, freeze, or dry. Pickle small bulbs.

Parsnip. If plastic-wrapped with the shoots twisted off, these roots last three weeks or longer in the refrigerator. Past-prime parsnips are flabby or discolored. For long-term storage, freeze, leave out in the garden under protective mulch, or root cellar* in damp sand.

Peas. Unshelled peas last one week in the refrigerator. Edible-podded types dry out within a couple of days if not wrapped in plastic. If overripe, peas lose their sweetness, become discolored, or grow so limp that they do not crisply snap open. For longer storage, freeze, can, or dry.

Peppers. These can take refrigeration for up to three weeks. United States Department of Agriculture (USDA) studies indicate that the refrigerator life can be even longer if you keep them at 50°F for ten days, and then at 32°F for eighteen days. If allowed to sit too long, they mold or get soft and dented. For longer storage life, freeze, can, pickle, or dry them.

Potatoes. Don't refrigerate potatoes. Keep them cool and dry in a dark location, such as a root cellar or basement. If spoiled, they become soft, discolored, or green. For longer-term storage, freeze new or cooked potatoes.

Pumpkin and winter squash. Don't refrigerate winter squash unless you have a cut, plastic-wrapped piece. Store whole winter squash near 50°F in a dry location. For longer storage, can or freeze the cooked pulp.

Radish. Twist the leaves off globe types and store plastic-wrapped for up to two weeks. Radishes should be crisp and firm to be fresh. Larger winter-storage types, like Daikon, can be root cellared for longer periods.

Rhubarb. Store about one week in the refrigerator. Keep the leaf attached and both the stalk and leaf wrapped in plastic. Cut off the inedible leaf when you are ready to cook the stalk. A fresh stalk is firm and crisp. For longer storage, cook and freeze or can. Or, dig and root cellar* the root, forcing new shoots in midwinter.

Shungiku. Treat the young shoot like a green. Wrap in damp paper towels, and store in plastic for a couple of days in the refrigerator. If you harvest the edible chrysanthemum head, you can store it for a day like other edible flowers.

Spinach. Wrap in plastic and refrigerate for up to one week. When no longer fresh, the leaves yellow, lose their shine, or grow bitter. For longer storage, freeze or can.

Summer squash. Remove the blossom, wrap in plastic, and store the fruit in the refrigerator for up to one week. Larger, thicker-skinned fruit may last longer. USDA studies showed a longer shelf life for zucchini when stored at 50°F for two days, and then 41°F for eight to sixteen days. Past-prime summer squash loses its firm-

MARK GRAF'S EASY REFRIGERATOR TOMATOES

Tomatoes are one of those crops that taste best without refrigeration. One contributor, however, has turned his refrigerator into a long-term storage place, and still ends up with better-quality tomatoes than those purchased in midwinter in the supermarket. Mark Graf has no time for freezing or canning, so he grows Pik Red, or when they are unavailable, Pik Rite shipping tomatoes, both of which store for a couple of months in his refrigerator. Graf says Pik Red has a thicker wall with more meat than other tomatoes, but it is not rubbery or tough. "I like the combination of good flavor and long-storing qualities, although it is not as good as a tomato like Celebrity," Graf says.

Here is his system: "I pick the tomatoes when not quite ripe, toward the end of the season, but before frost. I bring the fruits inside and wash them in the sink in cool water. Then, I pat them dry with a paper towel. I put them in the refrigerator totally dry and not touching or they spread fungal problems very quickly. They rest on a wire grid where they get cooled down quickly and have good air circulation. I have had fresh tomatoes until Thanksgiving and am now shooting for New Year's Day," Graf explains.

He sometimes wraps the tomatoes in newspaper and stores them in the basement. However, they do not last as long in the warmer temperature.

ness, shine, or fresh color. For longer storage, can, pickle or freeze.

Sweet potatoes. Do not refrigerate. Keep moist at 55° to 60°F. The roots do not store well and may become wet or soggy if kept too long.

Tomatillo. Tomatillos that have not fallen to the ground in the garden may be stored on a cool shelf or counter for a couple of days. For longer storage, pickle and can.

Tomatoes. Tomatoes lose their flavor and aroma with refrigeration. Do not refrigerate, therefore, unless you need to hold a ripe fruit up to a week or you wish to try Mark Graf's system (see box). Short-term freezing preserves better flavor. You can keep perfect green tomatoes in a cool, moist location for about a month. You will see that tomatoes are overripe when the fruit rots or develops soft spots. For longer storage, freeze, can, or dry.

Turnip. The roots can last several weeks in the refrigerator or root cellar. The greens can be refrigerated for about one week when wrapped in plastic. The tops should remain green and the roots firm. For longer storage, freeze, can, or dry.

Watermelon. A watermelon should last a week in the refrigerator. If overdue, the rind will develop sunken spots, or the flesh will become overly soft. For longer storage, freeze the flesh or pickle the rind.

Long-Term Storage in the Refrigerator

If you combine refrigerator cold with pickling, fermenting, or candying, you can extend the storage life of a perishable item from days to months. The refrigerator then becomes a time-saving alternative to canning. Here are some ideas:

◆ Hold on to perishable berry flavor for up to two months by storing them in fruit syrup. Combine 1 pint of ripe fresh berries with 1 cup sugar and ½ cup light corn syrup. First, microwave berries in a 2-quart casserole on High for 7 to 10 minutes. Strain to remove juice (discard pulp). Add sugar and corn syrup to juice. Microwave 4 to 6 minutes, until boiling. Stir every 2 minutes. Continue boiling another 1 to 1½ minutes. Pour into sterilized 1-pint containers. Use on pancakes, ice cream, or cake. Makes 1 pint. (From *Flower and Garden,* August 1991.)

◆ Marinate vegetables in vinegar. Renee Shepherd steams fresh vegetables until tender-crisp and marinates them in a vinaigrette sauce. Even cucumbers and summer squash last for weeks this way in the refrigerator.

◆ Make refrigerator cole slaw. Mary Keiser shares a recipe for Pepper Slaw, a Pennsylvania Dutch dish that lasts for weeks in the refrigerator or months in the freezer.

Pepper Slaw

Makes about 2 quarts

large head of cabbage
½ cup vinegar
½ cup hot water
1½ cups sugar
1½ teaspoons salt
chopped green pepper
shredded carrot

Chop the cabbage very finely, almost as if grated. Combine the vinegar and water, and mix the sugar and salt. Pour the vinegar mixture over the grated cabbage in a bowl and stir. Add some chopped green pepper and shredded carrot for color and flavor. Keep refrigerated up to two weeks or freeze.

◆ Make icebox pickles out of cucumbers or summer squash.

Summer Squash Icebox Pickles

Makes 2 quarts

7 cups thinly sliced zucchini, summer squash, or both
1 cup thinly sliced onions
1 cup grated carrot
1 green pepper, chopped finely
1 cup cider vinegar
2 cups sugar
1 tablespoon pickling salt
1 tablespoon dill seeds

Combine all ingredients in a large bowl. Mix well. Refrigerate overnight.

Pack vegetables tightly into quart jars. Cover with brine. Refrigerate. These pickles keep well in the refrigerator for up to 3 months.

From Andrea Chesman's
Favorite Pickles and Relishes
(Garden Way Publishing)

◆ Sugar green tomatoes and extend their refrigerator life to several months. Use as candied fruit in fruit cakes, candies, and cookies.

Candied Green Tomato Bits

Yield: 1½–2 cups

4 medium green tomatoes
2 cups sugar
1 cup water
Additional sugar for rolling

Cut the tomatoes into quarters. Scoop out the seeds and pulp and discard. Cut the fleshy outer shell into small pieces and drain thoroughly.

In a large skillet, combine the 2 cups sugar and water and bring to a boil. Reduce heat and cook to the soft ball stage (238°F).

Slowly add half the tomato pieces and simmer until clear. Remove the tomato pieces and drain. Reheat the sugar mixture to boiling and drop in the remaining tomato pieces. Repeat. When all the tomato pieces are cooked and drained, roll in sugar. Store in rigid plastic containers. The tomato bits will keep for several months in the refrigerator, or they may be frozen.

LONG-TERM STORAGE METHODS

Obviously, the size of your refrigerator limits how much you can refrigerate. If you have a big garden — or family — you may not be able to fit everything in and you will have to turn to longer-term storage methods.

Use long-term storage methods like freezing, canning, and drying to save your excess vegetables for the off season when produce prices are at a premium. You need to learn the pros and cons of each method, however, so you can decide which method or combination of methods to use.

The earliest forms of preserving produce were drying and salting, root cellaring, pickling, and fermenting. These methods are still used today but to a lesser extent than newer processes. Canning came into popularity in the late 1800s and has since been surpassed by freezing. The older methods have certain advantages. Once the produce has been processed, it lasts for months with no additional effort or expense. Canning, pickling, drying, and maintaining a root cellar all take time and effort, however. With the exception of root cellaring, they result in a product that is quite different from the fresh harvest. Freezing is the easiest way to preserve produce — and some frozen produce could pass for fresh — but a freezer requires electricity to maintain.

All of the above methods stop produce from aging by destroying enzymes and killing spoilers or by placing them in an environment in which they cannot function, but each step you take to preserve produce takes it further away from fresh flavor and texture. Here are some of the changes you can expect.

Texture. Changes in texture are especially striking. Frozen vegetables, herbs, and berries become softer, especially if they have a high water content, are tender fleshed, or freeze slowly. Canning softens produce because it requires extensive cooking and submersion in fluids. Dried produce loses most of its bulk. You can eat some dried berries, tomatoes, or summer squash hard or chewy, or reconstitute them to original size with water.

Nutrient loss. Although you do not see or feel vitamin loss, it happens whenever you heat or boil produce.

FREEZING OR REFRIGERATING

Freezing, a long-term storage method, can be best for short-term storage as well, because it captures fresh flavors. Imagine that garden produce is like fresh bread. If you bought three loaves because they were on sale and you knew you wouldn't eat them all within a week, you probably would not leave all three sitting out. If you did, two would be stale by the time you finished eating the first. After suffering through a couple of hard loaves, you would learn to stick the other two in the freezer for a couple of days until you were ready for them.

As with bread, quick-freeze extra beans, rhubarb, tomatoes, and peppers that you harvest in abundance, even if you expect to eat them in a week. Make freezing a standard procedure if you have a harvest that is highly perishable, like raspberries, sweet corn, or shelling peas.

Before freezing or drying, you usually prepare produce by blanching or quick cooking to destroy enzymes and some spoilers. It is a useful process but does reduce nutrient and flavoring levels. Vitamin C and the B vitamins may dissolve into the blanching water, given enough time. If you steam or microwave-blanch rather than boil, you can save most of these vitamins. Boiling and pressure cooking are likely to eliminate much vitamin C but not vitamin A, which does not cook off in boiling water or degrade under high heat or dehydration. See the table on page 187 for nutritional comparisons.

Flavor. You will certainly notice differences in flavor, variations that are most apparent after you have boiled produce. According to V. D. Arthey in *The Quality of Agricultural Products,* blanching can wash away as much as 30 percent of the sugars in peas, 70 percent in spinach, 8 percent in whole stringless beans, and 13 percent in carrots. These water-soluble elements also leach out into canning juices and permeate the entire container. You can still enjoy them if you include the fluids in your dish.

Preservation Options

Consider your options and take stock of which foods you like canned, frozen, or dried. Think about how much time you have and if the culti-

HOW FOODS CHANGE UNDER STORAGE

Compare for yourself some of the flavor and nutritional changes that come from boiling, freezing, and canning.

How Sweet Are They?

To let you imagine how sweet different produce is, compare grams of sugars: 1 cup of white sugar has 193.6 grams of sugar; 1 tablespoon of light corn syrup has 10.7 grams.

Crop	Grams of Crop	Preparation Method	Grams of Sugar
Artichoke, Jerusalem	75 (½ cup)	fresh, sliced	1.9
	75 (½ cup)	stored, sliced	7.2
Asparagus	90 (6 spears)	boiled	1.4
	60 (4 spears)	frozen, boiled	1.7
Beet	68 (½ cup)	raw	4.4
Broccoli	44 (½ cup)	raw, chopped	.7
	92 (½ cup)	chopped, frozen, boiled	1.8
Carrot	72 (1 medium)	raw	4.8
	78 (1 medium)	sliced, boiled	3.4
	73 (1 medium)	canned	2.4
	73 (1 medium)	frozen, boiled	4.2
Beans, baby lima	188 (1 cup)	frozen, boiled	9.0
Beans, Fordhook lima	170 (1 cup)	frozen, boiled	5.4
Beans, lima	188 (1 cup)	boiled	5.5
Onions, green spring	80 (½ cup)	raw	1.6
Onions, mature	80 (½ cup)	raw	5.0
Peas	80 (½ cup)	boiled	4.5
	80 (½ cup)	frozen, boiled	2.8
	85 (½ cup)	canned	3
Spinach	95 (½ cup)	frozen, boiled	1.1
	95 (½ cup)	raw	.34
Tomato	123	raw	3.4
	128	canned	3.2

How Nutritious are They?

Water-soluble vitamin C is more easily lost than vitamin A through cooking or processing in water. Here are some of the variations typical of different vegetables.

Crop	Grams of Crop	Preparation Method	Vitamin A (RE/IU)[1]	Vitamin C (mg)	Comments
Beans, green snap	62	boiled	41/413	6.0	
	68	canned	24/237	3.0	
	68	frozen, boiled	36/359	6.0	
Broccoli	44 (½ cup)	raw	68/678	41.0	Retains vitamin A but loses vitamin C with cooking and freezing.
	39 (¼ cup)	boiled	55/549.5	24.5	
	46 (¼ cup)	frozen and boiled	87/870.5	18.5	
Corn, yellow	82 (½ cup)	fresh, boiled	18/178	5.0	Vacuum-packed corn, with limited exposure to air, is more likely to retain vitamin C.
	82	canned	13/128		
	105	vacuum-packed	25/253	9.0	
	82	frozen, boiled	20/204	2.0	
Parsley	30 (½ cup)	raw chopped	156/1560	27.0	Notice parsley's large vitamin content and its water weight, both of which are lost with drying; much of the vitamin A remains.
	1.4 (¼ cup)	freeze-dried	89/885	2.0	

[1] Most adults need 5000 IU units of vitamin A and 60 mg vitamin C per day. RE refers to *retinol elements* — the total amount of vitamin A, including beta carotene (which does not entirely convert to vitamin A).

Nutritional information from *Food Values,* by Jean A. T. Pennington (Harper & Row, 1989).

vars you have grown will hold up better with a particular technique. You will find how-to information in chapter 8.

Freezing. If you work fast after harvesting, you can maintain good nutrient levels and flavor as well as put spoilers into suspended animation.

Best of all, you won't have to work too hard. Choose only fresh, top-quality, unblemished produce for freezing, and wash it well. Old, diseased, or dirty produce is teaming with spoiler spores. Blanch to deactivate enzymes, and then deactivate the remaining spoilers in the ultracold of your freezer. The spoilers are not destroyed, only immobilized, and if the produce thaws, they will be back in business.

To preserve vitamins, keep produce really cold and minimize soaking in water and exposure to oxygen. The best freezer temperature is 0°F. At 16°F, produce may lose up to 50 percent of its vitamin C content, according to Arthey. If the temperature fluctuates, Ohio State University research shows that frozen food can lose even more nutrients than a similar canned product.

Squeeze all of the air out of the package and keep it out with an airtight freezer container. Be certain the container stays closed. If it pops open even a crack, the contents will dry out, lose volatile flavorings, or pick up odors from other items in the freezer.

Keep the texture firm by picking produce slightly before prime and freezing it at very cold temperatures — down to –20 to –40°F. This keeps ice crystals small enough that they don't break cell walls; large crystals make what I think of as internal purée.

Know what results to expect from different crops and cultivars. When frozen, starchy vegetables like peas, corn, and lima beans stay the most like fresh. Brussels sprouts are particularly prone to softening after freezing and need only a touch of cooking or they are overdone. Snap beans sometimes contain two different layers of cells in the skin. When canned or frozen, one layer may slough off and leave a ragged, unappealing surface behind. Vegetables with high water contents, such as summer squash and tomatoes, lose their firmness when frozen and are best devoted to casseroles, stews, or the like. Berries often lose their already-delicate texture. For a fresher taste, Tom Eltzroth thaws them only partially, so they stay firm. Herbs are bound to get limp and in some cases darken, but they still maintain their fresh flavor for satisfactory cooking. For more cultivar information, see the table on pages 191–192, which recommends specific cultivars for different processing methods.

Canning. Canning eliminates spoilers and deactivates enzymes with high temperatures, an oxygen-free environment, and — when needed — high pressure. High-acid foods like tomatoes or pickles are inherently less attractive to spoilers, while low-acid foods need to be processed with even greater care.

Canning usually involves long cooking times with the produce submerged in water, pickling fluid, or natural juices. This can soften produce and leach out certain flavors and nutrients. Studies show losses of 30 to 70 percent of the vitamin C in peas, beans, spinach, and asparagus, and 20 to 50 percent of the vitamin C in root crops (from Arthey's *Quality of Horticultural Produce*). Some of the vitamin C, however, remains in the canned juice.

Although a well-processed jar should be sterile enough to keep for up to a year, you must provide a suitable storage facility in order to maintain quality. For instance, store jars in a cool, dark place. Sunlight fades produce. Heat destroys vitamins. Kept at 85°F, food loses 30 percent of the vitamin C that survives processing. At 45°F, nutrient loss is insignificant. Time also takes its share. If you store the jars over six months, expect to lose 10 to 20 percent of the existing vitamin C (from Ray Wolf's *Managing Your Personal Food Supply*).

Drying. Most spoilers need some moisture to do their work. If you remove much or all of the water from crops, you can stop spoilers cold. You need to dry plant tissues down to the last 18 percent of their fresh moisture level to limit bacteria, 20 percent for yeast, and 13 percent for molds, which are the biggest problem for dried goods.

Drying works best for crops that are naturally low in moisture, like fine-textured herbs or mature bean seeds. In arid climates, you can rely on the sun and the breeze to reduce moisture levels. In locations where the humidity is high, dry produce in the oven, in a food dehydrator, near a dehumidifier, or in the microwave. Each technique takes a somewhat different approach. See chapter 8 for more details.

Overwintering in the garden. People living in milder climates may be able to leave nearly mature plants outdoors with or without the protection of cold frames, row coverings, or plastic tunnels and harvest as needed. This is sometimes possible even in the North. You will probably have to experiment to find the crops that do well for you. They need to be hardy enough to survive winter lows and sturdy enough to withstand winter wet and humidity without rotting. Well-drained soil, a shape that encourages moisture to run off, or a plastic umbrella covering will help.

Oregon gardener Steve Solomon has devoted most of his book *Growing Vegetables West of the Cascades* to techniques for harvesting a winter garden in the Pacific Northwest. If you live in this region, look the book up — it is full of great tips. Contributors to *Harvest Gardener* also take advantage of the winter garden. Caroline Goodall harvests sweet Caramba carrots all winter in Oregon. Michelle Taylor devotes her California winter to growing perennial herbs and leafy vegetables. Oklahoma resident Sam

CULTIVARS FOR CANNING AND FREEZING

I surveyed recent catalogues of four seed companies to see which cultivars they recommended for canning and freezing and then asked them why.

Both Park Seed and Cook's Garden relied upon the recommendations of breeders and seed suppliers. Shepherd Ogden of Cook's Garden says these companies develop crops with extra amounts of whatever will be lost during processing, such as color or texture or vitamin content.

Renee Shepherd from Shepherd's Seeds freezes and cans most of the crops she offers in her catalogue. She looks for cultivars that will ripen in a short period of time, so you can put them all up at once. "There is no mystique," Shepherd says. "Pick cultivars for their good eating qualities. If it is good prepared fresh, it probably is excellent frozen. I use special varieties only when I make tomato sauce or pickles," Shepherd said. Among the cucumbers, she looks for cultivars bred to produce firmer, less hollow-hearted pickles. She freezes any overabundance of tomatoes but sticks to paste tomatoes when canning tomato sauce. She likes to freeze Royal Burgundy beans, which turn green after 2 minutes of blanching. When the color change comes, they are ready to freeze. Another preference is Mercedes broccoli, which divides neatly into florets for freezing; this makes the preparation work easier.

Robert Johnson from Johnny's Selected Seeds says the cultivars of some types of vegetables are all good for freezing or canning; which cultivar you choose thus does not make much of a difference. For other cases, a star variety stands out. Among the generally good freezers, he recommends broccoli, carrots, cauliflower, sweet corn, melons, peppers, parsnips, rutabaga, spinach, squash, and Swiss chard.

Among the superior cultivars, he mentions Sweetheart beet and Sweet Rondino and Ingot carrots; for tomato sauce, he suggests the meaty and less-juicy paste types, such as LaRossa and Bellstar. For a good freezing pea, Johnson looks for a cultivar with good flavor and easy shelling qualities, such as the medium-sized, podded Daybreak, Bounty, and Multistar.

Other Catalogue Recommendations

Crop	Storage Method	Cultivar
Beans, snap	canned, frozen	Blue Lakes, Tender Crop, E-Z Pick, Slenderette, Roma II
Beans, snap	frozen	Emerite (French filet bean), Royal Burgundy, Jumbo, Flambeau (French shell bean), Fortex, and Butterbeans (green soybeans)
Beets	canned, pickled	Red Ace, Little Ball, Kleine Bol (Dutch Little Ball)
Beets	root cellar	Long Season, Bolthardy
Beets	canned, frozen, root cellar	Sweetheart
Broccoli	frozen	Packman Hybrid, Mercedes
Cabbage	root cellar	Lasso early red, Danish Ball Head
Carrot	canned	Minicor, Planet baby carrots (also suitable for pickling), Parmex (can freeze, too)
Carrot	frozen	Rondino
Carrot	root cellar	Rumba
Cauliflower	frozen	Milkyway Hybrid, Andes
Corn	frozen	Seneca Chief, Early Sunglow, Tuxedo (Se), Honey, and Pearl (SH#2)
Corn	pickled, canned	Minor (baby corn)
Cucumbers	pickled	County Fair 87, Lemon
Eggplant	pickled, canned	Pingtung Long, Little Fingers
Lettuce	root cellar	Arctic King, North Pole, Winter Marvel, Rouge d'Hiver, Winter Density
Onions	long storage	Copra, Sweet Sandwich, Fiesta, Carmen, Giallo Di Milano, Di Milano (braiding), Rossa
Onions	winter growing (down to –20°F)	Sweet Winter
Peas	frozen	Norli snow pea, Daybreak, Bounty, Lincoln, Sparkle
Peas	frozen, canned	Waverex Petit Provencial

Other Catalogue Recommendations (continued)

Crop	Storage Method	Cultivar
Peas, field	frozen, canned, dried	Hercules, Mississippi Silver
Pepper	pickled	Early Jalapeno, Tam Mild Jalapeno, Pepperochini, Cherrytime
Pepper	frozen	roasted Anaheim chili peppers
Pepper	dried	Cayenne, Red and Yellow Cornos (sweet Italian heirloom), Serrano, Anaheim, Super Chili, Poblano
Spinach	frozen, canned	Melody, Vienna
Spinach	frozen	Italian Summer (a long season, so plenty is left over)
Squash, winter	long storage	Waltham Butternut, All Seasons (buttercup type), Cream of the Crop, Sweet Dumpling, Delicata JS, Ebony Acorn
Tomato	sauce, canned or frozen	Heinz 1439, Roma, Roma II, San Marzano, Milano

Forbes keeps carrots in the ground late into fall; he protects their exposed shoulders with a mulch and harvests them in perfect condition through Thanksgiving. Debbie Pruitt from southern Ohio leaves her parsnips outdoors and digs them when the ground thaws in early spring. Vermont's Shepherd Ogden plants winter seedling greens in fall for an extra-early spring crop.

Root cellaring. Where winters get cold, you can use the natural coolness and moistness of the earth to create a space ideal for vegetable storage. The beauty of root cellaring and similar methods is that you can store fresh produce in otherwise little-used space for no expense at all. The depths of the earth and cold weather handle the cooling for you. Monitor conditions outdoors and indoors to see which will be suitable for any particular crop. Even when you find the right location, you should expect some losses because it is hard to control the temperature or ventilation.

A neat cubbyhole molded into the ground or partitioned off in a damp cold cellar is ideal for holding roots and tubers that won't survive winter or be accessible outdoors.

The traditional root cellar used by our ancestors was an unfinished basement, the kind you would see in a century-old home. Cool and damp, it had an earthen floor and uninsulated walls — great for keeping vegetables and tree fruit but not so wonderful for a basement rumpus room. Today, many folks would rather use their basement as a living or working space. They insulate and dehumidify it to make it more comfortable. My own house, a 1950s model, has a concrete floor and walls without exceptional outside drainage. It is thus plenty damp but too warm to keep cold-loving vegetables long. Yet it is great for winter squash, pumpkins, and green tomatoes.

Even if you have a modern basement, you can still have a root cellar area. You don't have to give up the entire lower level. Adapt a corner room, preferably on the north side of your house, which is not as likely to be warmed by the sun. Insulate the interior walls to keep the warmth out, but do not insulate the outside walls, so some chill will seep through. The space will need a screen-covered window to bring in fresh, cool outside air, move out excess ethylene gas, and hinder spoilers. If your basement is dry, you can sprinkle water on the floor every couple of days, or leave open tubs of fresh water in each corner to raise the humidity levels. If the basement is too warm, store only winter squash

BERNARD PENCZEK'S ROOT CELLAR

If you are serious about storing produce for the winter, you may want to build your own root cellar. Here is what Bernard Penczek did at his home in central New York State.

"I dug out a 6-x-6-foot underground room by hand. The entry door cuts through the basement wall, and the cellar stretches out underneath the yard. The walls are concrete block, but the floor is soil and stays moist. I put a vent through the top to the outside. Since it gets to –30°F here in the winter, the vent has a trapdoor I can shut to keep the root cellar warm. I have a window screen under the trapdoor that I can open for ventilation when the weather is warmer. I try to keep the temperature around 35° to 40°F for winter potatoes, onions, and garlic. It all works well — the last of the onions just sprouted in May, and very few of the potatoes became wrinkled."

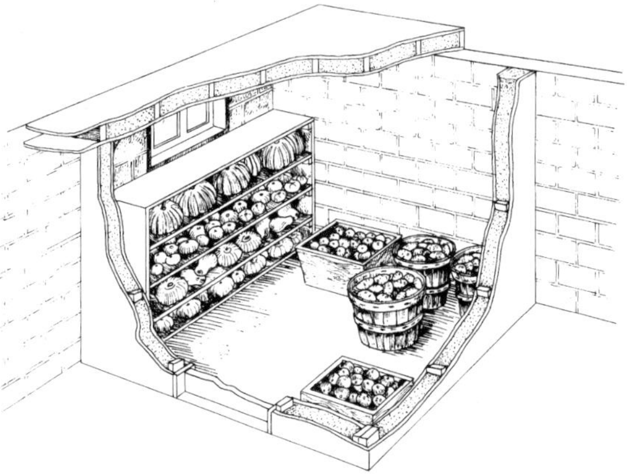

An unused corner of the basement can be walled off to create a root cellar.

and sweet potatoes there.

In addition to the basement, you may be able to adapt other areas for winter storage. Pack roots into a cooler and cover with 6 inches of leaves and a thick blanket, and store in a corner of a garage that is not prone to flooding with gas fumes.

You may be able to use a window well for root storage: line it with straw and cover containers with more straw.

Or, pack winter keepers into a dry, straw-lined window well. Top with foam packing peanuts, cover with pestproof wire mesh, and top with straw or leaves. Reach into this ministorehouse through the basement window when you need a few carrots for stew.

Use an unheated attic or bedroom for keeping onions and garlic, which need a cool, dry location. Because temperatures there can rise with the sun and fall at night, however, nutrient levels and keeping quality may be reduced. Watch out for mice, bats, or other pests that may hide in little-used places. Enclose all produce in nibble-proof packing.

You may also be able to keep vegetables outdoors. Your yard or outbuildings have potential, if winter temperatures drop near freezing. In my location, we can set buckets of roots and heads of endive and cauliflower buried in damp sand in the garden shed until the weather gets too cold around mid December. Roots can also stay outdoors during the more severe months if buried below the frost line or protected with heavy layers of mulch. Some crops, such as chicory root or parsnips, tolerate temperatures that fall below freezing. If you leave them until the soil freezes they are likely to be stuck in place in the garden, however, and you will have to wait for a February thaw before you are able to dig them out.

You will have better access to your vegetables in midwinter if you make an enclosed sunken storage pit. Sink a cooler, an angled barrel, or a large clay drainage tile in the ground. Or, dig a hole and line it with cement blocks; cover securely with a tight-fitting lid. If you leave a small opening for ventilation, cover it with wire mesh to keep the mice from feasting.

You can also mound layers of vegetables in shallow straw-lined trenches. Cover with pest-proofing wire mesh, 4 inches of soil, and 8 inches of straw or leaves. If possible, leave a small wire-covered opening for air circulation. Devote one trench to your longest keepers and the others to progressively shorter keepers. Tag different trenches, so you can unearth each in sequence. Dig the appropriate mound up and bring in the entire contents for short-term storage.

I sometimes adapt my cold frame for winter storage. I sink the frame about 6 inches deep in the soil and surround all sides with bales of hay. I top it with brown canvas and 8 inches of loose hay, which insulates and prevents sunlight from warming up the interior. I surround the produce within with rodent-proof wire mesh and fill in empty spaces with leftover foam shipping peanuts, a great insulator to recycle. Once the cold frame is secured from pests and cold, you can bundle the hay in the canvas, push it back, and prop the door open a bit to ventilate on warm days. Return the hay topping before nightfall.

A cement-block-lined pit works well as a root cellar.

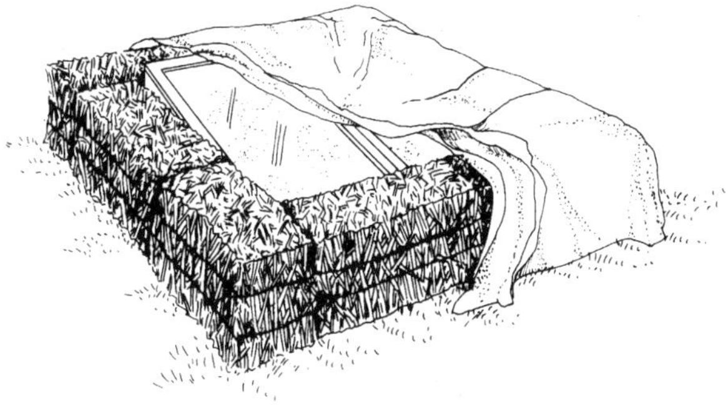

Adapt a cold frame for winter storage by surrounding it with hay bales and covering it with heavy canvas.

Root Cellaring Tips

◆ Whenever you put a bushel or more of vegetables together, separate them with a neutral layer of straw, shredded leaves, peat moss, or something similar that will not rot quickly. The neutral packing layer helps keep the entire hill or barrel from heating up as the produce respires. It is also a buffer that helps prevent one rotten tuber from spreading its disease spores to all the rest.

◆ Any subterranean root cellar must be free of standing water, which makes produce rot. Surround the cellar with drainage tiles or ditches to take away excess runoff. Put a thick layer of pebbles in the hole below to elevate the base above any potential puddles.

◆ If you store produce in the basement or garage, where you can see the vegetables relatively easily, make a point to check through the storage area once a month. Pull out and compost any bad roots or heads to discourage any further decay.

◆ Note on your calendar when you expect certain crops to require eating so you will be sure to get to them on time. Short-term storers include broccoli, cauliflower, turnips, kohlrabi, peppers, and celery. If the temperature is cold enough, roots, potatoes, and winter cabbages will last months.

◆ Be careful with many of the more odoriferous cole crops. They may be better for storage outside the house where their fragrance will not pervade.

◆ If you plant relatively late and let winter storage crops mature into the cool of fall, they will be toughened and last longer in storage. Take it easy on the fertilizer, especially nitrogen, so the plants will not grow soft and lush, and thus become prime targets for rot. Do not wait until a hard frost, however, to harvest the more sensitive crops, like winter squash or bulb fennel. Hard frost damages the protective skin, and they will surely spoil. Frost-tolerant parsnips and Brussels sprouts can and should stay outdoors, however, as they become sweeter with freezing. My Brussels sprouts stay fresh until temperatures fall into the 20s in late December.

◆ To keep well, produce must be of excellent quality without cuts or suspicious spots. Twist off vegetable tops, leaving about an inch of stub so you do not damage the root. If you leave the foliage on, the produce will rot. Don't wash winter keepers; moisture encourages decay organisms to get established. Instead, pull roots when the soil is dry so that little clings to the produce. Grow winter squash on top of mulch or on a trellis so the fruits stay clean. Use care that you do not scratch or dent their surfaces while handling them, especially if you try to brush excess soil off. Cure, if necessary. (See page 125.)

◆ Keep squash, onions, and garlic, which need good air circulation, in open mesh bags, peach crates, or woven plastic storage crates (the kind sold in toy stores). I like plastic best because I can disinfect it between each use.

◆ If maintaining air flow is a problem, don't store ethylene-producing fruits or aromatic cabbages with other crops. The ethylene is guaranteed to speed up spoilage, and cabbages share their aroma with all surrounding produce.

◆ You can leave Brussels sprouts, Chinese cabbage, kohlrabi, and cauliflower on the stalk. Simply uproot, replant into slightly moist soil, and leave in a cool place for a couple of weeks to a month, depending on temperature. For a solid-headed cabbage, such as Danish Ballhead, uproot the entire plant and cover with sand or peat moss in a cold outdoor pit, where it won't be too smelly. A sturdy cabbage head will last for two or more months.

◆ Root crops such as carrots, parsnips, and winter radishes are prone to drying out. Pack them in closed boxes, crates, or tubs of moist sand, vermiculite, or peat moss. Try to keep their surroundings lightly moist but far from wet. Amish gardener Emma Byler writes, "To keep root vegetables in the basement over winter, take 5 gallon buckets, one each for red beets, carrots, and turnips. Fill the buckets with roots and then top them off with sand loosely placed over the top. Set in a cool place in the basement, and vegetables will stay nice and crisp. The cover may be set loosely on the top."

Fearing Burr recommended leaving the roots on celery and endive before sending them to the root cellar. Specifically, he said to take celery out of the blanching pit, roots and all, and pack in moist soil in the cellar. Blanch the head of endive, tying up wrapper leaves around it like a cone. Remove dead or yellow leaves, and dig up the roots with a ball of soil. Set the endive in a pot of light soil in the cellar. If the head is perfectly dry, it will keep until spring.

Fearing Burr, Jr., 1863

◆ Potatoes, too, need high humidity but tend to rot or sprout if too moist or warm. Let these tubers cure thoroughly so the skin toughens before bringing them indoors. Caroline Goodall prefers to layer her potatoes in peat moss, which absorbs rot and may also have an antibiotic effect. She stores them in cardboard boxes, taped shut to keep out the light. Goodall has found that the longest keepers are those recommended in the Ronniger's Seed Potato catalogue, (see Appendix for address). "If it says good keeper, it tends to be just that. Eat the others first," she says.

Recipes for Food from the Root Cellar

Once you have this abundance of roots and cabbages, you may wonder what to do with them all. There are lots of good ways to prepare them.

Sweet Root Mix

4 servings

1 sweet potato, peeled and diced
3 sweet carrots, peeled and diced
1 rutabaga, peeled and diced
2 yellow, waxy-fleshed potatoes, peeled and diced
2 tablespoons dill weed
½ cup light cream
3 tablespoons margarine
salt and freshly ground black pepper, to taste

Preheat oven to 350°F. Steam all of the vegetables until tender. Chop in food processor until chunky. Mix with the dill weed, light cream, and margarine. Add the salt and pepper to taste. Pour into a casserole dish and bake uncovered for 15 minutes in the preheated oven.

Winter Squash and Tomato

4 servings

1 pint tomato sauce
2 cloves garlic, crushed
2 tablespoons olive oil
1 large nonsweet winter squash (such as Cream of the Crop), peeled and cut into 1-inch chunks
½ cup Parmesan cheese

Preheat oven to 425°F. Combine the tomato sauce, garlic, and olive oil, and cook until thick. Microwave the squash until tender about 10–15 minutes. Layer the squash on the bottom of a square casserole dish, and top with the tomato sauce. Sprinkle with Parmesan cheese and bake in the preheated oven about 25 minutes, or until the cheese browns lightly.

French-Fried Parsnips

Peel and thin-slice parsnips dug directly out of the garden after several frosts. Pat dry so the moisture on the slices won't make the oil splatter. Deep-fry several slices at a time for a couple of minutes until the oil foams around them.

Kohlrabi in Cream

Peel a young, tender kohlrabi and slice about ¼ inch thick. Layer slices on the bottom of a microwave-safe casserole dish. Pour light cream over kohlrabi to cover it, cover the dish with plastic wrap, and microwave on High about 8 minutes. Uncover and microwave again for 5 more minutes until the cream thickens.

Add 2 tablespoons chopped fresh thyme and salt and pepper to taste.

Cauliflower

Trim the stalk and green leaves from an entire head of cauliflower. Center the head in a microwave-safe casserole dish. Sprinkle with ¼ cup Italian salad dressing or vinaigrette and cover with plastic wrap. Microwave on High for 15 minutes or until tender. Turn occasionally while cooking.

Jerusalem Artichoke Bake

4 servings

6 Jerusalem artichoke tubers, washed, peeled, and sliced
½ teaspoon minced garlic
1 teaspoon onion, chopped
½ teaspoon dried lovage
½ cup mayonnaise
2 tablespoons prepared mustard
½ cup shredded Cheddar cheese

Dig Jerusalem artichokes from a mulched bed. Set prepared artichokes in a microwave-safe casserole dish, and microwave on High until tender. Sprinkle with garlic, onion, and lovage. Mix together the mayonnaise, mustard, and cheese, and spread topping over artichokes. Microwave on High another 10 minutes, until sauce bubbles and cheese melts.

eight

MAKING GOODNESS LAST

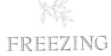

PRESERVING garden-fresh produce at home takes a little effort and organization but rewards you with top-quality, additive-free produce during times the garden is not productive. Freezing is the easiest preservation method, but drying, too, can be a snap if you own a dehydrator or a convection oven. Canning requires painstaking care to end up with an edible product. No matter which method you choose, the effort you put into preserving your crops in season will save you time the following winter. When you simply pull a package out of the freezer and drop it into a casserole in the microwave, or pop open a jar of tomatoes, most of the preparation has already been done.

For best results with all of these methods, you must work quickly after the harvest. For safety's sake, follow specific recipes, don't wing it, and maintain sanitary kitchen conditions. Get organized ahead of time so produce won't age as it sits idle. (See chapters 6 and 7 for more information about preparation tactics.) Gather together the know-how, modern and safe recipes, and the proper equipment for processing and storage. We can about once a year, and inevitably the tongs or jar lifters have been misplaced during that time. Finding them a day early sure beats frantically scouring the house while the canning water threatens to boil over.

Here are some of the tools and techniques you should have at your disposal. Pick and choose the methods you like best for each crop and cultivar.

FREEZING

If you have grown a sizable bed of beans or corn and it ripens at one time, you may find yourself with more than you can eat immediately. The tack you take toward preserving the extras will depend on whether you have a bushel basket or two handfuls.

Large loads. If you grow cultivars that ripen simultaneously, you may be able to save several month's worth of produce in a single day. Although you may have enough in the garden for a full eight hours of work, harvest only what you can freeze in the next couple of hours, thus keeping the rest fresh on the vine. When you finish processing the first batch, take a break from the kitchen and go pick some more.

To have everything work smoothly, make yourself comfortable. Have a tall stool handy and all the equipment you need. Organize separate areas for preparing vegetables, blanching, and packing so you can switch tasks easily when time allows. You also may want to invest in appliances that make the job go faster. Wire-mesh blanching baskets, a food processor, or a mechanical strainer will save you time and trouble.

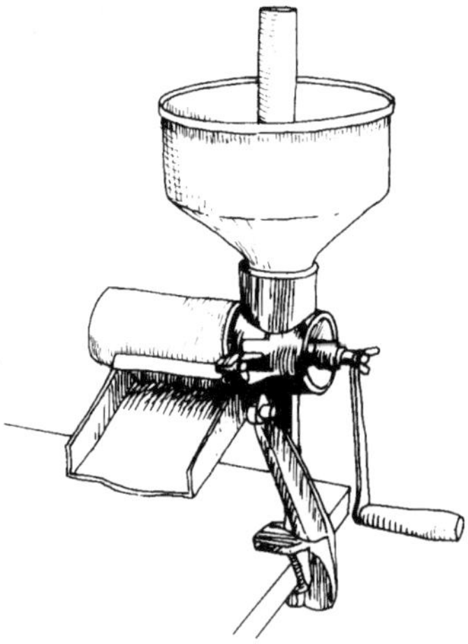

If you make a lot of sauces, a mechanical strainer is a good investment.

Small loads. This is my favorite, lazy way to fill up a freezer slowly and easily. I simply freeze whatever extra produce I cannot use for dinner or fit into the refrigerator. I do most harvesting just before dinner, which is a time of relative peace around my house. If I bring in more than I can use today or tomorrow, I freeze it. For instance, if we are having green beans for dinner, I blanch the extras in a separate pot while steaming the rest for our meal. I can cool and pack the freezer beans before the dinner beans are done.

Equipment

It pays to stock up on supplies. If you wait until everyone else is freezing tomatoes, too, you may find local stores are sold out of the supplies you need. Shopping early lets you evaluate the entire spectrum of containers and appliances and take some time to think about what would work best for you and what would provide the most value for the dollar. You may even find off-season price reductions. To avoid being caught short, buy a few more than you think you'll need.

Look for freezer-approved containers, including plastic bags, boxes, and jars. These have airtight seals, are moisture-, leak-, and vapor-proof, and do not have an unpleasant smell or taste. They stay supple at low temperatures and should be easy to seal.

Freezer bags. These are easy to use, presterilized, and transparent, so you can get some idea of what is inside. Just pull them out of the box and drop the produce in. Pick from self-sealing tops or twist-tie tops. Self-sealers are more expensive but worthwhile for such things as bags of berries, herbs, or peppers — from which you may want to remove only small amounts at a time. Some brands of self-sealing bags change colors when securely sealed, a guarantee against freezer burn.

For maximum convenience, pay a little more for "boilable" bags, which can be popped out of the freezer and into a pan of boiling water. Or, try microwave-safe freeze/cook bags, which hold the food while you use the microwave both to blanch and later to reheat the frozen package. Other food-storage kits heat-seal food-grade plastics, the ultimate in airtight packaging.

However sophisticated, freezer bags are good only for a single use. They are a product of our throw-away society and contribute, albeit minimally, to the landfill crisis. Furthermore, unlike sturdier containers, most are merely *resistant* to freezer damage, not immune to it. After long periods of storage, you may notice produce becomes drier, a condition called freezer burn. Also, bags will freeze into odd shapes that do not pack efficiently into a small freezer. (If you must use bags in spite of this problem, stack them in cardboard shoe boxes to reestablish some order.)

Reusable freezer containers. The most common reusable containers are made of thick, rigid, opaque plastic with sealable tops. Square or rectangular shapes pack more easily and efficiently than round ones. You can also use a standard canning jar for dry produce or a canning and freezer-proof jar for liquids, such as tomato sauce or vegetable soup. Although you pay a bit more for reusable containers, you save money in the long run. To keep soft plastic containers in good condition, do not put them in hot dishwashers, which can cause them to warp so that they don't reseal properly. Surround the seal of older containers with freezer tape to prevent leakage.

Container size. It's a good idea to have an assortment of container sizes at any given time. A 1-quart bag is great for frozen corn on the cob but generally too big to fill up with tomato sauce. Try to package just enough for one meal; produce can lose quality once you unseal freezer containers. I usually stick to the 1-pint size for beans, peas, corn cut off of the cob, green peppers, and berries; and the 1-quart size for summer squash and breaded eggplant chips. If you have a big family (or some big eaters), freeze a meal's worth in two packages rather than a huge one. The smaller two will freeze faster and maintain better texture.

Blancher. You need a big pot with a tight-fitting lid and a mesh or open basket inside to hold produce during blanching. You can buy a blanching pot or make your own with a pan big enough to hold a colander, strainer, fry basket, or a cheesecloth bag.

Knives. Avoid knives with high iron content, since iron can discolor produce.

Food processor or blender. If you do a lot of chopping, puréeing, or slicing, a food processor will do in two minutes what would take you half an hour with a knife. A blender or food processor is excellent for puréeing.

Labels. Be sure you can easily tell what you have frozen. You need large bright labels that will not deteriorate in a cold freezer. Use freezer tape or more decorative labels, as long as they are freezer-proof. If they are not, the adhesives may come unglued in the cold and fall off of the package. Write on the label with something that will not rub or fade off. A freezer marker is ideal, but you can substitute a permanent ink marker (choose one without an offensive odor) or a grease pencil. I like to use bright colors that contrast with the contents of the package, like a red marker on green beans or a black one on red tomatoes. If you use a different color for each type of vegetable, the colors will stand out in a crowded freezer.

How to Freeze

Assemble your supplies and garden-fresh produce. In order to stop enzymes, use procedure A to blanch most vegetables. If you are freezing produce that will be used for flavoring, skip the blanching and use procedure B (pages 211–212). Berries, too, require special handling, as described in procedure C (pages 212–215).

Procedure A

1. Wash. Wash ripe, perfect produce well to clean away microorganisms, grit, and debris. Dunk in a cold-water bath, and lift the produce out, leaving the dirt behind. If you have used pesticides, rinse produce under running water; you may also want to use a mild soap or vinegar. Repeat the process, if necessary.

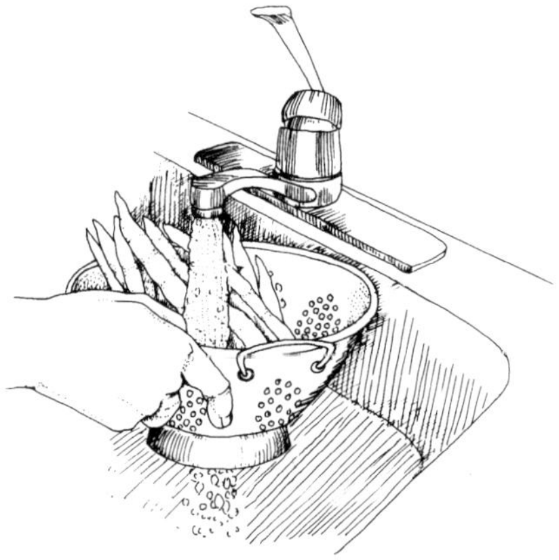

Wash produce well.

2. Trim. Trim off blossom ends, strings, stems, and other inedible

Trim into uniform-size pieces.

parts, and slice produce into uniform sizes that conform to blanching times listed below. You can cut off small bruised areas, but if a piece of produce is truly damaged or diseased, don't freeze it.

3. Blanch. Follow prescribed times precisely, so you will inactivate enzymes fully but won't overcook produce. You probably will boil most produce, although in some cases

STEAM AND MICROWAVE ALTERNATIVES

Steaming and microwave blanching can preserve nutrients and texture but may miss some spots. When you use these methods, you will get better results if you cut vegetables into small pieces and do not overcrowd blanching containers.

If you steam-blanch, suspend a single layer of vegetables over several inches of boiling water and cover the pan tightly. Increase the blanching time by 50 percent. For example, if you need 2 minutes of boiling, increase to 3 minutes for steaming.

To blanch in a microwave, follow the manufacturer's instructions that come with your microwave. You can also blanch in a covered casserole dish with ¼ to ½ cup of water for one-quarter to one-third of the non-microwave cooking time. Stir at least once. Look for green vegetables to turn a deeper shade of green or purple beans to change to green. It will take between 1 and 6 minutes, depending on the type of produce, size of container, and type of microwave. Let the casserole dish sit 1 minute, then cool and pack freezer containers, and freeze.

To blanch in a microwave- and freezer-safe bag, add a few tablespoons of water with the produce. Leave a 1-inch-long crack in the seal so steam can vent. Microwave on high, turning the package occasionally, until the vegetables reach 190°F. Check the progress with a temperature probe. It probably will take between 4 and 10 minutes. Once done, cool the entire package in ice, clean the seal, shut the bag, and freeze.

you may steam or microwave it instead. Boiling leaches out more vitamins and minerals than the other two methods, but it cooks each piece thoroughly and evenly. (For details on alternatives see page 205.) To get produce in and out quickly, blanch small loads, no more than 1 pound of produce per gallon of water. Begin timing the moment you immerse the load in boiling water. If you put the vegetables in a wire basket, weigh them down with a lid so they stay under water. Add an additional minute to blanching times if you live more than 5,000 feet above sea level. You can reuse the boiling water if it still looks clear after the first load.

Blanch only in soft, drinking-quality water. If you have a well, you might be smart to buy bottled water that is free of excessive amounts of iron, sulfur, or bacteria that can taint frozen goods.

Blanch small loads, and then plunge the blancher into chilled water to halt cooking.

4. Chill. Once you have inactivated enzymes and eliminated some spoilers, you must stop the cooking action quickly. Plunge the blancher basket into frigid water. Keep the water cold by adding ice (up to 1 pound of ice per pound of blanched vegetable) or by running cold tap water into the chilling tub. Because soft fruit and vegetables often cannot take additional soaking, spread them in a single layer in an uninsulated pan and set the pan in cold water.

When the produce is cold, drain off the extra water, blot produce with paper towels, and shake or spin dry.

5. Pack. Pack the produce into containers. The work goes faster if you use a stand or enlist a second pair of hands to hold bags open and containers upright. A funnel will help you pour soft ingredients into containers without smearing the sealing edges. Pack tightly to eliminate air holes. For crops with a fat head and slender stem, like cauliflower and broccoli, alternate floret and stem ends to pack more efficiently.

If you want to freeze a hash brown patty into a special shape or assure straight asparagus spears, broccoli, julienne potatoes, or some other fancy product, lay the vegetables out on a cookie sheet and place the sheet in freezer. Once the produce is solid, transfer it to a freezer container.

For most produce, leave extra

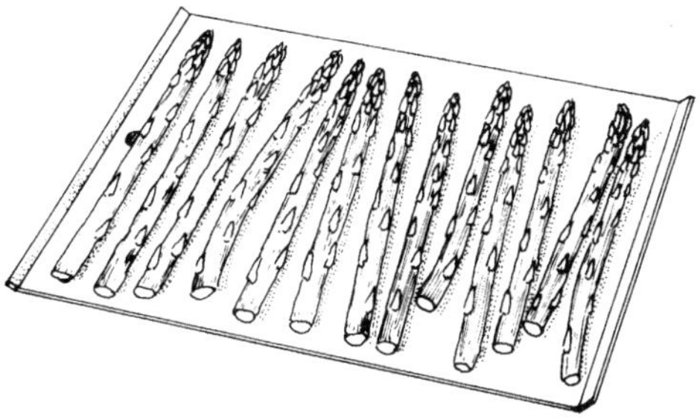

To maintain desired shape, arrange pieces on a cookie sheet until produce is frozen, and then transfer to sealed container.

headroom at the top of the bag. This space allows water to expand as it freezes without bursting open the seal. If a vegetable is not particularly wet, a ½ inch of headroom is generally safe. Leave extra room for juices or produce packed in water, especially in a rigid container. For tomato sauce, purées, or syrup-packed fruit, leave ½ inch headroom in a pint container and 1 inch in a quart container — even more if the container has a narrow mouth. Loose-packed things like broccoli and cauliflower florets or Brussels sprouts will not need extra headroom.

Once the container is packed, wipe the edge, put the lid in place, and either squeeze out the excess air, or suck it out with a straw. To be sure the container is airtight, put some freezer tape around any lids of questionable tightness. You can submerge the entire container in water to double-check the seal. If bubbles emerge, re-seal.

6. Label. Note on the freezer package such information as the contents, including the cultivar, date frozen, number of servings, any extra ingredients you have added, and any special thawing or use instructions. Sometimes I also add a short recipe to inspire me to use that particular package.

It is easier to label freezer bags *before* packing, when they are flat. If you are not sure how many bags you will need, however, label them one by one just before you fill them. To label a reusable container, attach a separate freezer-proof label.

If you keep an inventory of what is in the freezer, this is a good time to add these new goods to the list.

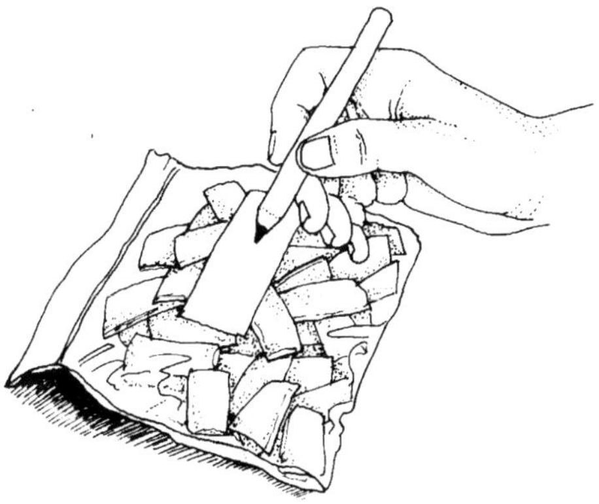

Label every package with contents, date frozen, and number of servings.

7. Quick-freeze. Once the produce is safely packed away, freeze it quickly to guarantee quality. Be certain newly packed produce is ice-cold and not warm enough to heat up the freezer or delay freezing.

If your freezer has one, use the extra-cold flash-freeze compartment. In other freezers, set new packages

BLANCHING TIMES

Vegetable	Blanching Time (in minutes)	Special Instructions
Asparagus		
small stalks	2	
medium stalks	3	
large stalks	4	
Beans, green shell	1	
Beans, green soybean	5	
Beans, lima and pinto		Before blanching, shell and sort by size.
small	2	
medium	3	
large	4	
Beans, snap	2–3	
Beets		
small	25	After blanching, chill, remove skin, slice, or dice (if desired).
medium	45	
Broccoli		
boiled	3	Split stalks length-wise. Soak in salt brine (4 teaspoons salt per 1 gallon cold water) for ½ hour to eliminate insects. Rinse and drain.
steamed	5	
Brussels sprouts		
small	3	
medium	4	
large	5	
Cabbage, standard and Chinese		
wedges	3	Suitable only for cooked dishes after freezing.
coarse shredded	1½	
Carrots		
diced, sliced, or strips	2	Scrape. Dice, slice ¼-inch-thick, or make strips.
whole baby	5	
Cauliflower	3	Prepare and brine-soak as for broccoli.
Celery	3	Cut into 1-inch pieces.
Corn, cut	4	After blanching and chilling (see pages 205–206), cut off about two-thirds of kernel. For cream-style (a good technique for overripe corn), cut off about one-half of the kernels, and then use the back of the knife to scrape off kernel hearts and juice.

Vegetable	Blanching Time (in minutes)	Special Instructions
Corn (on the cob)		
1¼-inch diameter	7	Before blanching, remove husk, silks, and ends.
1½-inch diameter	9	
over 1½-inch diameter	11	
Eggplant	–	Instead of blanching, peel, slice, dip in egg, and bread. Bake until almost tender.
Greens		Remove tough, discolored, or imperfect parts.
Beet greens, kale, chard, mustard greens, spinach, New Zealand spinach, and turnip greens	2	
Collards	3	
Young or tender leaves	1½	
Kohlrabi		
Whole baby	3	Peel before blanching.
½-inch cubes	1	
Okra		
small	3	Before blanching, cut off stems without opening pods. After blanching, leave whole or slice crosswise.
large	4	
Parsnips, ½-inch cubes	2	Use tender roots.
Peas, edible podded		
Chinese	2	Remove blossom ends and strings.
Sugar Snap	2½–3	
Peas, field	2	Use tender seeds; discard hard ones.
Peas, shelling	1½	
Peppers		
halves	3	Most peppers freeze well without blanching, but maybe blanched for use in stews, soups, and casseroles.
slices	2	
Pimientos and roasted chilis	–	Do not blanch. Instead, roast or broil. Remove charred skins before chilling.
Potatoes, sweet	–	See page 213.
Potatoes, white new potatoes	3–5	Peel before blanching. See also page 213.
Pumpkin	–	See page 213.
Rutabaga, ½-inch chunks	2	
Squash, summer		
½-inch slices	3	Shredded squash is blanched when it becomes translucent. See page 213.
shredded	1–2	
Squash, winter	–	See page 213.
Tomatoes	–	See page 213.
Turnips, ½-inch cube	2	

Adapted from USDA recommendations

in the coldest section, which is usually near the freezer coils or among already frozen goods. Separate packages so each is surrounded by cold. You can turn down the temperature to between –20° to –40°F until the packages are solid, and then return to the standard operating setting, around –5° to 0°F. Don't overload the freezer. Limit yourself to adding 2 or 3 pounds of produce per cubic foot of freezer space per twenty-four hours.

Lifetime of Frozen Produce

Most crops hold their quality in a freezer at 0°F at least eight months. By twelve months they probably won't be spoiled, but they may not taste as good as fresher frozen goods.

Expect a shorter lifetime in less-efficient freezers, especially combination refrigerator/freezers without a separate freezer door. Produce frozen in a small freezer tray may maintain quality for a few days. A separate freezer compartment does the job for a few weeks, and a side-by-side freezer keeps it a few months. A separate freezer stores goods for up to their maximum lifetime.

Potential Problems

After lengthy storage or improper preparation, frozen goods can develop the following problems:

Freezer burn. If food is not tightly sealed or is stored in a container that is not freezerproof, then air migrating through the compartment can pull moisture from the surface of the produce. Dry brown spots result, which may develop an off flavor. Freezer burn also may strike if you use part of a package and return the rest to the freezer for more than a week.

Mushy produce. Overly soft produce results from several causes. Blanching or cooking too long and using overripe produce are the most likely culprits. In addition, slow freezing or fluctuating temperatures encourage large tissue-rupturing ice crystals, which can soften even super-fresh, well-packaged produce. Vegetables and fruit with high moisture contents are especially prone to large ice-crystal damage.

Cultivars. Some cultivars and crops freeze better than others. Experiment by freezing a couple of trial packages of different things. Cook and evaluate the results. If you find an especially good cultivar, you will know what to grow next year.

Freezer or power failure. Freezers are well insulated and can hold the cold inside for about twenty-four hours if you don't open the door. If the power is off for longer than twenty-four hours, add dry ice, about 25 pounds per 10 cubic feet of freezer space. If fruits or vegetables thaw, you can refreeze them if they look and smell good or still contain ice crystals. Or, cook them in a soup, stew, casserole, jam, jelly, or pie, and then refreeze.

Thawing and Cooking Frozen Goods

Spoiler organisms become active once produce warms up, so it's generally a good idea to keep packages frozen until you are ready to cook them. There are some exceptions, however. Some frozen berries can be used as if they were fresh, if you thaw them at least part way immediately before use on ice cream, cereal, or cakes. To minimize cooking time, thaw greens until you can separate them.

Frozen produce that has already been blanched needs less cooking than fresh. Subtract the blanching time from your recipe and watch the vegetables closely. They are ready when thoroughly thawed and tender but still firm. To encourage quick, even cooking, break up frozen chunks before dropping into boiling water and continue to separate pieces with a fork or knife while the produce boils. In many cases, you will end up with a crisper product if you forsake boiling for steaming, microwaving, or stir-frying.

Procedure B

Use this method for unblanched produce, such as peppers, onions, herbs, and other flavorings. Freezing without blanching preserves flavorings, but tissues may soften or darken. Use produce frozen by procedure B in cooked dishes; add herbs only at the last minute in order to preserve their essential oils.

1. Wash. Wash gently and dry well as detailed in procedure A. Ground-hugging herbs often hide grit and may need repeated rinsing. Do not soak. Dry on paper towels or a clean towel washed in a pure, fragrance-free detergent.

2. Trim. Chop or slice into desired sizes. Pack chopped onions, leeks, or garlic into freezer containers. Lay pepper slices on a cookie tray and freeze; when solid, pack into freezer containers. [If you blanch peppers first (see page 209), you will be able to fit more into each container.]

You can treat herbs like peppers. Or, you can purée them by stripping off and liquifying their leaves in a food processor. Pour into an ice-cube tray and freeze. When solid, pack the cubes into freezer containers. You may be able to preserve herb colors better by quick-blanching them for about 30 seconds. Cool and freeze. Compare blanched and unblanched, and make up your own mind. Or, prepare easy-to-freeze herbs like basil in pesto. In a blender or food processor, blend the tender leafy sections of herbs with oil. Add the oil slowly until the herb takes on the consistency of a thick paste. Freeze the processed paste, and add chopped nuts, garlic, or cheese, as desired, before serving.

Procedure C (for berries)

How you freeze berries depends on their condition at harvest, what you intend to do with them, and how long you plan to keep them. Ideally, you should freeze fruit that is firm and ripe. For some jellies and jams, however, you may prefer slightly immature berries with a higher acid content. If a fruit is very soft and ripe, purée before freezing and use as a sauce. For short-term storage, freeze berries without adding extras. Fruit treated with sugar, sugar syrup, or acid tends to last longer in the freezer than fruit frozen dry.

The following techniques were taken from Ohio State University Extension Recommendations.

SUGAR SYRUPS

Solution Concentration	Amount of Sugar	Amount of Water
20% (light)	1 cup	4 cups
30% (medium)	1¾ cups	4 cups
40% (heavy)	2¾ cups	4 cups

1. Wash and trim. Follow instructions in procedure A, steps 1 and 2 (pages 204–205).

2. Sweeten. When using syrups, adapt the sugar concentration to your own preferences, as well as to the natural sugar and acid levels in the fruit. You may not want to sweeten fruit you intend to use for baking; on the other hand, for table-ready fruit, try a 40 percent syrup. Instead of using a syrup, you also can stir berries into dry sugar (known as a sugar pack) until it dissolves in their juices. The usual recommendation is ¾ cup of sugar per quart of berries.

To make the syrup, mix the sugar into lukewarm water, but let it cool completely before mixing with the berries. Save time by making syrup the evening ahead and refrigerating it overnight. For glossier-looking fruit, substitute light corn syrup for one-quarter of the required sugar.

3. Avoid darkening. Light-colored fruit, like apples and pears (and sometimes yellow raspberries and rhubarb), can darken with freezing. Blanching the fruit for a minute may help, if the fruit is not too soft. Or, add 1½ teaspoons crystalline ascorbic acid to 1 gallon chilled sugar syrup (or a similar amount to granular sugar, juice, purées, or dry fruit) just before packing. You may be able to find the crystalline acid at drug stores. If not, substitute finely ground vitamin C tablets. A 1500

OTHER PREFREEZE COOKING TECHNIQUES

The quality of some frozen vegetables, such as potatoes, winter squashes, and rutabagas, is better when the produce is precooked and mashed or puréed, rather than blanched. Here are some specific suggestions:

Potatoes, white. Cook until almost tender, then peel and grate. Form into shapes and freeze. *For french fries,* peel and cut into thin strips; fry until lightly golden. Use within a few months.

Potatoes, sweet. Cook until almost tender. Let cool at room temperature. Peel; cut into halves, slice, or mash. To prevent discoloring, dip pieces in 1 tablespoon citric acid or ½ cup lemon juice per quart of water. Or, mash with 2 tablespoons orange or lemon juice per quart of sweet potatoes. You can also roll them in sugar or cover with sugar syrup (see page 214).

Pumpkins. Boil, steam, pressure cook, or bake until tender and peel. Mash or purée pulp. Cool by placing pan with purée in a larger pan filled with iced water; stir pumpkin occasionally to hasten cooling.

Rutabaga. Cook in boiling water until tender; mash or purée. Cool purée as for pumpkin.

Squash, winter. Cook until soft, peel and then purée or strain. Cool as for pumpkin.

Tomatoes. Boil until skin slips loose, skin, and freeze. *For tomato juice,* simmer cut quarters 5 to 10 minutes; squeeze out juice and add 1 teaspoon salt per quart of liquid. *For stewed tomatoes,* peel and quarter. In a saucepan covered with a tight-fitting lid, cook tomatoes until tender, about 10 to 20 minutes. Cool by setting the pan with the tomatoes in a larger pan in cold water. *For tomato sauce,* blanch and peel whole tomatoes; quarter and cook in an open pan until sauce is thick.

Note: *If you intend to freeze vegetables in prepared dishes, wait to add black pepper, cloves, onion, or garlic until after thawing, since these tend to taste stronger after freezing.*

FREEZING BERRIES AND OTHER FRUITS

Fruit	Syrup Pack	Sugar Pack (per quart of fruit)	Comments
Blackberries, Boysenberries, Dewberries, Loganberries, Youngberries	40–50 percent	¾ cup	Use only fully ripe, glossy berries. Freeze unsweetened for pies or jams.
Blueberries Elderberries Huckleberries	40–50 percent		To serve uncooked, freeze whole in syrup. Steam a minute before freezing to tenderize skin. May be dry-packed: avoid washing in this case, if possible.
Currants	50 percent	¾–1⅛ cup	May be frozen whole, unsweetened. *For jelly,* use both ripe and underripe fruit; crush and warm, without boiling, to let juice flow; squeeze in jelly bag; sweeten with ¾ to 1 cup sugar, or freeze without sugar.
Gooseberries	50 percent		Cut off stems and tails. Freeze whole with or without syrup.
Melons	30 percent		Freeze ripe, firm flesh cut into cubes or balls. Or, crush (except watermelons) and add 1 tablespoon sugar per quart of fruit, if desired. Stir to dissolve.
Raspberries	40 percent	¾ cup	Freeze unsweetened or in syrup or sugar pack or purée with ¾ to 1 cup of sugar per quart of fruit. If very seedy, juice in a jelly bag; add ½ – 1 cup of sugar per quart of juice.
Rhubarb	40–50 percent	¾ cup	Trim into 1- to 2-inch pieces; blanch in boiling water for 1 minute. *For cooked purée,* boil 2 minutes; add ⅔ cup of sugar per quart. *For juice,* enclose stem pieces in jelly bag and submerge in a kettle of water; bring to a boil. Remove bag, press out juice, and add ½ cup of sugar per quart of juice, if desired.
Strawberries	50 percent	¾ cup	Best if frozen when ripe and sliced or crushed. If unsweetened, add 1 teaspoon crystalline ascorbic acid per quart of water; freeze in the treated water. You can also freeze whole berries in a pectin-and-sugar blend.

milligram tablet equals ½ teaspoon crystalline ascorbic acid. Note, however, that these may contain fillers that make syrup cloudy.

For a different flavor, use citric acid or lemon, pineapple, or lime juice to control darkening. None of these, however, is as effective as pure ascorbic acid. Other easy but more expensive alternatives are the commercially premixed antidarkening products containing sugars, ascorbic or citric acids, and other extras.

4. Pack. If you freeze fruit in syrup, cover the fruit and press floaters down into the liquid. You may need to crumble freezer wrap, waxed paper, or some other sterile, freezer-proof filler into the open space. For a dry sugar pack, cut fruit into similar-size pieces, and blend gently with sugar until the granules dissolve in natural juices. Pack into freezer containers. Leave headroom as indicated in procedure A, step 5.

Thawing and Using Frozen Fruit

Frozen fruit is great for cooking, juicing, jellies or jams, or eating like fresh fruit. To defrost, leave fruit in its original package at room temperature, submerge the package in lukewarm water, or thaw in a microwave. To maintain some firmness, leave a few ice crystals.

When cooking frozen fruits, note how much sugar or acid was added before freezing and subtract it from the recipe, or simply add sugar to taste. You are likely to need less additional sugar when you pick the berries sweet and fully ripe. Add crushed fruit or purées to ice cream, cakes, or jams. The juice is good to add to jellies, apple juice, or ginger ale.

DRYING PRODUCE

Drying is one of the less-common methods of preservation used today, but it is still an essential technique. Drying culinary herbs and legumes is a good place to begin. Once you perfect a system with these, turn small fruits into puréed fruit leathers that can be dried in strips or molded into shapes that kids like. Dry some vegetables for winter soup or for hiking, biking, and camping; food is easier to transport with most of the moisture gone.

Drying produce can take a little or a lot of energy, depending on the extent of mechanical aid you need to get the job done. You must dehydrate crop tissues quickly in order to preserve them before spoilers take their share. In hot, dry climates, nature can handle the job. Elsewhere, you will have to supplement with a dehydrator, oven, or microwave.

How to Dry Produce

Drying produce outdoors. In an

arid part of the country or arid season of the year, you may have good luck drying produce on screens or racks outdoors. Make the screens of an inert mesh like stainless steel that lets air circulate freely but doesn't stain or alter the flavor of produce. You probably will need to surround the edges of the mesh with wooden or plastic edging. Set the screen on a couple of chairs or between two sawhorses or other kinds of elevated legs. Situate it out of the sun where the breeze is steady. Cover with cheesecloth or floating row covers to keep birds and insects off. Bring the drying trays indoors at night to escape evening marauding animals and early morning dew.

Some naturally dry-fleshed herbs, beans, and popcorn dry when temperatures stay in the 80s or 90s(°F). Moister fruits and vegetables, however, usually need higher temperatures to dehydrate thoroughly. You could start them outdoors and finish in the oven. You can also use the oven to sterilize outdoor-dried goods

To dry herbs outdoors, lay them on a raised screen; cover with floating row cover to protect against insects.

before storing. (For more information, see pages 217–218.)

Drying produce indoors. If rain or humidity makes drying slow, bring produce indoors. Although your first thought may be to dangle bundles of herbs artfully around the kitchen, it really is not the best method. Kitchens get humid when you boil water and wash dishes. Furthermore, bunched plants do not receive good air circulation; those on the inside stay damper longer, often mildewing. The outer portions fade in the sunlight and shatter if bumped. Unprotected, the bundles are prime targets for oil splatters, food flings, and other unappetizing coatings. If you like the warm, country look of hanging herbs, evaluate their quality carefully before cooking with them.

I prefer to protect small herb clusters in perforated brown paper bags. The bags let air circulate through and catch falling leaves and seeds.

In parts of the house other than the kitchen, you may be able to leave drying goods uncovered. A little-used hot, dry attic can be a good place to dehydrate herbs, legumes, or popcorn. Be sure your attic is fairly clean and free of rodents, birds, and bats, however, which may eat or soil your harvest.

Basements usually are too damp for produce drying, but a dehumidifier can change that in a hurry. I sometimes place herbs on a cookie sheet on top of the dehumidifier.

The motor keeps the tray warm but not too hot, and the foliage dries quickly without losing much flavor.

Another alternative is the air conditioner. If your entire home is air-conditioned, humidity will be much lower than outdoors. You can select any out-of-the-way place to place goods to dry. I often perch parsley on waxed paper near my window air conditioner.

Note: When you dry produce in temperatures below about 140°F, pasteurize it before storing it. (Refer to page 221 for more information.)

Microwave drying. The microwave can dry some herbs successfully, but the technique is somewhat controversial. Part of the controversy stems from the difference in strength and mode of action between brands and models of microwaves. If you can fine-tune the procedure, the microwave can be a fast and effective drying tool. Check for instructions in the manual that came with your equipment. If there are none, try this procedure: Place a couple of small herb sprigs between two thick paper towels. Microwave on High for a minute or two. Move the herbs to a different place on the towel and repeat for 30–60 seconds. Continue to move the herbs and briefly microwave until the foliage and stems are crackling dry.

Oven. You can dry all produce in the oven, but the process ties up the oven for hours and heats up the kitchen. It is a good way to experiment with drying, but unless you have a gas or convection oven, oven drying is too tedious and time-consuming to make into a habit. A gas pilot light alone can provide enough heat to dry thin-fleshed herbs, and some convection ovens are outfitted for drying and do a good fast job.

If your oven is not already adapted for drying, make drying screens of teflon-coated fiberglass, stainless-steel screen, or cheesecloth (some other metals can stain or taint foods). Layer produce thinly on the screen, and set one or several screens on the metal racks in the oven. Set the oven temperature at 120° to 150°F. The exact temperature inside will vary depending on the sensitivity of the oven and how close a particular screen is to the heating elements. If the temperature gets a little too high, the produce will dry on the outside but not in the middle. If too low, it will take a long time to dry thoroughly. To monitor what is happening, use an oven thermometer. Stir food often and rotate trays to make drying more even.

Circulate fresh dry air through the oven the entire time. Leave the door open a few inches and use a fan to blow fresh air gently through the crack. Be careful not to disturb the pilot light on gas ovens. Expect to give fruit six to twenty hours to dry and vegetables four to twelve hours, depending on water content. Be especially attentive during the final few hours, when most foods scorch. You may want to turn the heat down, rather than run to the oven to check or stir every 5 minutes.

Drying with food dehydrators. If you intend to dry foods regularly, you may want to buy a dehydrator. This appliance is a self-contained electrical unit that circulates warm dry air over foods, crisping them regardless of what is happening outdoors. Most have slide-out screen trays that are easy to pull out and fill or check. A motor pulls in fresh air, heats it to a preset temperature, circulates it, and vents it out. Dehydrators work fast! Set at 120°F, my dehydrator dries tomatoes and zucchini overnight.

You may find an assortment of food dehydrators in department stores, specialty food outlets, and catalogues. Prices are quite variable. I have a small countertop model purchased years ago for about $20. Contemporary models run $30 to $400, depending on the size, quality of construction, and energy consumption levels.

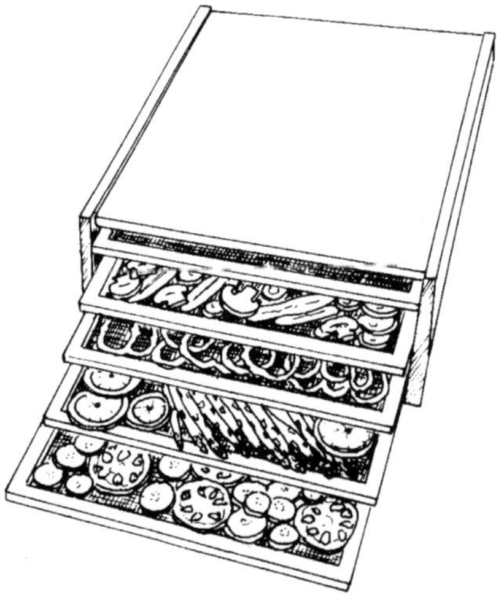

Food dehydrator

You can save a little money by making your own. Blueprints and instructions for dehydrators are included in a number of home projects books, Cooperative Extension Service brochures, and occasionally in gardening magazines.

Buy or make a dehydrator large enough to handle the maximum volume of produce you harvest. Ohio State University studies show that a square foot of drier space is needed to dry 1 pound of food. That can be a bagful of lightweight herbs or just a couple of plump-sliced tomatoes. The weight of tomatoes comes from their water content. Although they dry down to nothing but a sliver of flavor, they demand a large amount of dehydrator space when fresh.

What to Dry

Herbs. Herbs with fine, thin, or leathery leaves, such as rosemary, thyme, marjoram, oregano, savory, and sage, are a snap to dry using any of the techniques listed above. They maintain their essential oil content more readily at warm (not hot) temperatures — 95°F is ideal. Fleshier-leaved types, like parsley, celery, and basil, may need supplemental ventilation. For example, I use the dehydrator exclusively on basil cultivars like Green and Purple Ruffles, which have especially fat, moist leaves.

Herbs dry faster if you dry the foliage alone. Pull off and compost the succulent or woody stems. This is fairly easy for parsley, sage, bay, and other large-leaved plants but not for those with tiny leaves. Instead of spending hours plucking thyme leaf by leaf, for instance, dry sprigs on the stem and strip them off with a quick sweep of the finger when they are crisp.

In my humid Ohio climate, herbs pick up moisture from the air after they are dried and while they are waiting to be stripped, processed, and packaged. To counteract humidity, I recrisp the foliage by baking the herbs a few minutes in a warm (about 170°F) oven. I then pack the blender about one-third full and pulse to mix and coarse-grind the leaves into flakes. I pour them immediately into a jar, which I seal airtight.

Fruit. If you harvest fruit that looks good enough to eat, it probably will make a nice dried product. Freezing preserves its vitamin content and flavor better than drying, but you can use unique-textured dry fruit for baking or snacking. My kids love to eat crunchy, featherweight dried raspberries.

Light-colored fruit may darken with drying. You can treat it with ascorbic acid or blanch it to limit color changes. Or, try dipping the fruit in a 20 percent solution of honey and water, a method Cornell University researchers have found maintains natural flavor, texture, and color in dried white grapes and sliced fruit. Using a sulfite solution, which can cause allergic reactions in some people, is not necessary for berries.

You can turn fruit into dried fruit leather, a great snack with intense concentrated flavor. Wash, dry, and purée fruit. Add sugar to taste if you wish. Spread the fruit in ¼-inch thick strips on a small, shallow greased pan — a pie tin will do. Dry in a dehydrator or in an oven on low heat until the surface of the fruit is stiff. Flip the slivers and repeat the process on the other side. When the fruit is done, pull the entire piece off the pan. Roll it up between sheets of plastic wrap and store it in an airtight container.

Vegetables. Like fruit, a dried vegetable looks and tastes far different from the fresh original. Some, like zucchini chips, dried tomatoes, and onion and pepper slices, are a delicious gourmet treat. A few vegetables, like broccoli, cauliflower, collard, mustard, cucumber, eggplant, radish, lettuce, spinach, and winter squash are unappetizing dried; use another storage method on these vegetables. Others, like dried beans, peas, carrots, corn, parsnips, rutabagas, turnips, and potatoes, can be reduced in size for convenient, energy-free storage. When dried, these

GUIDE TO DRYING VEGETABLES

BLANCHING TIMES FOR DRYING VEGETABLES

Produce	Preparation	Blanching Time	Comments
Artichokes	Cut hearts into ⅛-inch strips. Boil in ¾ cup water and 1 tablespoon lemon juice.	6–8 minutes	
Beans, green	Cut into short pieces or thin strips.	2 minutes	Freezing for 30–40 minutes after blanching may improve dried texture.
Beets		Cook fully	Cut into thin strips after cooking.
Cabbage	Cut tender central part of the head into ⅛-inch strips.	1½ to 2 minutes	May also be steamed until wilted, instead of blanched.
Carrots	Cut slices or strips ⅛ inch thick.	3½ minutes	
Celery	Slice stalks.	2 minutes	
Corn		4–5 minutes	Cut kernels off the cob *after* blanching.
Eggplant	Cut into ¼-inch slices.	3 minutes	
Garlic	Peel and chop finely.		Dry without blanching.
Horseradish	Peel roots and grate.		Dry without blanching.
Okra	Slice into ⅛- to ¼-inch-wide slices.		Dry without blanching.
Onion	Slice peeled bulb ⅛ to ¼ inch thick.		Dry without blanching.
Peas	Shell.	2 minutes	
Peppers, hot	Dry ripe hot peppers, such as cayenne, chili, and paprika, whole; may string for drying.		Grind into flakes or powder to store and use.
Peppers, sweet	Trim off outer shell, and cut into ⅜-inch-wide and -long slices.		Dry without blanching. These may still feel pliable when dry.
Potatoes	Peel and cut into ¼-inch-thick strips or ⅛-inch-thick slices.	5 or 6 minutes	

Produce	Preparation	Blanching Time	Comments
Squash, summer	Cut into ¼-inch-slices.	½ minute	These may still feel pliable when dry.
Tomato	Dip in boiling water for 1 minute, peel skin, and cut into slices ¾ inch wide (lengthwise slices make a prettier end product). Cut smaller tomatoes in half.		These will still feel pliable when dry.

Adapted from USDA and Georgia Cooperative Extension Service recommendations.

vegetables are easy to make into soup, stew, baked beans, or casseroles, replumping readily if soaked or boiled. When my upright freezer failed one summer, I quickly converted to drying most of my garden extras.

The drying process is simple. Clean and trim fresh, top-quality vegetables; blanch as indicated in the table at the left and above. Chill in ice water to stop the cooking. Blot off extra moisture with paper towels or cloth towels washed in an additive- and fragrance-free detergent. I prefer to use my dehydrator for fleshy vegetables; see pages 215–218 for other alternatives. Most vegetables are dry when they feel crisp or are brittle enough to shatter if you hit them briskly with something hard. Tomatoes, however, become leathery.

If properly dried, most vegetables can be stored for twelve months. Onions, carrots, and cabbage may spoil more quickly.

Storing Dried Produce

If you are concerned that insect larvae or eggs may remain hidden in or around dried produce, kill them before packaging and storing the produce. Put the produce in a plastic bag in the freezer for no more than forty-eight hours or heat it on a cookie tray at 175°F for 15 minutes or 160°F for 30 minutes. Whichever way you do this, return produce to room temperature as quickly as possible and package.

DELICIOUS TOMATO LEATHER

Harvest meaty tomatoes, cook into a very thick sauce, strain, and taste. Add 1 teaspoon lemon juice or wine, if the tomato sauce needs more zip. Spread in a greased pie tin and dry until leathery, flipping occasionally. Roll up the strip, and store airtight.

Most containers suitable for freezing or canning also work for dried goods. The most important criterion is that they seal air and humidity out. I prefer canning jars, since once I screw the lid on, I know the jar is sealed. Plastic bags are harder to seal securely, and they can tear or be punctured.

Check the container frequently a few days after you pack it. This is the time when the dried goods are conditioning. Moisture migrates from slightly fatter or more succulent tissue to thin or dry areas. If there is excess moisture, the container will fog up and mildew will follow. If you see a little cloudiness in the jar, recrisp the dried goods immediately. Spread herbs, vegetables, or fruit in a 175°F oven from 5 to 20 minutes, depending on the product. Repackage with a small cloth bag of white rice, which absorbs any stray moisture.

Once the contents stabilize, store the container out of light in a cool, dry place. If you have room in the refrigerator or freezer, you can extend the shelf life even longer.

Using Dried Produce

Crumble dried herbs into any dish. Be aware that newly dried herbs have more concentrated flavor than fresh herbs. One teaspoon dried can equal 3 teaspoons of fresh. With age, however, the pungency wanes, and you must use more to get the same effect.

You can eat fruit leather and many berries as is or bake them in muffins or cake, or try replumping berries with a couple of teaspoons of water in a covered microwave dish. Microwave on High for several minutes until the water is absorbed. To restore to full size, soak in room-temperature water for several hours.

Return vegetables to their fresh size by soaking 1 cup dried vegetables in 2 cups boiling water. Cabbage, okra, asparagus, beans, beets, carrots, corn, and green peas may use more moisture. Asparagus, lima

CROPS THAT IMPROVE WITH PROCESSING

While vine-ripened produce that you pick, cook, and eat within minutes offers the best flavor, texture, and nutrition, processing some products can give you an exciting alternative. For instance, you can sweeten, spice, pickle, or concentrate flavors, or even tenderize slightly large root crops after processing and canning them.

Cucumbers and zucchini. Turn these into sweet, sour, dill, or garlic pickles, and store the finished product in refrigerator, freezer, or jars.

Cabbage and turnips. Both may be stored in a root cellar but not for long periods of time. To extend their shelf life and take an edge off their mustardy flavor, you can pickle these in salt brine and freeze or can the results.

Carrots and beets. If you have an overabundance of fairly large carrots and beets, store them in damp sand in the root cellar, if it is near freezing. For longer storage in locations without suitable cellars, process both and store in canning jars. They remain sweet, flavorful, and even more tender than fresh. Freezing does nothing to improve the texture of these crops.

Berries. Dry berries to concentrate their sweet flavor and use them in muffins or cakes. Purée them and dry as fruit leather for eating fresh. Freeze or can in a sugar syrup for a table-ready dessert.

Culinary herbs, onions, and hot peppers. Dried, these have more zing.

Horseradish. Develop the bite by blending with water and vinegar (2 parts water to 1 part vinegar). Store in the refrigerator and serve with roast beef or add to cheese spreads.

Alpine strawberries. Capture and concentrate the flavor and pectins of this small berry in jellies or jams.

Tomatoes. Canned tomatoes have a rich, sweet taste. Canned dry-fleshed paste tomatoes can even be superior to fresh. Paste tomatoes also make flavorful dried products.

CONTRIBUTOR'S FAVORITE PRESERVATION METHODS

Doc and Katy Abraham. "We can, freeze, and also dry many crops. All systems are good, but with tomatoes we can less and freeze more."

Sharon Carson. "I freeze more than I can, but I do can beets, sauerkraut, relishes, jellies, and fruits. I like to freeze raspberries, cook them down, and use their pulp for wine and their juice for jellies, sodas, and popsicles. It is so concentrated that a pint will go a long way."

Alan Cook. "I give a medium-size tomato 1 minute in boiling water, remove the skin, and freeze it whole, with four or five to a plastic bag. They are great for soup in the winter."

Dave DeWitt. "Freezing is best for fresh chilis, as it preserves color, texture, and flavor fairly well. There is no need for blanching before freezing. If chilis are mature and turn red, drying on strings works well. Canning is useless, in my opinion."

Gail Harrigan. "I put tomatoes through a Squeeze-O [mechanical strainer] to remove skins and seeds; no precooking is necessary. I boil the squeezed tomatoes down to half their volume and freeze as is."

Susan C. and Harvey E. Moser. "Our major method of preserving is canning. My husband says I can anything that does not run away from me, so he keeps moving. With his help, we put up about 600 jars of food. Canning offers a long storage life with no expense after the produce is canned. The jars can be used many times. We know what's in each jar, and what's not, including salt. We dry herbs, onions, peppers, celery, tomatoes, and blueberries in the microwave or the convection oven/dehydrator. Pinto or October beans dry on the plant. Popcorn dries on the stalk; we then store it in the freezer or make cornmeal with our Vita Mix. Everything we dry that is stored on our shelves is vacuum-sealed in canning jars with our food saver. This means no bugs, no spoilage, and an almost indefinite shelf life. Freezing works well for peas and strawberries."

Bernard Penczek. "We like the flavor of Sweet Illini corn especially well after it is frozen."

Rachel Snyder. "Freezing is the fastest and easiest method for busy people. Fruits like cherries and gooseberries do not even have to be blanched; just pour them into freezer bags and transfer to the freezer. Gooseberries can be stemmed after they are frozen. Roma tomatoes are good for freezing whole; it's best to blanch them first to remove skins."

David Stern. "I grind garlic, freeze it in olive oil in small jars, and use it as needed."

Hazel Weihe. "I freeze just about everything — it is so easy. You just blanch and put the vegetables in containers. I like to put fully cooked beets on a bed of chopped beet tops. They freeze beautifully. If you run out of time to defrost them, you can put them in a double boiler.

"I used to can tomatoes, but with freezing the taste is so fresh I like it better. I drop whole tomatoes in boiling water until the skin is loose, peel the skin, and then cut into the side to take a peek just to be sure it is okay. Then I drain off extra juice because tomatoes get so watery when frozen."

Rose Marie Whiteley. "I do a tremendous amount of preservation, but limit my canning to those foods for which there is really no truly satisfactory alternative — pickles, jellies, relishes, chili sauce, tomatoes, etc. (I freeze my tomato juice.)

"I freeze the largest percentage of my crops. There's no question that freezing provides the retention of the most fresh flavor, nutritive value, and color.

I have a small dehydrator, so I do some drying. I enjoy using dried tomatoes, so I grow a few paste tomatoes strictly for drying. I usually have an abundant harvest of potatoes, and I dry a few potato slices. It never fails that I find a soup recipe that I simply must try, and it requires potatoes — when there is a raging Nebraska winter blizzard outside and, horrors, not a potato in sight. I dry a few onions for the same reason. I also freeze a small quantity of both onions and peppers for adding to prepared dishes."

beans, and beets will take about 1½ hours to replump; green beans, carrots, and cabbage will take about 1 hour; corn, okra, onions, green peas, spinach, and sweet potatoes will take ½ hour or slightly longer. Soak mature beans overnight.

CANNING

Canning takes second place to freezing in most households today. The amount of time you must spend processing produce and the danger of eating improperly canned foods turns many gardeners to other preservation methods. On the other hand, once the food is safely sealed in canning jars and stored away in a cool location, it will keep for months, energy-free. Since canning involves cooking for extended periods at elevated temperatures, most produce becomes soft, and less flavorful, with fewer vitamins. On the other hand, processing makes some vegetables and fruits extra delicious. Canned tomatoes steeped in their own flavorful juices may taste richer than when fresh. Sweetened canned berries make delightful sauces, jellies, and jams. Vinegaring or brining canned pickles and sauerkraut gives a whole new dimension to cucumbers and cabbage.

If you decide to try canning, remember that cutting corners may result in contaminated canned goods. Unless you destroy all spoiler organisms by following proven procedures to the letter, you may get food poisoning, including deadly botulism poisoning.

Highly acidic foods, like tomatoes, pickled or fermented produce, berries, and rhubarb, are the easiest to can safely using a simple boiling-water-bath canner. Pressure canning is not necessary, because botulism spores cannot grow below pH 4.6. You can test the pH of your canned goods with pH indicator strips. These change color when dipped in a solution of a certain pH. In this case, look for indicator strips in the acid range. Jellies and jams are also good for beginning canners. The sugar, combined with natural fruit acids, acts as a preservative. It thwarts bacteria but not yeasts and molds. If a jar is not well sealed, you will see them form a white crust on the surface or side. The pH of these acidic items, however, varies. Read the following sections for more information on pH and safety.

Most other vegetables are lower in acid and must be processed in a pressure cooker that elevates temperatures to 240° or 250°F, high enough to kill spores of botulinum. The processing time required for thorough heating and sterilizing varies depending on the kind of produce, size of pieces, and volume of the jar.

Herbs are not suitable for canning. They lose flavor and fragrance when processed.

CANNING WITH DEBBIE PRUITT

Canning remains more popular in rural areas like southern Ohio. There, Debbie Pruitt saves all the extra harvest from her 100 x 100-foot garden by canning. "You can just let the food sit on the shelf and don't have to worry about it going bad," she says. Pruitt is a student of traditional ways. She learned how to can from her seventy-year-old neighbor, who has canned produce her entire lifetime. She neither freezes nor refrigerates vegetables. Debbie says, "I try to pick what I need for each meal."

◆ Pruitt prefers Blue Lake snap beans for canning. They mature quickly and stay tender, even larger sizes. "The seeds of some others can get tough, if you can't pick the beans fast enough," she says.

◆ She likes a corn relish recipe in the Ball Blue Book. Occasionally, she substitutes different vegetables but always checks the required processing time for the newcomer. "You have to process it as long as necessary."

◆ Since carrots are hard to harvest in midwinter, she cans Danvers Half Long after cutting them into chunks. "They stay sweet and are excellent to open and lay next to a roast or marinate for tabouli."

Tips for Safer Canning

◆ Follow only specific modern recipes. Older ones may not meet current safety guidelines.

◆ Always use soft water for blanching, precooking, or processing. If you have well water, or even municipal water that occasionally clouds or leaves white flakes in your ice cubes, buy bottled water or use a friend's truly soft water. Mineral deposits in hard water can cloud or discolor canned goods, symptoms hard to distinguish from microbial contamination. Such water may also shrivel or harden fruits and vegetables.

◆ Avoid cooking or working with iron, copper, brass, aluminum, galvanized zinc, or tin pans, which may give canned produce an off color and flavor.

◆ Work quickly after harvest and between canning steps, so produce does not sit around aging and collecting mold and bacteria spores.

CAROLINE GOODALL

Hillsboro, Oregon, resident Caroline Goodall grows most of her own vegetables, fruit — even ducks, geese, and beef — and saves her produce by canning, freezing, and drying. Preserving her own foods also allows Goodall to tailor their contents to family tastes. Low sugar has become a high priority. All of this preserving is a big job, so Goodall has fine-tuned the process to make it faster and easier.

Caroline likes to make jams out of marionberry, boysenberry, cascade berry (a tart local berry), Fall Gold yellow raspberry, and a mixture of strawberries and rhubarb. She often freezes the berries after harvest and cooks them later. "Who wants to make jam in the middle of summer when it is so hot, and there are so many other things to do? I freeze the berries and make them into jam during a cold, wet day in November. It warms up the house and makes it smell wonderful," says Goodall.
She also notes the following:

- Yellow raspberries have a milder flavor than red varieties and make a more muted jam, which everyone likes.

- Red raspberries are best picked fully ripe. Cook them only for a few minutes with pectin, so the color doesn't darken.

- Wild blackberries make a nice jam, but after the effort involved in picking them, they make more of a splash featured in a pie. She layers Granny Smith apples on the bottom of the pie and tops them with blackberries, which release their nectar over the apples as they cook.

Although she has tried making jams with low-sugar recipes, she doesn't think they tasted especially good. So, she returned to the full-sugar recipes, taking comfort in the fact that nobody in the family actually eats that much jam at a single sitting.

Berries that are not reserved for pies or jams go into the freezer, a method that has taken priority over canning. "I think peaches, nectarines, plums, and cherries are better canned, but strawberries can be just as good frozen." Here are some of Caroline's favorite recipes.

Caroline's Frozen Strawberries

Slice strawberries and place them in a small plastic freezer container, about 4 inches square and 3 inches high. Cover the berries with about 2 tablespoons of a sugar and pectin mixture (see below), more or less according to your taste. Let the berries sit on the counter for half the day, so the flavors blend. Freeze. The resulting berries have a thick sauce, ideal for pies, gelatins, or ice cream toppings.

◆ If you freeze a lot of berries, blend the sugar and pectin in bulk, mixing 2 pounds of sugar with 1 package of pectin. Store it in an airtight jar and use as needed through the growing season.

Caroline's Frozen Bramble Berries

Wash the berries if appropriate. If you do not spray pesticides or fungicides, you may not need to wash them. This is helpful, because ripe berries are delicate and fall apart easily. To remove a little dust or a few bugs, Caroline recommends floating berries in a bowl of water and rolling them out on a paper towel to draw out the excess moisture.

Once they are clean, set the berries on waxed paper on a cookie sheet and cover with plastic wrap. Freeze overnight, and then put berries in a freezer bag. Each berry will freeze separately rather than in a mass.

Caroline dries salmon, beef jerky, herbs, and produce in a food dehydrator. Her favorite is the Montmorency pie cherry, which resembles a tart red raisin when dry. "It makes a nice snack or substitute for raisins in baking." Before she dries apples, pears, or other fruits that brown after they are cut, she dips them in pineapple juice instead of lemon juice. "It prevents browning without the kickback of lemon juice," Caroline says.

She dries sage, thyme, chives, and dill weed but prefers to freeze basil. "I purée it and then freeze it in ice-cube trays. I then put the cubes in self-seal freezer bags, so I can pull one or two out as needed."

When she does can, she has a great system for storing the jars so they are easy to find. Drawers in the pantry open to reveal vertical tiers of canned goods, every one easily within view. "I don't have to stretch to the back of the cupboard to get a jar, and I use the entire cupboard efficiently," Goodall says.

Goodall also stores winter produce in her greenhouse and the garden. Winter squash, green tomatoes that are individually wrapped and boxed, clumps of chives and parsley, and sealed boxes of potatoes nestle between greenhouse benches. The area is heated just enough to stay above freezing.

Caramba carrots and Jerusalem artichokes stay out in the garden, covered with 6 inches of mulch. Cole and salad crops nestle in the cold frame. The winter low occasionally drops to 19°F, but it is not enough to freeze the well-insulated roots.

◆ Can only ripe, perfect produce. High-acid fruits and tomatoes are best picked slightly immature rather than overmature. When overripe, their acidity falls. You can cut out tiny bruises, but don't try to can anything infected with diseases or molds. They are teeming with spores that will remain in high numbers on surrounding surfaces, even if you cut out the bad spot. Remove the stems and blossom ends of vegetables, if possible. They are more likely to spoil.

◆ Disinfect all canning utensils, cutting boards, and whatever the food may touch. Use 1 part liquid chlorine bleach to 9 parts water. Wash your hands, pull long hair back, and avoid sneezing or coughing into the preparations.

◆ Older recipes have instructions for canning puréed winter squash or sweet potatoes. Newer research has shown that thick purées are hard to can safely. Without fluid to circulate heat uniformly through the jar, the center is hard to sterilize adequately without overcooking outer layers. A safer way is to slice the flesh into strips and pack into hot water.

◆ Adjust processing times according to altitude. Water boils at lower temperatures as elevation increases and will not be as effective in eliminating bacteria. When using a boiling water bath, add 1 minute to the processing time for every 1,000 feet of elevation above sea level. If the recipe calls for processing over 20 minutes, add 2 minutes to the time. Double the 2 minutes with every additional 1,000 feet in elevation.

◆ Before eating anything canned at home, make sure the lid is tight and well sealed. There should be no leakage or signs of mold on the lid, in the food, or on the jar. The top should not bulge. The liquid should not spurt or foam when you open the top. The produce inside should smell just as it did when you filled the jar and look firm with a clear liquid at the top. It should not be spongy, slippery, or shriveled. If something is out of order, dispose of the entire container where no person or animal can reach it. Sterilize anything the bad produce has touched, including the countertop, pan, washcloth, and your hands.

◆ To destroy toxins released by unseen bacteria that may have survived processing, boil canned goods before you eat them. Boil high-acid canned goods for at least 15 minutes and low-acid goods for 30 minutes. If you live at a high altitude, increase boiling time.

◆ For more information and recipes, refer to books such as *Keeping the Harvest, Putting Food By,* or *So Easy to Preserve* (see Appendix for details). Or, contact your local Cooperative Extension Service for their inexpensive recipes.

Canning Jars

Use canning jars approved for canning, not jars recycled from store-bought mayonnaise, apple juice, or other commercial products. Be certain the jars, ring bands, and lids are perfect, not dented, discolored, or chipped. Wash the jars in hot soapy water or the dishwasher and rinse well. If you are using a boiling-water bath, sterilize jars inside and out by submerging them and boiling for 10 minutes. You don't have to bother sterilizing if you are going to process jars in a pressure cooker or for longer than 10 minutes in a boiling-water bath.

Always use approved canning jars for home canning.

Modern jars are topped with a lid with a rubber seal and a screw-on band. Throw away the rubber seal after one use; it will not seal tightly a second time. You can reuse the band if it looks clean, round, and new. Read the manufacturer's directions on the lid package for instructions on how to prepare and sterilize lids.

Hot and Cold Packs

Canning involves packing produce into the jars cold (cold packs) or precooking it and packing it hot (hot packs). Cold packing works better for soft produce like berries, which would dissolve with additional cooking. Hot packing softens vegetables and makes them easier to settle securely into jars; less air is trapped so the seal is more likely to remain tight.

Cold pack. Fill jars with prepared fruit, and cover with hot syrup, juice, or boiling water. Start processing in simmering water, so the jar will not break with the temperature change. Once the water heats up to a full boil, start timing.

Hot pack. Boil produce as indicated in the recipe you are following, and pack it into the jar with the cooking water. This will save a portion of the water-soluble nutrients. However, some mustards and greens like shungiku, cardoon, or asparagus often leave bitter compounds in cooking water; in these cases, you may want to replace the cooking water with fresh boiling water.

For both hot and cold packs, fill the jars full of produce (not just liquid), so produce is unlikely to float to the top. Leave a little headroom; the amount varies with the recipe. Starchy vegetables, like lima beans, corn, or new potatoes, swell and need more elbow room, so you may leave them 1 inch of headroom. Leave ½ inch of headroom for acid vegetables and fruit and ¼ inch for pickles and relishes.

After packing, run a plastic spatula around the sides of the jar to release any air bubbles trapped inside. Clean the jar top, so the lid can seal tightly. Screw on the lid as tightly as possible and start processing.

Processing

To kill any spoilers inside, you must heat-treat the sealed jars. Follow recipe specifications for the type and length of processing. It is a vital part of the preservation process.

To use a boiling-water bath on acidic produce, buy a boiling-water canner or use any large, deep metal pan with a tight-fitting lid. It must be tall enough to submerge jars and a jar rack in boiling water. The jar rack holds jars slightly above the bottom of the pan and away from each other so boiling water can circulate freely around them.

Boiling-water canner

For low-acid vegetables, buy a pressure cooker. By applying 10 or more pounds of pressure, pressure cookers raise water temperatures above boiling, high enough to kill botulism-causing bacteria. Just how many pounds of pressure you need varies with the type of pressure cooker, the kind of gauge, the size of jar and its contents, and the altitude. Read the manufacturer's instructions carefully.

Pressure canner

At the start of each canning season, check the gauges and be certain your pressure cooker is working properly. You may be able to have them tested at the local Cooperative Extension Service.

Care After Processing

Once the jar has been processed, remove it from the boiling water with jar tongs and let it cool on a cake rack in a draft-free area. Check to see if the lid is tightly sealed. Look for suction pulling the top of the jar in. Feel the lid to see if it is secure. Once the jar is cool and you remove the screw band, you should hear a clear ping if you tap the top with a spoon. If you find the lid comes loose during the twenty-four hours after processing, you must repeat the entire sequence again. The produce, however, may lose additional quality.

If the lid is secure, move the jar to a cool, dark location for long-term storage. Check the seal occasionally to be sure it is still tight. Discard the entire jar if it loosens. Even one tiny gap is enough for spoilers to slip in and contaminate the entire jar.

Canning Specifics

Tomatoes. When harvesting, select only perfect fruits that are nearly ripe, fully red, and blemish free. Don't can any tomatoes picked from dead or dying vines.

Some of the newer sweet or mild varieties, regardless of color, may have less acidity and may not qualify as acid crops. To be safe, you can process tomatoes in a pressure cooker or treat them with an extra ¼ teaspoon citric acid or 1 tablespoon lemon juice per pint, or ½ teaspoon citric acid or 2 tablespoons lemon juice per quart. You may want to add extra sugar to counteract acid taste and ½ teaspoon salt for flavor.

MARY KEISER'S PRESERVING TIPS

Mary Keiser of Mifflinburg, Pennsylvania, prefers canning bulk loads of produce to many other forms of preservation. "If you are going to go to the trouble of washing six canning jars, you might as well wash twelve," she says. "If you are going to bother with boiling down tomatoes into sauce, you might as well boil down a bushel."

She acknowledges that canning is not widely popular today but responds, "Canning is not bad to do, as long as you follow instructions. Once you get used to it, you can do it almost with your eyes closed."

Canning Tips

- Get a mechanical strainer that separates tomato flesh from juice.
- Use a food processor, which spares you from hand chopping.
- Try meaty Roma tomatos for sauce; they don't need as much boiling.
- If time runs short, accept a sauce that is not quite as thick as you ultimately want. "I do a bushel at a time and have to have it all cooked and canned in one day. So when I get sick and tired of simmering the sauce, I can it and boil it down later when I am ready to use it," Mary says.
- Keep the processes simple and individual ingredients separate. The resulting canned goods will be versatile enough for a number of different uses, and you can add extras as you cook with them.
- To give extra body and flavor to meatless tomato sauce, Keiser preserves tomatillos, a sweeter, less-acidic cousin of the tomato. She chops the fruit into a chunky liquid in the food processor, and cooks 7 to 8 quarts with about 2 cups of vinegar. She sometimes drops in pickling spices or hot peppers. She cooks the salsa down until it is fairly thick and then cans it in pint jars. "The smaller jar is better because the relish gets moldy unless you use it quickly after you open it," she says.

◆ Even though peppers are a snap to freeze, Keiser prefers canning them. She preserves hot Ancho peppers in a sweet vinegar mixture, a blend of 1 cup water, 1 cup vinegar, and 2½ tablespoons honey. She dices sweet peppers and cans them in plain hot water. The result is a milder flavor and a softer texture than comparable frozen peppers. "In the winter, when peppers cost $1 each in the store, they are just fine."

Freezing Tips

◆ Keiser freezes spinach, peas, and broccoli. She recommends chopping up zucchini in the food processor and freezing it in small containers for zucchini bread or stir-fries. "If you rinse the thawing squash well and pat it dry, you can put a little more body back into the squash," she said.

◆ Keiser slices freezer strawberries extra-thin — ¼- to ⅛-inch-diameter — and dry-packs them in freezer containers. At that size, they don't get mushy, Keiser says, and they can be used like fresh strawberries in strawberry shortcake.

Drying Tips

◆ Dried beans are standard fare, as Mary and her husband Dennis eat little meat. They harvest dried kidney, pinto, adzuki, and heirloom beans when the vines are dead and the sun has begun drying them. Mary finishes drying them on a screen in the attic or a spare bedroom. The door is always closed to keep the cat from napping on the beans. The finished beans go into recycled screw-top glass jars, which are boxed and set in a little-used corner.

Crushed Tomatoes

Note: Never supplement juice with water or you will lower acidity levels.

Wash tomatoes, and dip them in boiling water for 30 to 60 seconds, or until their skins split. Chill in cold water, slip off skins, and remove cores. Trim off any bruised or discolored portions, and cut into quarters.

Heat one-sixth of the quarters quickly in a large pot, crushing them with a wooden mallet or spoon as they are added to the pot; this will draw off some juice. Continue heating the tomatoes, stirring to prevent burning.

Once the tomatoes are boiling, gradually add the remaining quartered tomatoes, stirring constantly. You need not crush these remaining, as they will soften with heating and stirring. After all the tomatoes are added, boil gently for 5 minutes.

Add bottled lemon juice or citric acid to jars (see above for amounts). If desired, add 1 teaspoon of salt per quart to the jars. Fill jars immediately with hot tomatoes, leaving ½ inch of headroom.

Adjust lids and process jars in a boiling-water bath: Give pint jars 35 minutes (40 minutes if you are from 1,000 to 3,000 feet in altitude). Give quart containers 45 minutes (50 minutes at higher altitudes).

Or, process pint containers for 20 minutes in a pressure cooker at 6 pounds pressure for dial gauges, 5 pounds for weighted gauges, or 10 pounds above 1,000 feet of altitude. For quart jars, process for 15 minutes at 11 pounds for dial gauges, 10 pounds weighted, or 15 pounds above 1,000 feet of altitude.

Ohio State University
Extension Service

Green beans. Select cultivars noted for retaining quality when canned. Many of the older cultivars, like Blue Lake or Kentucky Wonder, are good examples. Beans slightly past prime for fresh eating and those with a swelling seed and tougher pod may keep a firmer texture. Newer, more tender-podded, beans are better frozen.

Wash beans, and trim off both ends. Cut into 1-inch pieces or leave whole. *To cold-pack,* place raw beans in jars leaving 1 inch of headroom (add 1 teaspoon salt per quart, if desired) and cover with boiling water, again leaving 1 inch of headroom. Adjust lids. *To hot-pack,* place jars in a kettle, cover with boiling water, and boil for 5 minutes; loosely fill jars, leaving 1 inch of headroom. Adjust lids.

In a pressure-cooker, process pint containers for 20 minutes and quart containers for 25 minutes. Maintain 240°F with 11 pounds of pressure on a dial gauge or 10 pounds on a weighted gauge; use 15 pounds between 1,000 and 2,000 feet elevation. These times and pressures are based on Ohio State University Extension Service recommendations.

Pickles. Pick small, unblemished pickling cucumbers, preferably in the morning when they are more crisp and cool. Discard any with mold. Process the rest immediately. If you miss harvesting the cucumbers small enough for standard dill pickles, you can slice them and make them into bread-and-butter pickles or dill chips. Wash cucumbers thoroughly and remove the blossom ends. Enzymes released there can make the fruit softer.

◆ Many old pickle recipes are out of date and not always safe. Pick a modern recipe, and follow it closely. Maintain necessary acidity levels to process pickles in a boiling-water bath.

◆ Use unadulterated canning, pickling, or kosher salt. Low-sodium salt is adequate for quick-process pickles but not for brine.

◆ The vinegar should be 5 to 6 percent white distilled vinegar (which does not distort the color of white vegetables) or darker cider vinegar.

◆ White sugar helps preserve the color, but brown sugar adds interesting flavor.

◆ Use fresh whole pickling spices, such as fresh-picked garlic and dill out of your own garden. Ground or old spices can make pickles dark and musty.

Quick Dill Pickles

Yield: 3 quarts

3 cups white vinegar
3 cups water
⅓ cup canning salt
4 pounds cucumbers, washed and cut into spears
6 heads dill or 6 tablespoons dill seed
3 peeled cloves garlic (optional)
9 peppercorns

Combine liquids and salt, and heat to boiling. Pack cucumbers into hot, clean quart jars. Add to each jar 2 heads dill or 2 tablespoons dill seed, 1 clove garlic, and 3 peppercorns. Fill the jars with the hot pickling syrup, leaving ½ inch of headroom. Adjust lids. Process in a boiling-water bath for 20 minutes.

For the best flavor, let the pickles stand and mellow for several weeks before eating.

Keeping the Harvest by Nancy Chioffi and Gretchen Mead

Berries (including blueberries, blackberries, dewberries, huckleberries, loganberries, elderberries, gooseberries, raspberries, and currants. Strawberries generally are better frozen or used for jelly). If you sweeten berries, they hold their flavor and color better. They are also easier to use — just pour them out of the jar onto ice cream or pancakes. Use granulated white sugar, or substitute up to 25 percent light corn syrup for a better shine on the berries. If you want to add low-calorie sweeteners like saccharine, wait until you are ready to use the berries; cooking gives saccharine an unpleasant taste. To can without any sugar, heat and stir the berries to release natural juices, or add boiling water instead of syrups.

Raw-pack softer bramble berries, gooseberries, blueberries, and huckleberries to preserve their firmness. Expect delicate raspberries to soften into sauce or juice after processing. Hot-pack firmer berries like currants and elderberries. Boil each quart of clean, prepared berries with ½ cup sugar, stirring gently until they are surrounded with juice. Let them sit at room temperature several hours. Reheat before packing.

Canned Berries

Wash berries in cold or iced water to firm the fruit. Use scissors to snip off heads and tails of gooseberries. Drain. Prepare and boil syrup, if desired. For table-ready berries, use the medium syrup given on page 212. Add ½ cup syrup, juice, or water to each jar. Pack berries into jars; leave ½ inch of headroom. Shake jars while filling to get a full pack. Fill jars up to about ½ inch from the top with boiling syrup or water. Process in a boiling water bath 15 minutes for pint containers (20 minutes for 1,000 to 3,000 foot elevations) and 20 minutes for quart containers (25 minutes for 1,000 to 3,000 foot elevations).

Ohio State University
Extension Service

Jellies and jams. To make jelly, boil the berries until the juice begins to flow, and squeeze the juice out in a jelly or cheesecloth bag. Those with fine pulp will yield a clearer juice if allowed to seep out with minimal pressure or if strained a second time. For jam, crush the berries and add sugar and pectin, if desired. Recipes requiring added pectin shorten the cooking time and thus preserve fresh flavor and color better than recipes that require longer cooking.

Berry Jam with Powdered Pectin

Yield: Eleven or twelve half-pint jars

This recipe can be used to make jam with blackberries, boysenberries, dewberries, strawberries, youngberries, loganberries, red raspberries, and gooseberries.

6 cups crushed berries — about 3 quarts of fully ripe berries (grind gooseberries instead of crushing)
1 package powdered pectin
8½ cups sugar

Measure crushed berries into a large saucepan. Add powdered pectin and stir well to dissolve. Bring to a hard boil over high heat, stirring constantly. Add sugar all at once. Continue stirring and bring to a full rolling boil (a boil that cannot be stirred down). Boil hard for exactly 1 minute. Remove from heat and skim off foam with metal spoon. Stir and skim for 5 minutes to cool slightly and prevent fruit from floating. Ladle into hot, sterilized containers, leaving ¼ inch of headroom in jars. Seal and process canning jars in a boiling-water bath for 10 minutes.

Keeping the Harvest by Nancy Chioffi and Gretchen Mead

nine

Encyclopedia of Crops

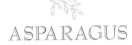

ARTICHOKE, GLOBE

Although not frequently grown in home gardens, this bristly, 5-foot-tall member of the thistle family can be interesting and delicious to try. In California and other areas with a cool growing season and mild winter, one plant can be productive for several years; it peaks in the second year and fades near the fourth. You may be able to grow it as an annual in the North. For a fast start, begin the seed indoors early or transplant a division from another plant. Plant seedlings in a well-drained but evenly moist soil of good fertility. Harvest the scales on the flower buds and eat the succulent bases or pickle the inner heart.

Green Globe Improved is the standard cultivar. Violetto has handsome purple buds.

ASPARAGUS

The succulent shoots of a vigorous perennial asparagus bed return to tempt your taste buds year after year. To resprout reliably, the crop requires a period of winter dormancy and a touch of special care. In the past, asparagus was planted quite deeply, but new studies show that more shallow planting is just as productive — and much easier. The shoots are thinner when they emerge but they appear in greater numbers.

Begin a new asparagus bed by enriching the entire area with abundant compost and rotted horse or cow manure, so the roots can grow into soil of good fertility. Buy large and healthy year-old bare-root clumps, and spread them in trenches 1 foot wide and 6 inches deep — shallower in heavier soils.

Grow the new higher-yielding, disease-resistant cultivars, like Jersey Centennial, which surpass the productivity of the old-fashioned Martha and Mary Washington types. All-male types such as SYN 4–56 (formerly Jersey Giant) are more prolific, because they do not expend energy in seed production.

Traditionally, a three-year wait was imposed before any new plantings of asparagus were harvested, so that the roots could grow strong and vigorous. New research shows, however, that yields actually improve with early harvesting if you live in an area with mild winters. More new buds develop if you harvest lightly the first year after planting. Harvest for two weeks the first year, four the second, and six the third and following years. In northern climates, you are still wise to wait at least two years before the first light harvest. When you do harvest, look for the most tender spears. These usually are relatively short, with a tight tip, and are wider than the size of a pencil but not excessively obese.

To keep the crop healthy and control weeds, do not hoe deeply, as you may damage asparagus roots. Continue to fertilize by adding a layer of compost or composted manure to the bed every spring. During the first couple of years, irrigate during dry spells. In the North, mulch before winter. Destroy old asparagus spears if asparagus beetles feed on the new shoots, which often makes them grow crooked.

BEANS

Homegrown beans are healthful for you, and they are good for the soil. High in protein, fiber, and vitamins, beans also add nitrogen to your garden soil. Try a couple of cultivars of all the following types before you pick favorites. In each case, the flavor and texture of extra-fresh snapping or shelling beans will be quite different from what you probably have come to expect from supermarket beans.

Bush beans of all kinds grow and yield better if you plant them in double rows in a wide bed. Treat the soil with a nitrogen-fixing bacteria inoculum for faster germination. If you keep the soil nitrogen-poor and allow the beans to grow long enough, the bacteria will form round pink nodules on the roots to capture their own nitrogen (see page 114).

All immature beans that you pick for their tender pods need regular harvesting. Once seeds mature, the plant stops producing new beans. You can leave mature shelling beans on the vine until they are dry or ready for supplementary drying indoors.

Green or Snap Beans

If you browse through seed catalogues, you will find a diversity of what you may once have thought of as plain, ordinary green beans. A variety of shapes, textures, flavors, and colors are available exclusively to gardeners. Try mild, golden wax beans; buttery, heirloom Roma beans; magical purple Royal Burgundy or Purple Teepee beans; or superlong, podded, climbing Kentucky Wonder or bush Jumbo beans. Tiny Bush Baby beans are a delicate treat, quite unlike any other cultivar.

Grow bush beans for a short but intense harvest of tender pods. You can extend the season and safeguard against yields lowered by heat or insects if you plant successions every couple of weeks. Some great bush bean cultivars to try include Blue Lake Bush, Derby, Kentucky Wonder (bush), Romano (bush), and the new slender French filet beans.

For a longer harvest season and up to three times greater yield, plant some pole beans. These need support on a trellis, fence, net, cornstalk, or the like, but they will be easier to harvest for the initial effort. Many of the above bush bean cultivars are extra good in their pole-bean form. Another cultivar to look for is Kentucky Blue, a very tender-podded offspring of Kentucky Wonder and Blue Lake. Check out some of the catalogues of heirloom seeds for even more unusual offerings.

Most snap beans can be attacked by the Mexican bean beetle, which riddles the leaves and gnaws on the pods. The adults look like brown ladybugs and leave behind soft-spiny, yellow larvae that cling beneath the bean leaves. To keep their damage under control, clean out all bean residues once the plant is done cropping, and rototill the area to eliminate overwintering beetles. Use predatory spined soldier bugs or the parasitic wasp *Pediobius faveolatus* for nontoxic control or dust with insecticides.

Lima Beans

These buttery and, when fresh, nutty-tasting beans are said to be finicky growers in the North. If northern gardeners stick to bush baby limas with some cool soil tolerance, like Geneva and Eastland, however, they can still enjoy the best lima beans can offer. Southerners can revel in large-seeded vining limas, like King of the Garden.

Dry Beans

Of the great variety of different dry beans, many are heirlooms with colorful seed coats. Choose from bush or vining forms. Some, like Black Turtle, Dwarf Horticultural, Buttergreen or cool-season broad, or fava, beans (Broad Windsor Long Pod, for instance), double as green snap beans if picked early. (A few people may be allergic to broad beans.) For fully mature dried beans try Jacob's Cattle, Black Turtle, Red Mexican, Great Northern, Adzuki, or pinto. (See chapter 8 for more on harvesting and drying beans.)

Soybeans

If you don't have rabbits nearby, try some soybeans for a welcome change. (Rabbits love the new shoots and will vaccuum them up as they emerge.) Brought to maturity after a fairly long, warm growing season, garden soybeans have the high protein and vitamin content of field types with a great nutty flavor. The cultivar Butterbeans is ideal for eating moist and green. Pick when the beans are green and about the size of a pea, boil in the pods until the beans are easy to evict, around 5 to 15 minutes, and then boil or steam until the beans are tender enough to eat. The green seeds lose quality fast, so don't let them sit around. You can also let the seeds mature and dry in the pod and treat them like a dried bean. Try to gather the pods up before the seeds escape.

BERRIES

Although you may not have room for an orchard in your yard, you probably can squeeze in some of the small fruit crops. You simply cannot buy berries that are as delicious as those picked perfectly ripe and eaten promptly. Furthermore, the space and time you contribute to berry production is well spent; these are among the most costly produce items you can buy. Try thorny bramble berries like blackberries and raspberries, low-growing strawberries, and bush-forming blueberries, gooseberries, and currants. If you plan ahead, you can

have a succession of berries all summer. Start with June-bearing strawberries, progress to currants and gooseberries, summer-fruiting blackberries and raspberries, day-neutral and alpine strawberries, blueberries, late-season elderberries, everbearing brambles, and everbearing strawberries.

Plant bare-root berry plants in the spring. If you can find them grown in containers, you can plant in early fall in mild areas of the country. Wait until spring elsewhere. Choose a location in full sun, if possible, or in partial shade in hot climates. The soil should be well drained and fertile but not excessively high in nitrogen. Since most berries are perennials, look for cultivars suitable for your climatic zone. Space new plants according to package instructions or plant them slightly closer to create an informal hedge. Each plant will produce fewer berries, but overall, the planting can bring in higher volume.

All berries can fall victim to hungry birds. This is especially true of red-fruited kinds, although birds also find blues, blacks, and to a lesser extent yellows. If birds are a problem, enclose bushes in bird-proof cages or wrap them in bird nets once the berries start to ripen.

Bramble Berries

This group of small fruits is named for their thorny stems and tendency to spring up in large thickets. The majority of brambles grow best in the northern portion of the country, but a few cultivars have been bred to take the heat and humidity of the South. Here are some choices:

Blackberries. Quite hardy and vigorous, blackberries are large, succulent, and sweet. Give them plenty of room to spread and keep a clipper handy. A good early cultivar is Raven. Ranger comes in midseason and Dirksen, a thornless cultivar, produces over much of the summer. Dirksen represents one of a new class of thornless blackberries, a revolution in berry growing. They grow upright, since they are self-supporting, and they do not need trellising. They are not hardy enough for northern states, how-ever; the northern limit for the hardiest thornless cultivar, Chester, is zone 5.

Raspberries. The most fragile-fruited of the bramble berries, raspberries are not high yielders, but what you do pick is delicious. Some cultivars fruit heavily in summer. Other cultivars, the everbearers, double up with a second harvest in fall. In all, you might expect to pick about 2 pounds of berries from a healthy plant of either type of raspberry. In general, this group needs a cold winter and long cool spring, but tolerances vary depending on the species and cultivar. Growth habits also vary. Red- and yellow-fruited bushes grow on upright canes and spread by suckers. Black and purple are more trailing, root on shoot tips, and usually need trellising.

Red raspberries are the standard against which other berries are judged. Some commonly grown cultivars include Taylor, a midseason producer; Latham, which is somewhat resistant to viral diseases; and everbearing Heritage. Latham is hardy as far north as zone 3. Dorman Red is suitable for southern zones 7 to 10. Southerners also should try the new Bababerry, which is everbearing, thornless and reputed to have better flavor than other southern varieties.

Black (or blackcap) raspberries tend to have small- to medium-size berries with intense flavor but a greater percentage of the berry is taken up by seed. They also can be more susceptible to disease. Some good cultivars include Allen, Bristol, and Cumberland.

Purple raspberries are hybrids between red and black, with larger, more acidic fruit. Some good cultivars are Brandywine and early-cropping Clyde and Amethyst. For the ultimate in versatility, try Royalty. You can pick the berries when immature and red, tart and purple, or overmature black and sweeter.

Yellow raspberries, a pigment-free red type, produce fewer berries, but they are soft and sweet. Everbearing Fall Gold and Amber are good choices for the North.

Lesser berries. These hybrids of blackberries or raspberries and other bramble species combine virtues of both with new blood. The *tayberry* is a hybrid blackberry and raspberry that grows like a blackberry. *Dewberry* (or trailing blackberry) is good for the South and looks like an early-ripening blackberry. *Youngberry,* a hybrid between blackberry and dewberry is available in thornless plants for zones 5 to 8. The *loganberry* is an August-fruiting hybrid, thought to include parentage of dewberry and red raspberry, though it is hardy enough to survive only along the California coast and in the Pacific Northwest. The *boysenberry* is a large-fruited plant, though a fussy grower, that comes from loganberry, blackberry, and raspberry parents.

Bramble care. On all brambles, you must cut back canes that have borne fruit to allow new ones to grow. However, different types of brambles will fruit on different-age canes. Those that fruit early in the summer will bear on longer canes that sprouted the year before; later ones will bear on new growth that sprouted in spring. In either case, you will be safe to cut back old canes after you have harvested their fruit or see them turn brittle and brown.

After tackling old, spent canes, remove any other shoots that are damaged, diseased, or obviously overcrowded, and then decide how thick to leave the remainder. If you want large, choice berries and don't mind fewer of them, you can thin to two or three of the best canes per foot. Alternatively, for more but smaller berries, leave most of the new canes. You can vary your pruning plans even further. Traditional advice is to cut back fruiting shoots of black and purple raspberry and blackberry by about one-third their total length to encourage them to develop productive side branches and more berries. If you do this, however, the fruit develops later, and if you are raising everbearing fall producers, it may be too late for short-season areas.

You can let red raspberries and thornless blackberries grow without support, but other types, including the red Heritage raspberry, trailing blackberries, and most cultivars with canes over 24 inches long, need trellising. Tie them to a sturdy trellis in a fan or concentric V shape.

Keep the soil fertile enough for steady growth, but don't overfertilize and force excessive growth. Use a balanced fertilizer in spring or slow-release minerals in fall. If in doubt about how much fertilizer to add, have the soil tested and get professional recommendations.

Bramble berries share many diseases and insect pests. You can avoid some of these by planting only certified virus-free plants. Don't plant brambles anywhere that the soil may be infested by verticillium wilt, a problem of tomatoes, eggplant, strawberries, and other edible crops. Eliminate nearby wild bramble berry stands if they are infested with pests or diseases. Isolate black raspberries 300 to 700 feet from red raspberries because the reds can carry a mosaic virus that will damage the blacks. Keep the old canes clipped off so they will not spread disease. For fungus problems, spray with lime sulfur in spring as the first leaves open.

Shrub Berries

Blueberries, currants, gooseberries, and elderberries are the small-fruit high-performers. A mature bush can produce up to 10 pounds of berries. In return for this bounty, they ask little of your time. For instance, you need only prune mature bushes lightly: Remove dead or diseased wood; thin out overcrowded growth and crossing or shaded branches by cutting the branches off at the base or origin on a mother branch; limit height by cutting upward-growing branches back to outward-facing branches or shoots. When well shaped, all of the following shrubs can double as handsome ornamentals *and* delightful edibles.

Blueberries. An American native with glowing red autumn foliage, the blueberry grows in sandy but moist, acidic soils from zone 3 to zone 10. You may be able to adapt marginal sites by adding extra sand, peat moss, pine needles, and wettable sulfur to lower the pH. If you have quite alkaline or heavy soil, blueberries are probably not the crop for you. If the leaves start to yellow from lack of nitrogen, fertilize with sulfate of ammonia; blueberries cannot use many other forms of nitrogen. Plant two compatible cultivars that can cross-pollinate. Buy two- to three-year-old plants, and do not prune for the first three years except to remove dead branches. After that time the shrubs should begin to produce fruit and you can begin maintenance pruning.

Find a cultivar suitable to your climate. For the South, try the smaller-fruited rabbiteye types, such as

Centurion, Premier, Tifblue, and Woodard. In the North (zones 5 to 7), stick to highbush cultivars like Bluecrop, Blueray, and Jersey. For the far North (zones 3 and 4), try extra-hardy lowbush or hybrid highbush cultivars like Northland, Patriot, and Northblue, which is a half-highbush that is 2 feet tall. Northsky is a good pollinator for Northblue.

Within each range, you can select cultivars that fruit early, midseason, or late in order to have ripe berries over a period of several months. Among the rabbiteye types, for example, Woodard ripens in early June, Tifblue and Premier in late June, Delite in early July, and Centurion in late August. Among the highbush types, Earliblue and New Blueray ripen first, Bluecrop and Berkeley midseason, and Jersey and Dixie late.

Currants, Gooseberries, and Elderberries. These unusual but tasty fruits are members of the genus *Ribes*. They have lost favor because they can be alternate hosts for pine blister rust, a devastating disease of white pine. Do not plant within 900 feet of a white pine, therefore. Cultivation is banned in some states. In locations where rust is a problem, look for new rust-resistant cultivars, such as Coronet, Crusader, or Consort.

Except for disease, both *Ribes* fruits are exceedingly easy to grow. They are self-pollinating, so one shrub produces a full quota of berries. They also tolerate heavier soils than most shrub berries. They do bloom earlier than most bush fruit, however, and the flowers can be damaged by late frosts. To minimize loss, don't plant in low areas that are more prone to frosts. The berries are especially delicious in baked goods, jellies, or jams; when very ripe, the berries can be good for eating fresh.

Among the currants are milder-flavored white types, such as White Grape; red varieties, such as Red Lake, which are attractive to birds and very tart; and black types, which are the least cultivated, the tallest, and the most susceptible to rust.

Thorny-stemmed gooseberries produce tart-sweet berries that are not as tempting to birds. A crop for northern areas, gooseberries suffer in heat. Try them in zones 4 to 6; plant in light shade where summers are warmer. The fruit is quite tart but you may be able to eat them right off the bush when they are extremely ripe. The Japanese wineberry (*Rubus phoenicolasius*), tastes sweeter and muskier than most gooseberries. The cultivars Pixwell and Poorman ripen to a blushing red. Downing ripens a week later, but the fruit stays green. Welcome is a thornless variety.

Gooseberries bear their berries on young, one- to three-year-old wood. To keep the compact shrub putting out new growth for future crops, remove old, weak, or damaged branches while the plant is dormant in late spring.

The elderberry, another American shrub, grows to be about 8 feet tall, bearing clusters of small berries that are good for cooking or winemaking. They are attractive and hardy and will grow in most well-drained soils. For the largest amount of fruit, plant two different varieties. York and Nova are most commonly sold. They ripen in late summer from zones 4 to 8.

Strawberries

Everyone loves a sweet red strawberry, but how seldom they come that way in the grocery store. You will have nothing less than the ripest and best if you let a few plants grow in a sunny location at home. Choose from cultivars that bear heavily in June only *(June bearing)*, lightly throughout the summer into fall *(day neutrals)*, or in spring and again lightly in fall *(everbearing)*. Under ideal circumstances, you can expect to get a total of 1 quart of berries a season from each plant.

June bearers produce the largest fruit, but they are finished soon after the start of summer. They sprout more runners than the rest and can be hard to keep up with if you intend to pinch runners off. Protect the flowers from late spring frosts with floating row covers or mulch. The first spring after planting, remove flowers to strengthen the plants for future crops. Especially in the South, try disease-resistant Surecrop, Blakemore, Cardinal, and Red Chief. For the North, sample flavorful Honeoye, late-fruiting Redstar, and later-flowering Abundant Sparkle.

Day neutrals are the newest of the bunch. These flower and fruit continuously from spring to fall, but tend to be weaker plants than the others and require special care. Plant virus-free bare-root plants as early as possible in spring. The longer you wait, the smaller the harvest will be. Stagger them in rows about 12 inches apart. They can grow this closely because the plants stay small and put out few runners, which you should remove anyway. Pinch off flowers for the first six weeks.

Day-neutral plants struggle where summers are hot, but they do better when mulched with a light-colored plastic or straw to keep the soil cool. Shade them lightly, and irrigate often. Fertilize these shallow-rooted, heavy feeders once a month throughout the summer with composted manure or a balanced 10-10-10 fertilizer. Cultivars Aptos, Brighton, and Hecker are for the California coast and other mild regions. Yolo grows well in the South. For the East and Midwest, stick with vigorous but less intense-flavored Tribute or the excellent-flavored Tristar. The latter two fruit from January through August in milder climates.

Everbearing strawberries produce a large spring crop and a smaller autumn crop. They do well in California and other areas where seasons are long and mild. Plant the bare-root plants in spring and remove the flowers for the next three months. They can produce their first crop in fall and continue normally in the spring and fall the next year. Try cultivars such as Ozark Beauty and Superfection.

The alpine strawberry has a more intense-flavored but less sweet fruit that is thick with pectin. My family loves it. It grows beautifully in the rock garden and fruits all summer long, a treat for the kids. Look for Alexandria, Baron Solemacher, Ruegen Improved, and Pineapple Crush, which is a yellow-fruited type.

You can buy alpine strawberry plants or start your own from seed. Mine started easily in the basement light garden where the temperature hovers at about 60°F. They also can self-sow, though not invasively. They seldom spread by runners.

Strawberries are susceptible to a number of diseases. Gray rot is common on berries. Remove any berries that are infected. Buy certified disease-free plants and grow them in well-drained soils to escape verticillium wilt and red stele root rot. For the longest productive life, give each plant ample room to grow without crowding into neighbors, and don't apply too much fertilizer. You may want to start new plantings in different locations every two or three years to replace older crops. Day neutrals may be best treated as an annual crop.

Strawberry patches that become a tangled mat of plantlets and weeds are a hard situation to remedy. If you remove runners to keep the mother plants producing larger berries, you can plant individuals 1 foot apart, cultivate, and mulch around plants to keep out weeds. If you leave a few of the young runners on, give the plants 2 feet of space on all sides and weed by hand in the openings. Alternatively, you can let the plantlets root into organic mulches or openings in plastic sheeting. Cover with several inches of loose mulch in winter to prevent frost from heaving up the shallow root systems. Remove the mulch when leaves begin to turn green in early spring.

BRASSICAS

The *Brassica* genus encompasses a large number of vegetables, including broccoli, cauliflower, Brussels sprouts, cabbage, and Chinese cabbage. (Related leafy greens like kohlrabi, turnips, and rutabagas are discussed under separate entries.) All are full of vitamins, some of which are reputed to fight cancer, so they make a healthy addition to the garden. Although the most common of the *Brassicas* are inexpensive at the grocery, you can grow gourmet varieties that are more exciting.

Many of these plants are in the same species, *Brassica oleracea,* and thus very much alike. Not surprisingly, they have similar growing requirements, nutritional needs, pests, and even flavorings. The biting mustard component is a chemical called *glucosinolate*. This compound can be present in greater or lesser extents depending on the cultivar, weather, growing conditions, and season; it often increases with stress or slow growth.

Brassicas need abundant calcium to produce well. They are all susceptible to club root, cabbage maggots, cabbage loopers, and flea beetles, though the amount of damage possible varies with the crop, even cultivar. Spray with *Bt* for the loopers. Secure the crop beneath floating row covers for maggots and flea beetles. Rotate planting areas with unrelated crops and lime the soil to avoid club root. For harvesting and preserving information, see chapters 5, 6, 7, and 8.

Broccoflower

This green cauliflower shares traits of both broccoli and cauliflower. The light green head is shaped like cauliflower but requires no blanching. The plant has some of the hardiness and vigor of broccoli but a mild flavor reminiscent of cauliflower. Alverda is one of open-pollinated types available in America. When I grew it, the heads took much longer to mature than advertised, but when they cropped, they were great — full and sweet.

Broccoli

Broccoli is easy to grow in spring and fall, or, in mild climates, even winter. Choose from broccoli cultivars that produce a single large head or a smaller central head with an abundance of later-emerging side shoots. For the former type, try Premium Crop; for the latter form, grow Bonanza Hybrid. If summer strikes quickly, use a heat-tolerant cultivar like Premium Crop or Saga. Or, go with a more exotic variation on standard broccoli. Romanesco broccoli (sometimes listed in seed catalogues under cauliflower) is an Italian heirloom with a spiraling, cone-shaped head and florets of lime-green. It is open-pollinated, especially variable in its performance, and takes a long time to mature. The resulting head (if you get one), is astonishing and

beautiful, however. Broccoli raab, or rapa, grows quickly, rather like a mustard, and sends up a succulent but bitter-flowering shoot. Harvest before the buds break and the stem becomes stringy.

Plant broccoli and Romanesco as a four- to six-week-old seedling — a healthy, quickly growing plant that has not dallied in the six-pack. Sow raab seeds directly in the garden. Wait until the weather is consistently above 40°F, or larger seedlings may bolt or button without heading. If you set them out extra early, cover with a plastic tunnel or floating row cover, which also will protect the seedlings from insect pests later. If your cool season is long enough, plant new seedlings two and three weeks later for a succession of harvests. For an autumn harvest, start in summer in a cool area, lightly shaded by neighboring plants or shade cloth. As the weather moderates in fall, give the plants full sun.

Brussels Sprouts

Among the most frost-hardy of the *Brassicas,* these unusual-looking plants produce edibles under their leafy arms. In fact, frost makes the flavor of the sprouts milder and sweeter. Consequently, Brussels sprouts are best planted in summer for late autumn harvest, or in mild climates, in fall for winter harvest. Give them three or four months to mature be-

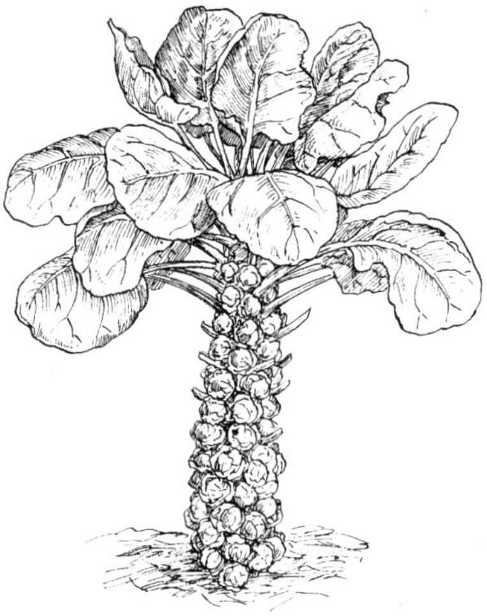

fore the onset of steady cold. Here in Cleveland, I plant them from April to June and harvest in late September through November — even December, if the weather does not drop into the teens.

Until recent years, Americans have been limited to the shorter- and earlier-maturing American hybrids like Jade Cross E and Long Island Improved. These have round, plump sprouts along a 2- to 3-foot stem. Now, specialty catalogues carry European types that grow taller and bear more slender sprouts. Among them is Rubine, which has a handsome bluish red tint and slightly spicier sprouts.

Cabbage

Good-quality cabbage is available inexpensively in groceries and is no longer the staple it was a century ago. It is worth including in your garden, however, if you prefer organic methods, unusual cultivars, or homemade sauerkraut, or you wish to store quantities in a root cellar. Choose from lovely red cabbages, pungent savoy types, mild early types, and long-storing late cultivars. Try the heirloom Early Jersey Wakefield, late-maturing Danish Roundhead for winter storage, and the long-growing and heat-tolerant Savoy Queen.

The size of the cabbage head depends on the cultivar, as well as how closely you space the plants.

The heads will be smaller if you space them closely, but you may harvest more from a given space. If you have a long cool season, you may be able to cut the main head and harvest small, later-sprouting miniheads.

Like other *Brassicas,* start seedlings in consistently cool weather, above about 50°F. Keep them growing quickly and well fertilized.

Cabbage, Chinese

There are two main groups of Chinese cabbage — Pekinensis and Chinensis (which is also called pak choi, bok choi, and celery mustard). Pekinensis, similar to western cabbages, has relatively thin leaves in

long slender or short stocky heads. Pak choi looks a bit like a large Swiss chard with broad white stems that are succulent and sweet.

In many parts of the country, Chinese cabbages are not easy to grow. They bolt easily as days grow longer in spring and they are prime targets for flea beetles and cabbage loopers. Look for newer cultivars that tolerate a wider range of temperatures and resist diseases. For spring growing, plant Two Seasons Hybrid or quick-cropping miniature pak choi cultivars like Mei Quing Choi. In the fall, try Dynasty or disease-resistant Blues Hybrid.

You may not be able to find prestarted plants of these better cultivars in garden centers and greenhouses. Start your own indoors four to six weeks before spring planting, or direct-sow in midsummer.

Cauliflower

Cauliflower, the primadonna of this group, is rather picky about growing conditions. It does not take much frost or heat but thrives in temperatures that hover around 60°F. Plant just a few weeks before your last spring frost date, or during the end of winter in the South.

If you buy seedlings, stay away from short, stunted ones with overly compacted roots, which are already stressed and not likely to do well. Keep the seedlings growing quickly with plenty of nutrients and moisture. When a head begins to develop, loop nearby leaves over it and secure them with a rubber band. This will shade and blanch the head, and thus keep the vegetable mild flavored and creamy colored.

Find the cultivar that will survive in your temperature range. Ask your neighbors who garden what cultivars have worked well for them. If your season has a short ideal growing period, look for the very quick-cropping early types, like small-headed White Corona Hybrid or standard-size Milkyway Hybrid. Snow Crown Hybrid is a little later but more tolerant of changes in the weather. Andes takes about a week longer to mature but can be self-blanching.

In the fall, try purple-headed cauliflowers, which need no blanching but do require cool weather to develop the color. As a rule, they are more weather tolerant and thus easier to grow than white types. The purple changes to green when cooked. Look for Sicilian Purple, Violet Queen, or darker Burgundy Queen.

CARROTS

Carrots first hit the culinary scene as coarse woody-rooted animal fodder, and many of those sold commercially are not far removed. Today, homegrown carrots have come a long way. There are gourmet miniature carrots like Little Finger and Baby Spike, and long slender supersweets.

Try all-purpose carrots like Touchon, Nandor Hybrid, Danvers Half Long, and Nantes Half Long, which are sweet and tender but not grown for mechanical harvest or long storage and shipping.

Carrot breeders have also been releasing a new generation of carrots with increased vitamin A content, deeper orange color, more sugar, and less bitterness. You will find all these advantages in cultivars like A+ Hybrid and Ingot. These carrots, however, mature only in deep loose soils. Elsewhere, stick with the shorter-rooted types.

When planting carrots, avoid recently manured locations, which make roots split and grow hairy. Lay the seed out in more efficient staggered double or triple rows. Since germination can be precarious, warm the soil up with clear plastic in early to mid-spring just before planting. Cover the seed with no more than ¼ inch of fine soil, peat moss, or compost. Make sure the soil stays extra fine so the seedlings can rise. Interplanting with radishes or under floating row covers (which help prevent the soil from compacting in hard rain) can help. Keep the seed bed moist for two weeks, at which time the seedlings should emerge. (See chapter 3 for more on germinating carrot seeds.)

As carrots grow, they first dig deep to their mature length, and then they swell. The first stage is the critical one for good carrots. Make sure they are not stunted by drought or nutrient deficiencies. Wait until the roots develop full orange color to harvest, or they won't be worth eating. (For more on determining when carrots are mature, see chapter 6. For storage ideas, see chapters 7 and 8.)

> "Young Carrots are popularly regarded as a delicacy and fit for invalids. In common with all immature fruit and vegetables they are unwholesome. So far as having a delicate flavour, that of young carrots is, I think, merely raw, whereas that of fully mature specimens is rich, sweet and nutlike."
>
> *Eleanour Sinclair Rhode, 1938*

CORN

Corn takes a lot of space, a highly fertile soil, good pollination, and protection from raccoons and caterpillars. Standard sweet corn, moreover, which many gardeners still feel has the best flavor, loses quality every minute it is off the stalk; for this reason, homegrown corn has long had the upper hand over commercial offerings. The tide is starting to turn, however, as sugar-enhanced and supersweet types enter farm fields, because these newer types hold their sugar for days, even weeks. They can thus handle shipping and marketing without a dramatic loss of quality.

Traditional sweet corn, a mutation from starchy flour types, has a rich corn taste and is pleasantly sweet when freshly picked at just the right stage (see chapter 5). White kernels tend to be sweeter, yellows are higher in vitamin A, and bicolors combine the advantages of both. Some of the best sweet corn cultivars include Silver Queen, Golden Cross Bantam, Honey and Cream, and the open-pollinated ancient Mexican variety, Black Aztec, which you can eat like corn on the cob at the milk stage, or let it mature to use as cornmeal.

Sugar-enhanced may be the best of the new sweeter corn types. These have tender kernels with some corn flavor, plus sugar levels that last four days in the refrigerator. Like regular sweet corn, these start growing in a cool soil and fruit true, despite nearby patches of other types of corn. Some cultivars include early yellow Sugar Buns, midseason Kandy Korn, bicolor Kiss 'n' Tell, and white Summer Pearl.

Supersweets abound in sugar, perhaps to the detriment of the corn flavor. They stay sweet as long as fourteen days in the refrigerator and are good canned or frozen with no added sugar. The seed does not germinate easily, since there is so little starch in the kernel to nurture the young seedling. Seed rot is also a problem, especially in cool soils. Wait until the garden soil is at least 70°F to plant. Separate supersweets from other types of corn by 25 feet or plant them ten days apart so they don't cross-pollinate and adulterate the supersweet kernels. If you are willing to pamper them, try yellow Illini Xtra-Sweet, the original supersweet; white How Sweet It Is; or bicolor Honey 'n' Pearl.

Homegrown popcorn can be fun to grow, although it is hard to cure to good popping quality. Harvest when the kernels are dry on the outside with a little moisture trapped inside. When heated, the moisture expands to make the corn pop. When the kernels appear to be dry enough, try popping a few. They should pop quickly and be fluffy. If mushy, the kernels are too wet and need more drying. If too dry, nothing will happen. Mist the kernels lightly with a hand sprayer; let the moisture soak in, and try again. Once the kernels are just right, strip them off the cob and store in an airtight container.

If you can't perfect kernels that are good for popping, grind the kernels for cornmeal or keep the colorful ears as decorations. The pretty miniature Strawberry ornamental popcorn looks so good that it's almost a shame to eat it.

CUCUMBERS

A bounty of succulent cucumbers is enough to fill pickle jars and salad bowls, as well as expand into unusual soups, sauces, and stuffers. Choose long-vined cultivars for maximum productivity or plant compact plants for smaller gardens.

Grow burpless, or bitter-free, types, like Sweet Slice Hybrid, Sweet Success Hybrid, Euro-American Hybrid, Marketmore 80, and County Fair 87. Or, try new super-productive all-female plants, like Pickalot Hybrid, Pioneer, and Burpee Hybrid II. Because they lack the unproductive male flowers, they pack more fruit on each vine. Keep harvesting to keep the vine producing. Pollen has to come from somewhere, of course, so seed packets include a few seeds of a standard variety.

Some cultivars are also *parthenocarpic,* meaning that they produce fruits without fertilization. These cultivars set few seeds and thus have more energy to produce additional fruit. These include Sweet Success and County Fair 87. You can also find an unusual heirloom called Lemon, which is sweet and prickly and is harvested when lemon size.

Many newer cultivars have resistance to diseases. Look for these where summers are humid or disease is a problem. Unfortunately, no cultivars are resistant to a wilt disease carried by cucumber beetles. Eliminate the beetles to prevent the wilt.

Plant and care for cucumbers as you would for squash and other members of the Cucumber Family. (See Squash, pages 275–276.)

EGGPLANTS

I enjoy growing and using handsome, versatile eggplants, which make low-calorie fillers for casseroles or a breaded alternative to pasta. Tiny eggplants make a super pickle.

The large purple-skinned globelike fruit is most often sold in markets. Some of the best of these cultivars include Early Bird Hybrid for short-season areas or the standard Black Beauty. These eggplants are large and meaty, producing few but bulky fruit. Early-season oriental types, like Pingtung Long and Ichiban Hybrid, are smaller but more prolific. In addition, heirloom enthusiasts can find green, yellow, pink, striped, red, white, and lavender fruits of all different sizes. Dourga and Casper are readily available white-skinned types. See the *Garden Seed Inventory* (Seed Saver Publications) or heirloom seed catalogues to find other colors. In my garden, Casper is not as prolific as purple-skinned types, but it is still a delightful novelty.

Grow eggplant much the same as tomatoes. Eggplants differ in that they thrive in warmer temperatures and reasonably long frost-free seasons. Start seedlings indoors eight to ten weeks before the last frost date. For the best texture and flavor, pick the fruit young, before seeds mature and while the skin is glossy. Older cultivars may require soaking in salt water to remove bitterness, but this is seldom necessary for newer types.

Like tomato, eggplant is susceptible to wilt diseases. Unfortunately, no resistant eggplant cultivars have yet been developed. To escape wilt, rotate planting areas with unrelated crops that do not suffer from soilborne wilt disease. You can also grow eggplant in containers, if you water and fertilize often. Flea beetles and Colorado potato beetles can be a problem. Use floating row covers while the seedlings get established and insect deterrents whenever you see insect damage.

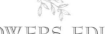

FLOWERS, EDIBLE

I have sampled many edible flowers and have decided that often people classify a flower as edible simply because it is not poisonous (rather like wild mushrooms). They don't necessarily mean the flower tastes good. Edible flowers can, however, add color to a dish, and a few are particularly delicious. Use them promptly after harvesting because the tender tissues are ephemeral. Most wilt and discolor if cooked. Two exceptions are daylilies and squash buds, which are often used in tempura.

These fragrant and flavorful culinary additives can perk up salads, casseroles, and vegetable dishes — in fact, just about anything. Grow them in a well-drained sunny bed, or scatter the more adaptable ones amid other ornamentals. Plant annual types in containers. Perennials may overwinter in pots where winters are mild; elsewhere, they need additional insulation.

The flowers of all culinary herbs are edible. When interplanted in a vegetable garden, herbs may help repel insect pests. (For more on harvesting and storing herbs, see chapters 5 and 6.)

Nasturtiums

These peppery-tasting flowers and their foliage are excellent as garnishes or toppings to salads, soups, and casseroles, or use them to flavor and color white wine vinegar. The pickled seeds taste like capers. Nasturtiums grow easily from seed. You can plant small seedlings, but larger plants seldom transplant well. If you want plenty of flowers, give them full sun in a soil that is only moderately fertile. Watch out for aphids; they love the plant.

Chive Blossoms

These round purple globes taste like onions. You can break the florets into pieces and scatter them on an already-cooked dish or serve the flower whole at the side of a dish. These flowers emerge on perennial chive plants every spring. Be sure to pick off all the blossoms or you will have a garden of self-sown chives. (For more on chives, see page 278.)

Shungiku

An annual chrysanthemum with small yellow flowers, shungiku has a mild, interesting, mumlike flavor. Grow the plant as a quick-cropping, cool-season annual. Harvest leaves while they are tender before flowering, and flowers when newly opened.

Calendula

Similar in flavor to shungiku, calendula is a fuller flower with a broader range of warm orange, gold, and yellow colors. This, too, is a cool-season annual, which can self-sow to return in later seasons. You can start it from seed or seedlings. Plant in full sun and well-drained soil of reasonable fertility.

Squash Blossoms

For a pretty, mild-flavored shell that is useful for an assortment of stuffings, pick squash blossoms just before they open. Use the swelling bud right away, before it wilts. If you especially like squash blossoms, plant Butterblossom, which produces only oversize male flowers and no female fruits.

Other edible flowers include beebalm, lavender, marigold, rose petals, sunflowers, pansies, and violets, basil, runner beans, broccoli, mustard, peas, fennel, and dill.

GARLIC

Grow garlic for its flavor, which is especially good ultra-fresh, or for its medicinal qualities. These plump, paper-skinned bulbs are full of vitamins, antibiotics, and perhaps even agents that lower blood pressure.

Choose from topset types, which put up a flower stalk in early summer, or soft necks, which have no flowers and bear minicloves where other types have a stalk. If you let topset stalks grow, the cloves will be smaller, but the stem will produce minibulblets. Plant these bulblets and you will get small but perfect bulbs next year. Most growers snap off the young stalks to serve as a delicacy.

Garlic seldom sets seed, so it is usually propagated with the cloves. The biggest cloves produce the biggest bulbs, but medium-size cloves give the largest increase in size, notes the Garlic Seed Foundation.

It is not easy to find good garlic cultivars. Garlic varieties vary in their hardiness and the day length that inspires bulbing. You need a long-day cultivar for the North and a short-day for the South. Furthermore, soil type, moisture levels and temperature and other factors alter bulb size, shape, and character. When you find a cultivar that you like, save some cloves to start your own climatically attuned garlic.

The Garlic Seed Foundation (listed in the Appendix) and the Cornell University Department of Vegetable Crops recommend the following varieties in their *Vegetable Crop Report #387*. In New York, topsets German Red and Valencia grow well. For the West Coast, try Silver Skin and Susanville. For a variety, try purple-skinned and Rocambole, a topset with a curved flower stalk. When left with no other choice, you can try healthy looking cultivars from the grocery. These are likely to be California Early or California Late, not ideal but perhaps passable for the East Coast.

Elephant garlic is listed in more seed catalogues than true garlic. It is actually a species of leek that produces four to six giant but mild cloves.

Plant garlic in the fall about six weeks before the first frost and harvest the following summer. You can also plant very early in spring, but you probably will harvest smaller bulbs. In either case, garlic needs about two months of cool (40°F) weather to break dormancy. Plant early enough to satisfy this requirement. Like onions, garlic grows best in moist, but not wet, well-drained fertile soil in full sun. Keep it separated from other onion species. Set the cloves 3 to 4 inches apart — further for extra-large ones — and twice as deep as the clove is high, and in rows 12 to 18 inches apart or staggered in a wide row. Fertilize several times during the nine-month growing season with fish emulsion or 5-10-10 fertilizer. Mulch over winter and keep weeds down. Remove the flowering stalk of topsets as soon as you see it. Provide plenty of water as the bulb develops, but cut back several weeks before harvest to harden the bulbs for storage.

Cure for one to two weeks in 60° to 70°F temperatures, 60 to 70 percent humidity, out of the sun, and in good ventilation. Peel off dirty outer layers and cut off roots. As soon as the bulbs are dry, you can braid the semidry stalks to create a string of garlic bulbs. For more information, see chapters 4, 5, and 7, and contact the Garlic Seed Foundation.

GREENS

For a quick-maturing crop packed with vitamins but low in calories grow one of the many greens. Because they are ultra-fresh and pesticide-free, even the standard types are a vast improvement over commercial greens. You may wish to try one of dozens of cultivars with different flavors, textures, and colors — don't limit yourself to standard iceberg lettuce.

Most greens thrive in cool (50° to 60°F) weather, but a few succeed in summer. Work them into your succession and interplanting schemes. All greens have a similar need for rich soils or frequent feeding with a nitrogen fertilizer to keep them growing fast and sweet. Generally, full sun in spring and fall and partial shade in summer is ideal, yet most greens can tolerate light shade better than fruit-bearing crops. To eliminate most pests, top the crop with floating row covers.

Amaranth

A good summer crop, this fast-growing weed relative is fine-tuned to produce abundant leaves. Other strains yield nutritious grain. Select from red, green, yellow, or striped leaf types, with some varieties taller than others. All leaves taste best harvested when young and tender.

Chicory, Endive, and Escarole

This group of plants produces edible loose heads of thick and sometimes bitter greens. Moderate the bitterness with blanching, early harvest, and exposure to cold.

Chicory. Chicories are deeper rooted than lettuces and more resistant to drought or weeds, but they take longer to mature — an average of eighty to ninety days to harvest size. Grow most cultivars for autumn harvest or stick with slow bolters for spring.

Endive. Curly-leaved endive includes commonly grown large and rugged Salad King or more delicate European Tres Fin Maraichere types.

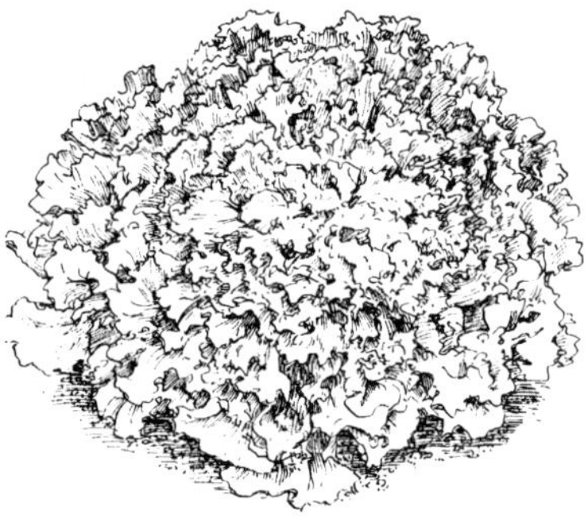

Endive, Belgian. Another of the chicory clan that can be fun to try is Belgian endive. Plant Witloof Improved or Large Brussels in late spring. Dig the roots in fall, remove all but 1 inch of the foliage, and store the sturdiest 1- to 2-inch-wide roots in a box of moist soil. If you can find Witloof Zoom or pink Witloof Robin, you can force them without soil. Hold in cold storage, and then move the box to a dark 60°F location. Water often and in several weeks look for the mild white heads to appear.

Escarole. Larger leaves and a more upright growth are characteristics of escarole. The standard, Florida Deep Heart, is susceptible to basal rot, especially in warm weather. Where rot is a problem, grow Full Heart Batavian. Self-blanching Nuvol is an alternative for spring planting.

Radicchio. A miniature cabbagelike vegetable with a ruby and white head, radicchio is a biennial that grows long rough leaves most of the season. These may hide the small head or the head may sprout after you cut the foliage back in summer or fall. Sow Italian heirloom cultivars like Red Verona in spring and cut the leaves back around Labor Day for sprouts in fall. Where winters are mild, plant in fall and harvest the heads in spring. The newer cultivar Giulio may produce heads without cutting back the leaves. Pan di Zucchero yields a light green romaine-like head.

Corn salad

Cultivars like Fetticus Broad Leaved are commonly eaten in Europe. They grow easily in early spring and fall, producing delicate leaves with mild flavor. The foliage needs gentle but thorough washing to remove grit and spoils quickly once harvested.

Lettuce

Lettuce sets the standard for greens, yet a visit to the grocery lettuce counter barely hints at the diversity of lettuce varieties available to gardeners. Lettuce may be tall, short, rounded, or frilly, pink, red, or green, and it can have a solid head or open rosette. Nearly all types bolt to seed when they mature or the days grow long. Harvest promptly. Sow lettuce seed directly in the garden when the soil is dry enough to work. For an earlier crop, especially with longer-growing types, start the seed indoors in peat pots four weeks before planting out.

Head lettuce. Where the cool season extends a bit longer, you can grow larger heading types. For Boston or butterhead lettuces with loose heads of tender leaves, try early Cindy, warmth-tolerant Buttercrunch, or red-tipped Pirat. Less-common

Bibbs grows nicely from English heirloom Tom Thumb and ruby-tipped Four Seasons. Stiff, upright cos or romaine lettuce includes slow-bolting Parris Island Cos, red-leaved Rosalita, mildew-tolerant Valmaine Cos, and winter-keeping Winter Density.

Leaf lettuce. Quick-maturing leaf lettuces are easy to grow in nearly any climate with even a brief period of cool weather. Some of the best are lobed Oak Leaf, slow-bolting ruby Red Sails, frilly red Lollo Rosso, super-early Black-Seeded Simpson, and slow-bolting Salad Bowl.

Mesclun

This term refers to a mixture of greens that are clipped when young and blended for salads. Many of the above-mentioned plants are included in mesclun mixtures. Some seed companies have developed mixes of different flavors, colors, seasons, and nationalities. Grow them as an interplanted assortment, or give each green its own space and mix after harvesting. Cut the greens down and let them come up again with a smaller return, or harvest and replant with something else.

Mustard Family Greens

In addition to heading and root crops, the *Brassicas* sport a number of edible greens: mustards, collards and kale, turnip greens, roquette (arugula), cress and mizuma. These tend to be spicy flavored, especially if grown in heat or drought. Most are susceptible to cabbage loopers, flea beetles, and other typical *Brassica* pests.

Arugula. With a taste like a pleasant combination of garlic and mustard, arugula (roquette) is a quick-growing salad spicer for cool weather. Harvest young while the leaves are still tender and relatively mild.

Collards and kale. Highly nutritious and also quite hardy, both collards and kale have rather leathery leaves that are best cooked. Dwarf Blue Curled Vates kale, preferred in the North, is frillier. Variegated and colorful ornamental types are edible but not as tasty. Collards like Georgia, a southern favorite, have oblong, rounded leaves.

Cress. Both curly and broadleaf cresses (also sold as Peppergrass) are very quick growing and quite hardy. Harvest when they sprout, or let them reach a couple of inches in height. In mild areas, watercress can be a perennial grown in fresh-flowing water.

Mizuma. A quick-maturing annual with lightly spicy, feathery leaves, mizuma is also best harvested young. I like it on cream-cheese-and-chive sandwiches.

Mustard greens. Well-liked in the Orient, mustard greens should grow quickly to stay mild. Try handsome Red Giant; mild, drought-resistant Tendergreens; or long-holding Savanna Hybrid.

Turnip greens. Pluck turnip greens off swelling bulbs, or grow cultivars like All Top Hybrid, which is bred for its large, smooth greenery. Small, tender greens are choicest.

New Zealand Spinach

This tangy-leaved climbing vine looks great twining up a pole tepee or over a fence. The fleshy, furry leaves are good, though they take some getting used to. Because the plant takes a couple of months to begin vigorous growth, it's best to start it indoors early in cold climates. Harvest the young tips or individual leaves throughout the summer until frost.

Purslane

Both the succulent creeping weed and a cultivated, more upright alternative have edible stems and leaves that are juicy and mildly tart and grow well in summer.

Sorrel

This relative of rhubarb has a lemony flavor that makes great sauces or additions to chicken, fish, cream soup, and salads. In minutes, the leaf cooks down to nothing but a bit of green paste and lots of flavor. It is a perennial that can be harvested all season long, though the leaves are a bit tougher in the summer.

Spinach

This familiar nutritious green is more succulent and sweet when harvested at home and eaten garden-fresh. Choose from cultivars with varying degrees of savoying, or crinkling, on the leaves. The standard spinach cultivar is the disease-tolerant, semi-savoyed Melody, which bolts quickly with maturity and lengthening days. Cultivars like the savoyed Tyee bolt more slowly, but some have thicker leaves with a slightly stronger flavor. Smooth-leaved Nordic is more tender than most slow-bolting cultivars. Olympia's plain leaf is easy to clean.

Spinach is shallow rooted and heavy feeding. Water and fertilize often. Grow far from Cucumber Family members because the two crops share viral diseases. Spinach is also susceptible to a variety of fungal diseases, although newer cultivars such as Tyee and Vienna have multiple disease resistance. Rotate to avoid relatives like beets and Swiss chard.

Swiss Chard

This bulbless cousin to the beet is a green for all seasons. It grows in both heat and cold (above freezing), staying sweet and mild regardless. Harvest young for salads or large for steaming. Boil thick stalks like asparagus. I like red-stemmed Vulcan or Rhubarb best. You can also find Fordhook Giant, which can reach 4 feet tall. For similar flavor in a smaller leaf, try a perpetual spinach (which is actually a leafy beet), such as MacGregor's Favorite.

HERBS

For information on the culture, cultivars, and uses of herbs, see the chart on pages 278–281.

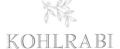

KOHLRABI

This is another of the *Brassicas,* but rather a unique one. Grow it for the swollen stem, which is crunchy and sweet — milder than turnips. Kohlrabi grows well in rich soils, full sun, and cool weather. If stressed be-

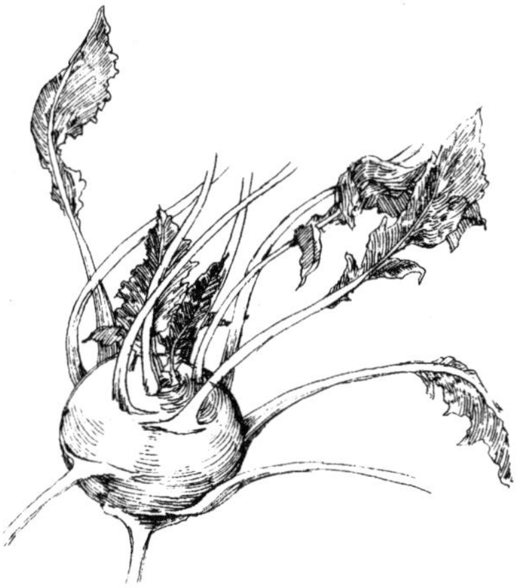

cause it lacks any of these, the bulb can be strong tasting or tough. Kohlrabi may bolt after producing a long narrow bulb, but in my experience this is rare. For best results, harvest kohlrabi small and pare off the fibrous skin layer. Look for some of the newer hybrids, like Grand Duke, that produce tasty globes nearly every time.

MELONS

These members of the Cucumber Family require much the same care as other *Cucurbita*. See the Squash entry {pages 275–276) for more detail. In short-season northern areas or humid southern climates, melons can be frustrating to grow, because they are plagued by many diseases and pests. You may also have a hard time telling when they are ripe. If you can get past these problems, you can grow a better-tasting melon than you can buy.

There are several types of melons, such as, muskmelon, true cantaloupe, and watermelon. Muskmelons are the brown-netted melons we often call cantaloupes. True cantaloupes are actually a group of European melons that includes honeydews and French Charentais. They can be harder to grow than muskmelons and require different criteria to tell when they are ripe (see chapter 5). If you are game, try extra-sweet green-fleshed Passport or an early cultivar for short-season climates.

Among the muskmelons, choose from cultivars developed specifically for the East or West Coast, early or late harvest, and disease resistance. For the West, stick to heat- and sun-tolerant Top Mark, Starship, or Ambrosia. For the East, try Burpee's Hybrid, short-season Earlisweet, or cool-tolerant Earligold. Saticoy Hybrid has a broad disease resistance. Sweet Bush and Musketeer are more compact.

Watermelons take a long growing season to reach full size. Where seasons are shorter, grow miniature melons, such as Sugar Baby and Mickylee. You also can find seedless melons, like early Jack of Hearts Hybrid, but they are a special challenge to germinate. If you keep the seeds warm and uniformly moist, they may emerge in a peat pot indoors. Move the seedlings outside with at least one vine of a pollinator that will be included in the package.

If you like watermelon, you can find all different sizes, colors, and disease resistances in the Willhite Seed Company catalogue (see Appendix for ordering information).

OKRA

This warmth lover from the South produces tasty pods with mucilage inside, a traditional thickening in gumbo recipes. Those unaccustomed

to okra's texture may find this vegetable an acquired taste. Okra makes a handsome, tall, productive plant for areas with long growing seasons and abundant space. Try Clemson Spineless, Annie Oakley, Burgundy, and dwarf cultivars such as Dwarf Green Long Pod and Lee. Harvest young for a more tender pod.

ONIONS

There are many pungent *Alliums* available for gardens. All of them thrive in cool weather, need light but fertile soil, and often share pests and diseases. Rotate with other unrelated crops.

Bulbing onions. When you select bulbing onions, remember that they fall into one of two classes — long-day types that bulb in midsummer in the North and short-day types that bulb in early spring, fall, or winter in the South. Northern types are often more pungent and store well. Southern cultivars tend to be sweeter, with a short storage life. Beyond these important distinctions, select cultivars for their color, bulb shape, and other special characteristics.

Some good onions for the North include Sweet Sandwich, which gets sweeter with storage; extra-early but short-storing Norstar; yellow-skinned Ebenezer; red Carmen; and hardy, long-storing Copra. Southern onions include Walla Walla, Sweet Spanish, Red Burgundy, and Granex 33.

For an early start, grow seedlings, divisions, or sets. Contrary to what you may think, a large set will not produce a bigger bulb — it probably will bolt to seed or split into two. For a large bulb, growing time is the most important factor. Plant early in the cool season, but not so early that the young plant will be subjected to temperatures below 40°F, which may cause bolting.

Pickling onions. If you grow small pearl or pickling onions, you will find they become larger in the South and progressively smaller the further north you live. Try early Spanish onions, super-early Snow Baby, or red-skinned Purplette.

Scallions. Harvest green, bulbless scallions from larger onion sets, or sow onion seed thickly to harvest before bulbing. You can also try scallion cultivars like the standard Evergreen White Bunching, Japanese Bunching, pungent Welsh Onion, or White Lisbon. Chives are discussed in the Herb entry.

Leeks. Try leeks for mild onion flavor. Plant leek seedlings in spring to harvest in late summer or fall. In the South, you can plant in fall to harvest in spring or summer. Set the seedlings in a small trench, so you can hill soil around the plant base to blanch the lower stem. Wrap the stem with paper or surround it with a toilet-paper tube before blanching to keep the grit out of the stem. The later-maturing cultivars, such as American Flag, store better and may even last in a mulched bed over winter, after which they will flower. When you cut the flower stalk off, bulbs form at the base. Early-maturing cultivars, like King Richard, are tender without blanching, but they are also more vulnerable to spoilers and not especially hardy.

Eleanour Sinclair Rhode felt the need to defend leeks: "Unduly despised by the lofty folk, the leek is nevertheless a most delicately flavoured vegetable, and if it were possible to grow it free of grit it would probably be universally popular." Nowadays, the leek is considered a gourmet crop.

Eleanour Sinclair Rhode, 1938

Other onions worth trying include small-bulbed but perennial multiplier onions, topsets, potato onions, and shallots, all suitable for both Northern and Southern gardens.

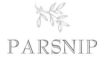

PARSNIP

The parsnip is one of the crops of antiquity that is much neglected today. The uniquely sweet roots take most of the growing season to mature. Sow in spring to harvest in fall or, where winters are mild, in the fall for spring harvest. Plant in very deep, well-drained soil that has not been manured recently. Give the seeds plenty of time to germinate; they can be somewhat irregular. Harvest spring-sown crops as needed through the fall. Mulch to overwinter in the garden. If you store parsnips in a root cellar, keep away from ethylene-producing fruit, as the gas makes this root vegetable bitter. Long, slim, smooth Harris Model is one of the better cultivars.

PEAS

If you have never plucked a newly swollen pea out of a succulent pod right in the garden, you don't know how good peas may be. And if you have not browsed through seed catalogues lately, you cannot know just how many different and delicious types are available to gardeners. The old-fashioned shelling peas are now available in different forms. Daybreak is super-early, Maestro is disease resistant, and Knight is quick cropping and compact. Both of the latter are resistant to most pea diseases. You can grow tiny-podded Petite Pois or, for larger yields, longer-season Green Arrow, which is resistant to several diseases. Some produce two sets of pods at nodes where older types had only one, and they can yield a third more. Novella, a leafless type, is said to be self-supporting, but they have never put on a good show in my garden.

Beyond shelling types, you can grow sugar snap peas with edible pods and fat sweet seeds. They may take slightly longer to mature, but they present much more to eat (although they usually need stringing). In my opinion, Sugar Snap, which was the first of these cultivars, still remains the best; it is prolific but long vined and without disease resistance. Running close behind is the more compact Super Sugar Mel and stringless, disease-resistant Sugar Daddy.

You also can grow edible-podded snow peas like the disease-resistant Oregon Sugar Pod II. Harvest these pods younger than sugar snaps, before the seeds inside swell.

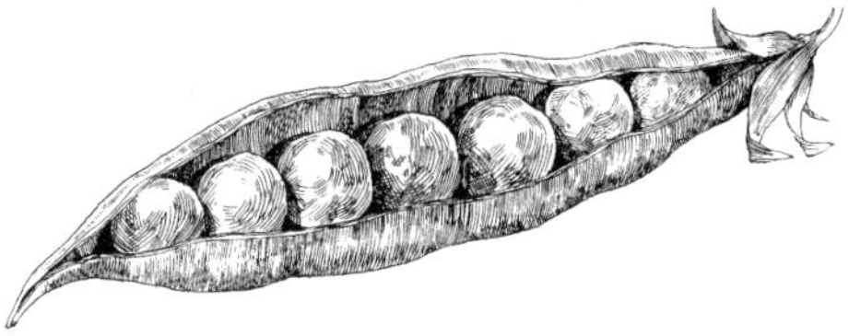

Try growing starchy field peas or smooth-seeded types for drying and using in pea soup. One cultivar is Alaska, which is more cold-tolerant than most sweet peas. See southern, farm, or heirloom catalogues for the best cultivar selection.

Peas are cool-season crops that stop fruiting when the temperature rises much above 80°F. If heat is inescapable, try the cultivar Wando, which is more heat tolerant than most others. Plant all peas in spring once the soil warms above 40°F or preferably 50°F. If it is too cold and wet, the pea seeds will rot. You may be able to slip in several early succession plantings and another one or two in the fall. In the Northwest, plant early or plant disease-resistant cultivars to escape the enation mosaic virus. All peas perform better if planted with nitrogen-fixing bacteria and supported with a trellis or some other upright structure.

PEPPERS

For some special flavoring with lots of vitamins, grow spicy or savory peppers. Both sweet and hot peppers require similar growing conditions. They differ in the length of their growing season, as well as the shape and hotness of the fruit. Start both types indoors under lights six to ten weeks before the last frost date. Transplant into a light, well-drained soil that is fertile but not too rich. Most peppers tolerate close planting, because they can mature elbow to elbow, as long as water and nutrient requirements are met. Peppers set fruit best when days are 65° to 80°F and nights are down to 55°F. Above and below this range new fruit production will be slow. Peppers are susceptible to viruses, wilts, fungal diseases, and certain caterpillars. These problems are seldom serious, however, especially if you rotate with unrelated crops to minimize pest or disease build-up.

Sweet peppers are tangy when harvested green. They turn fruity-sweet once they mature to red, yellow, purple, or orange. The traditional sweet pepper has a broad bell shape, but today you will find a greater diversity of forms, including wedgelike Gypsy; long, thin Sweet Banana Whopper Hybrid; and tiny upright Sweet Pickle.

Hot peppers, most of which are variations of the chili pepper, can be challenging to grow. Most require a long, warm, growing season, typical of the Southwest. A few cultivars are now available for the North, however, including Super Chili Hybrid, Mexibell Hybrid, and Early Jalapeño.

How hot the peppers get varies greatly depending on both genetics and climate. In general, the smaller fruits, like cayenne and bird peppers, are the hottest ones. Whether they reach full potency, however, depends on growing conditions. They get hotter as they mature and if they are exposed to hot weather or drought. The chemical responsible for the heat accumulates in the white interior ribs and can rub off on the seeds. Remove both ribs and seeds to moderate heat. When you prepare hot peppers, use gloves; the hot chemical can burn your hands or, if you rub your eyes after touching hot peppers, it can burn your eyes. Even pepper fumes from ground dried fruit or cooked fresh ones may bother some people. For a milder hot pepper, look for Tam Mild Jalapeño, Poblano, MexiBell, and Numex Big Jim.

Dry chilis, serranos, cayennes, and anchos, and pickle jalapeños, pepperoncini, and Hungarian Wax. To freeze chilis and other thick-walled peppers, roast them until the skin chars and separates, and then let them sweat in a paper bag. Remove skin and freeze.

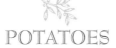

POTATOES

Once considered a survival staple, potatoes are being elevated to a gourmet food, as heirlooms and other unusual cultivars emerge. You can choose from red, yellow, purple, and blue skins, with white, yellow, or purple flesh of varying textures and flavors. Interesting cultivars to look for include petite Lady Finger; early purple-skinned Caribe; and blight-resistant Yukon Gold and lav-

ender Peruvian Blue. You will find these and many others in specialty potato or heirloom vegetable catalogues (see Appendix for details).

You probably will propagate your crop from a seed potato that is a certified disease-free tuber. To be double-safe about planting clean stock, you can pay considerably more for tissue-cultured minipotatoes. Explorer is the potato available from a seed packet, and it performs irregularly, producing small yields of little potatoes. It is best to stick to vegetatively propagated tubers.

Plant the potato whole to grow more medium-size tubers. For fewer but larger tubers, cut seed potatoes into sections, each with a couple of eyes or sprouts. Grow in rich but not recently manured soil. The soil should be deep and well drained or mounded into a raised bed. Hill the soil up repeatedly over the section of tuber you planted, because this is where the new tubers will develop. Some gardeners plant on top of the soil and cover the tubers with a thick layer of straw. In either case, keep the soil acidic to eliminate scab, and watch for Colorado potato beetle, flea beetle, aphids, and leaf rollers. Rotate with crops from unrelated families. Plant in spring about a week before frost or in successions through early summer (although potatoes may not tuber well in heat). For harvesting information, see potato entries in chapters 6 through 8.

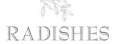

PUMPKINS

This group of large squash relatives can be fun to watch swell, to carve into jack-o'-lanterns, and to bake into pie or muffins — a big order for a single crop. Grow them as detailed under the Squash entry (pages 275–276). A few cultivars, such as Big Moon and Ghostrider, can grow into mammoths, if you give them rich soil and plenty of water and pinch off all other pumpkins on the same vine. I'd rather have a smaller, sweeter cultivar that is good for baking and decoration. A couple of really good ones are Spookie, Autumn Gold, and Small Sugar. For a tiny pumpkin on long vines, try 3-inch-wide Jack Be Little. In small gardens, look for cultivars with compact vines, such as Spirit or Bushkin. Pumpkins generally do not keep as well as most winter squash. Cook and freeze the flesh of extras.

RADISHES

These can be the fastest-maturing crops in the garden; they are thus good for interplanting and succession sowing. If you grow them in cool weather and light soil of reasonable fertility, you can harvest within three or four weeks. Grown in heavy or very sandy soil or in heat or drought, however, the root may stay skinny, woody, or highly pun-

gent. If the soil is too wet, the globe is likely to crack. Root maggots can be a problem in many areas; escape them by covering radish beds with floating row covers. Some of the best of the small-globe radishes include multicolored Easter Egg, early Cherry Belle, larger Crimson Giant, and long-tapered French Breakfast and White Icicle. Some people grow radishes specifically for their seed pods, harvested once seeds have swollen but before they bulge in the pod.

Where you have a long, cool growing season, you may be able to grow the larger-rooted Daikon or winter radish. Some are long and carrotlike, white, pink, or black skinned; others are shorter, round, and green. All require a deeper, well-drained soil and are exposed to more pests because they take longer to mature. Among the Daikons, Mino Springs Cross and Spring Leader are bolt resistant; for fall, try stump-rooted Miyashige.

The pungent black Russian or Spanish radishes are older types similar to turnips. They overwinter in milder winters and are used similarly to horseradish.

RHUBARB

If you like tangy sweet rhubarb pie or jam, even simple stewed rhubarb, you should grow your own at home. The stalks taste best ultra-fresh. In addition, the plant is bold and handsome, a nice addition to a perennial garden or mixed border. Rhubarb grows best in full sun and well-drained, rich soil. Fertilize in spring with rotted manure or a complete granular fertilizer with a ratio like 10-10-10. Water regularly if the weather becomes dry. To be perennial, rhubarb needs a cold dormant period — although in the far South, you can grow it as an annual. In the North, wait until the second year after planting to harvest lightly. During the following years you can cut stalks from the time the foliage expands through midsummer when new stems begin to emerge thinner. Don't take more than about one-third of the stems. Eat only the stalk; the leaves are poisonous.

Most cultivars have similar flavor. What differs is their color, disease resistance, and climatic tolerances. For a bright red stalk that stays red with cooking, try Valentine or Chipman's Canada Red. Green Victoria has green stalks that cook to brown; its main virtue is that it can be forced indoors in the winter to sprout into tender, light pink shoots. To force, let the plant fall dormant and rest outdoors for several weeks. Then, bring indoors to a dark place with 50° to 60°F temperatures. Plant in a box of moist sand and harvest the sprouts that emerge.

ROOTS

An abundance of unusual roots may appeal to your appetite. Most need deep, well-drained, moderately fertile soil. See also separate entries for Beets, Carrots, Parsnips, and Radishes.

Celeriac

Celeriac swells into a sweet, celery-flavored bulb. After spring weather has moderated, direct-sow the seed heavily; germination percentages are low and the seeds that do sprout develop slowly. Let the plant grow

all summer, fertilizing frequently and irrigating during dry weather. Harvest in the fall after a light frost. Store in a root cellar away from ethylene producers; exposure to the gas creates a bitter chemical in celeriac.

Salsify

Known as the creamy-rooted oyster plant, salsify needs a long, relatively cool growing season; it takes up to four months to mature. Direct-sow in a deep, moderately fertile soil; too much nitrogen will make the roots split. You can leave salsify in the ground through a couple of light frosts, and then store in a root cellar. The flavor that many writers describe as "oyster" dissipates quickly after harvest.

Turnips and Rutabagas

Two fleshy-rooted *Brassicas,* turnips and rutabagas grow well under conditions similar to those of their leafy cousins. Because they are grown for their roots rather than for their leaves or fruits, however, they need less nitrogen and more potassium and phosphorus for good growth. A 5-10-10 fertilizer is suitable. Direct-sow turnips about a month before the last spring frost or two months before the first frost in fall. Plant rutabagas in mid June to harvest in fall. For a mild tender root, both need to grow in moist soils. Rutabagas can take a bit of heat, but turnips will taste hot if exposed to tempera-

tures over 80°F. Harvest turnips when roots are a couple of inches across. Rutabagas can get to 4 or 5 inches in diameter and still remain mild. Both grow on top of the ground and are not particularly winter hardy, unless the weather is mild and the roots are heavily mulched. They are, however, sweeter if exposed to several light frosts.

Among rutabagas, Altasweet is especially sweet; Laurentian is also popular. For turnips, the purple-topped types, like Purple Top White Globe, are less appealing to root maggots than mild white Japanese hybrids, like Tokyo Cross. All Top produces a healthy rosette of greens.

For more harvest and storage information, see chapters 5 and 6 and the *Brassicas* entry.

SQUASH

There are a multitude of different squash types, most of which are quite easy to cultivate. Grow summer squashes for their soft, moist, mild, and prolific immature fruit. Try easy-to-harvest Gold Rush Zucchini, beautiful Sunburst Hybrid, prolific Scallop Peter Pan Hybrid, and versatile Kuta Hybrid and Gourmet Globe Hybrid.

Let winter squash mature fully to a hard outer shell and enjoy the sweet rich flesh within. Try big-fruited Waltham Butternut, Buttercup, Turban, Sweet Mama Hybrid, or smaller Sweet Dumpling. Acorn is tasty but doesn't keep long. White-skinned Cream of the Crop is not particularly sweet. Spaghetti squash is actually a summer squash, but should be allowed to mature to develop mild, noodle-like flesh. It will keep three months or more in my basement.

The members of the Cucumber Family share many problems. They all can be attacked by cucumber beetles, which may carry a wilt disease. Squash vine borer tunnels into stems just above ground level and causes wilting or death. Protect young plants with floating row covers and plants in flower with insect predators and insecticidal soaps. To limit damage from mildews, rots, and other fungal diseases, look for cultivars with resistance to fungus, rotate crops, and give plants plenty of air circulation and sun.

You can train squash, melon, and cucumber vines to a trellis if you begin when the vines are young and flexible. Work them through the supporting grid or strings. Support larger-size fruit with slings made of nylon stocking.

If your growing season is fairly long, you can sow the seed directly when frost is past and the soil is warm. For better germination and an earlier start, plant the seed in peat pots indoors two or three weeks early. *Cucurbitas* need rich warm soil and plenty of water and fertilizer to support their vigorous growth. A mulch of black plastic can help.

Most squashes bear separate male and female flowers, both of which are necessary for fruit development. A bee or similar pollinator must carry the pollen from one to the other. Male flowers tend to outnumber females when a vine is small or fruits are already developing. Harvest often to encourage more female flowers and thus more fruit. For more information, see chapters 6–8.

SWEET POTATOES

This vine is somewhat of a mystery, as it is not an Irish potato nor is it the super-moist tropical yam. Sweet potatoes like Nuggett can have sweet and dry flesh. Others, like the popular Centennial and early Georgia Jet, are moister and do not store as well. Porto Rico is compact for smaller gardens.

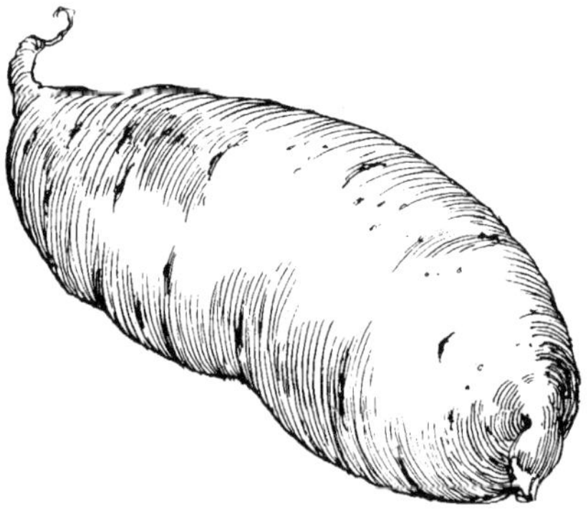

Start sweet potatoes from slips or stem cuttings. Plant after the last frost passes in spring in deep, well-drained soil with good fertility. A black plastic mulch will help warm the soil, prevent weeds, and stop vines from rooting as they spread. Do not give them too much nitrogen, or they will produce all vine and little root. Sink the slips so only the top couple of sets of leaves emerge. If autumn is wet, dig the roots before the soil is saturated and they begin to rot. Elsewhere, dig before the last frost or once the vines begin to die back. Cure for several days in 80° to 85°F darkness then store at about 55° to 65°F in moderately moist humidity.

TOMATOES

No other crop is as widely grown in home gardens, and for good reason. Allowed to ripen on the vine, tomatoes are sweet, flavor-rich, and very versatile in the kitchen. You have a lot of tomato types to choose from.

Determinate tomatoes stay smaller and produce their fruit in one quick burst. *Indeterminate tomatoes* continue growing and producing fruit on their new growth. They crop longer and yield greater amounts, but they take up more space and

need staking or caging. Choose from cultivars that bear early, midseason, and late; plant some of each for a succession of fruits. The early ones, like Early Girl Hybrid and Oregon Spring, tend to produce small tomatoes, but are so welcome because they are the first of the season. Midseason types include Better Boy Hybrid, Floramerica, and Lemon Boy. The larger and meatier Beefsteak types come late. If you live in the South, check with your local Cooperative Extension Service to see what will grow well. Your selection may be more limited.

For smaller gardens, you can get new indeterminate dwarfs, which are more productive than dwarf determinates. Some cultivars to seek out include Husky, Heartland, and Better Bush. If you want to can or dry tomatoes, grow Italian or paste tomatoes like Roma and La Rossa, which have more meat and less moisture; these tend to have less flavor than the others. Cherry tomatoes, small and juicy-fruited, with their long rangy vines and abundance of fruit, are most similar to wild tomatoes. Choose from red-, orange-, yellow-, and pink-skinned and -fleshed types. I like Sweet 100 and Sun Cherry. For even more variety, seek out some of the heirlooms.

Because disease can be a problem, look for resistance to verticillium and fusarium wilts, indicated as *V* and *F* on the package. *T* indicates resistance to tobacco mosaic virus. Nematode resistance is indicated by *N*. Celebrity is resistant to all of the previous.

Give tomatoes a moderately fertile soil. Too much nitrogen will result in rambunctious growth and few fruits. The fruit will be sweeter in warmer weather and more intense-flavored with only moderate moisture. To avoid blossom end rot, maintain an even moisture level; a mulch helps. Above about 95°F, flowers will drop rather than develop. You can get by this in the South with the cultivar Heatwave. For cooler climates, try Oregon Spring. For more on caging, harvesting, and processing, see chapters 3, 6, 7 and 8.

SOME FAVORITE HERBS

Herb	Life Cycle	Part Used	Uses	Culture	Types
Basil	A	Leaves	With tomatoes, meats, vinegars, and vegetables	Full sun to light shade; moderately fertile; keep seed heads pinched off	Sweet (classic); Bush (mound-forming); Dark Opal (purple-leaved); Purple Ruffles (purple-leaved) Lemon; Licorice, Cinnamon, and Holy (grown for scent rather than culinary uses)
Celery	B	Leaves, stalks, seed	With fish; in stews and casseroles as salt substitute; in potato salad	Direct-sow or transplant very young seedlings; fertile soil; full sun/light shade; lots of moisture and fertilizer	Utah 52-70 R Improved (disease-resistant)
Chives	P	Leaves	With sour cream, vegetables, salads, casseroles	Moderately fertile, moist soil; full sun or light shade; spreads by fleshy root clumps or self-sown seeds; clip spent flowers	*Allium schoenoprasum* (purple-flowered); *Allium tuberosum* (Oriental or garlic)
Cilantro	A	Leaves	Like parsley; salsa	Full sun; moderately fertile soil	Santo (slow-bolting)
Dill	A	Leaves and flowers; mature seeds	With fish, cream cheese, cucumbers, salads	Full sun; modertely fertile soil; succession plantings	Bouquet (slow-growing); Dukat (slow-bolting): Dwarf Fernleaf (sturdy-stemmed)

Herb	Life Cycle	Part Used	Uses	Culture	Types
Horse-radish	P	Root	Grate or slice fine with salt and vinegar for sauce with meat, cheese, seafood, sushi; seal airtight	Start cuttings in spring; well-drained, moderately fertile, moist soil; needs cold winter dormancy; harvest in October and November; spreads aggressively	
Lovage	*P	Leaves	With fish; in stews and casseroles as salt substitutes; in potato salad	Direct-sow or transplant very young seedlings; offsets; moderately fertile soil; full sun or light shade Plenty of moisture; cold period	
		Stalks	Straws for tomato juice	For winter dormancy; grows to 6 feet	
		Seeds	As substitute for celery seed		
Mint/ Lemon balm	P	Leaves	In teas and fruit salads; with fish and chicken	Moderately fertile soil; full sun to partial shade; spreads vigorously by runners — plant in slightly raised contrainers to limit invasiveness; deadhead to avoid self-sowing	Lemon; Candy; Apple; Curly; Orange; Ginger Silver; Peppermint Spearmint
Oregano	P	Leaves	Italian dishes; with tomatoes, cheese, and meat	Lightly fertile soil; full sun; can spread aggressively	Greek (other cultivars are weedy and less flavorful)
Parsley	B	Leaves	Garnish, in salads, stews, and casse-roles; with baked or boiled potatoes	Full sun; fertile soil	Curly-leaved; Flat-leaved Italian (intense flavor); Hamburg (edible roots); Parsnip-rooted (edible roots)

Herb	Life Cycle	Part Used	Uses	Culture	Types
Rosemary	TP	Leaves	With lamb; in vinegars and stews	Lightly fertile soil; full sun; in North, bring indoors for winter and place in bright, cool location; keep evenly moist	Arp (extra tall) Forresteri (creeping)
Sage	P	Leaves	With pork; in stuffings (use with restraint)	Lightly fertile soil; full sun; cut back older stems to encourage new growth at base	Silver Variegated and purple species (less hardy and not as flavorful); Dwarf (18 inches); Tricolor (ornamental, variegated); Aurea (golden); Purpurea (purple-leaved)
Savory, summer	A	Leaves	With beans and other vegetables; in casseroles	Full sun; lightly fertile soil; start indoors early or direct sow	
Savory, winter	P	Leaves	Same as summer savory	Full sun; lightly fertile soil	
Sweet marjoram	TP	Leaves	In chicken dishes and stews; with eggs	Lightly fertile soil; full sun; direct sow or start indoors	
Tarragon	P	Leaves	With fish, poultry; in vinegar	Full sun (or light shade in South); moderately moist, fertile soil; divide every 3 years; in North, mulch over winter; grow from cuttings or division	French (licorice-flavored); Russian (poor flavor)

Herb	Life Cycle	Part Used	Uses	Culture	Types
Thyme	P	Leaves	With meats and vegetables; stews and vinegars	Full sun; adequately fertile soil; start from cuttings or division; may spread and need cutting back; remove seed heads to strengthen foliage	French (choice); English (vigorous); Lemon (less hardy); Silver; Woolly (creeping, gray leaved); Mother-of-thyme (low ground cover)

Key:

A=Annual
B=Biennial
P=Perennial
TP= Tender perennial
*Moderately hardy

appendix I

North American Hardiness Zones

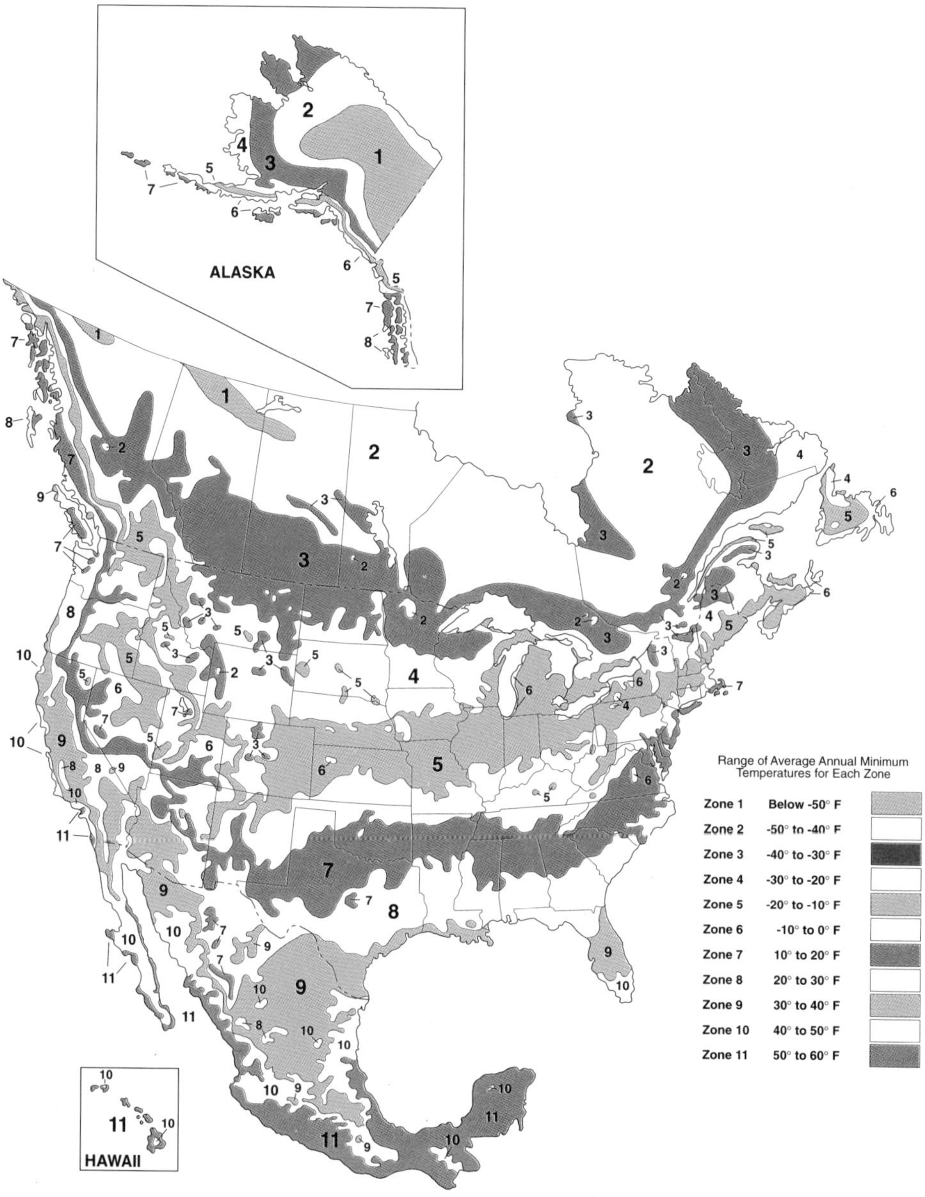

appendix II

Contributors

Doc and Katy Abraham. New York-based gardeners; hosts of "The Green Thumb" on WHAM TV, Naples, NY; and authors of many gardening books.

Millie Adams. A nutritionist from Ohio, Millie enjoys experimenting with produce from her garden and with new recipes.

Suzanne Ashworth. California-based curator of eggplants and other crops for the Seed Savers Exchange, author of a book on saving seeds, and a teacher.

Helen Atthowe. Organic farming consultant in New Jersey. She has recently relocated to the West Coast.

Elizabeth Berry. Organic market gardener and rancher in the canyons of New Mexico. She's recently begun selling heirloom bean seeds that are good for cooking or growing. (For more information, send a self-addressed, stamped envelope to 144 Camino Escondido, Sante Fe, NM 87501.)

Jan Blüm. Owner of Blüm's Seeds, a mail-order heirloom seed company in Idaho.

Bill Bricker, Sr. Owner of Bricker's Organic Farm, Georgia-based gardener, and writer and radio show host.

John Bryan. Horticultural consultant, garden book author, video and broadcaster from Sausalito, California.

Emma Byler. Amish gardener and author of *Recipes and Remedies for Plain and Happy Living* (Goosefoot Acres Press).

Sharon Carson. Organic subscription gardener from Delaware with ¾-acre market garden.

Tim Closs. Researcher for the National Pesticide Telecommunications Network at Texas Tech University Health Sciences Center.

Eliot Coleman. Author of *The New Organic Grower* and market gardener in Maine.

Alan Cook. An Ohio-based gardener on the staff of the Dawes Arboretum.

Dave DeWitt. An editor of *Whole Chili Pepper Magazine* and a New

Mexico resident, DeWitt grows about thirty varieties of chili peppers from around the world each year.

Deb and Paul Doscher. The Doschers are former organic market gardeners from New Hampshire and winners of an *Organic Gardening* contest. Deb says now she enjoys her garden more because she grows for just herself and her family.

Irma Dugan. Gardener and retired garden editor for the *Cleveland Plain Dealer.*

G.M. Dunn. A New Hampshire gardener.

Tom Eltzroth. Horticulture teacher and garden photographer in California.

Lloyd Evans. A Master Gardener in Ohio.

Kathleen Fenton. A Gardener and co-owner of Peaceful Valley Farm Supply in California. She desires "to support organic and sustainable agriculture and to help heal the planet."

Sam Forbes. Organic market and Master Gardener from Oklahoma.

Peter Gail. Director of Goosefood Acres Center for Wild Vegetable Research and Education in Ohio. For his publication list, write P.O. Box 18016, Cleveland Heights, OH 44118.

Carolyn Goodall. Gardener, cook, and preserver in Hillsboro, Oregon. Carolyn has been featured in *National Gardening* magazine.

Mark Graf. Flower seed department manager for Harris Seeds and a New York home gardener.

Gail Harrigan. A Connecticut-based gardener.

Betty Hofstetter. An Ohio resident, active member of North American Fruit Explorers, and the daughter of Mennonite farmers. She spent part of her wedding gift money on fruit trees and a vegetable garden. "I guess, perhaps, I gardened at first to save money, but it has become more of a vocation for me. I love to be outside and I love to eat and I love the physical labor involved in gardening. Sometimes I think I want to grow every kind of fruit and vegetable there is. Fortunately, we have fewer than 2 acres here so there is a limit to what I can do. Even so, I have collected over 200 fruit varieties."

Dennis and Mary Keiser. Pennsylvania-based residents with an edible-ornamental landscape. Mary is a teacher, and Dennis works with Walnut Acres, an organic farm and natural foods company.

Leopold Klein. Author of *100 Pounds of Tomatoes Out of an Inexpensive Foam Box* and a New York gardener. For a copy, write to P.O. Box 1237, Valley Stream, NY 11582; $10.95.

Lies Kobbe. Staff member of the Kimberton Hills Biodynamic Community in Pennsylvania.

Wendy Krupnick. Trial garden manager for Shepherd's Garden Seeds in California.

George Kuepper. Agronomist formerly on the staff of the Kerr Center for Sustainable Agriculture, and now an independent consultant from Oklahoma.

Robert Johnson. Owner of Johnny's Selected Seeds, in Maine.

Judy Lowe. Garden editor of *Chattanooga News-Free Press.*

Jeff Lowenfels. An Alaska-based attorney, gardener, and host of "Alaska Gardens with Jeff Lowenfels" on WAKM-TV.

Susan C. and Harvey E. Moser. Gardeners from North Carolina. "What started out as a hobby when my husband and I married has become a major part of our lives. It is so rewarding to see what can be produced from a small seed and God's help. We now enter four fairs each year (two local, one regional, and the state fairs). This past year we won 451 ribbons."

Virginia and Ed Nix. Tailgate market gardeners from North Carolina and past winners of a *National Gardening* contest.

Shepherd Ogden. Owner of the Cook's Garden, a mail-order seed merchant, former market gardener, and book author living in Vermont.

Eliot Paine. A home gardener and director of Holden Arboretum in Ohio.

Bernard Penczek. A New York resident, engineer, the 1988 winner of a "Victory Garden" contest, and member of the Men's Garden Club. "I've hunted and fished and I still like those sports. But I especially like to see things grow."

Nancy Pippart. Museum gardener at the Landis Valley Museum Heirloom Seed Project in Pennsylvania.

Debbie Pleu. Owner of Earthly Goods, an organic and sustainable agriculture and garden supply company in Oklahoma.

Debbie Pruitt. An Ohio-based gardener who prefers traditional ways.

Rob Ringer. Owner of Ringer and Safer's, organic garden products manufacturers.

Renee Shepherd. Owner of Shepherd's Garden Seeds and an avid cook.

Rachel Snyder. Former editor of *Flower and Garden* magazine and Kansas-based gardener.

David Stern. Organic market gardener, who concentrates on sustainable agriculture at Rose Valley Farm in New York. He is an active member of the New York State Garlic Seed Foundation. "May your bulbs swell and breath stink," Stern writes.

Donna Swansen. Past president of the Association of Professional Landscape Designers and Pennsylvania resident.

Michelle Taylor. Gardener and owner of Taylor's Herb Garden in California.

Victor Thompson. Retired apiarist at Ohio State University and gardener in Columbus, Ohio.

Hazel Weihe. Garden writer, lecturer, and radio host from New York.

Chris Werronen. Organizer of an organic and biodynamic subscription garden in Lake County, Ohio, who works with handicapped youth during the school year.

Kent Whealy. Founder and director of the Seed Savers Exchange in Iowa.

Rose Marie Whiteley. Former home economics teacher, gardener, and Nebraska-based test gardener for the National Gardening Association.

Wilfred Wooldridge. A retired physician, garden writer, and Missouri gardener.

Lori Zaim. Formerly connected with the restaurant trade, this Ohio resident likes to grow herbs and to experiment with cuisine.

appendix III

Mail-Order Suppliers

Your local nursery or garden center is likely to carry a variety of plants and equipment. To order by mail or to obtain product information, consult the companies listed below. This is only a partial listing. *The Complete Guide to Gardening by Mail* is available from The Mailorder Association of Nurseries, Dept. SCI, 8683 Doves Fly Way, Laurel, MD 20723. Please add $1.00 for postage and handling.

Abundant Life Seed Foundation, P.O. Box 772, Port Townsend, WA 98368

A & L Eastern Agricultural Lab, 7621 White Pine Road, Richmond, VA 23237

Bountiful Gardens, 5798 Ridgewood Road, Willits, CA 95490

W. Atlee Burpee and Co., Warminster, PA 18974

Bricker's, 824-K Sandbar Ferry Road, Augusta, GA 30901

The Cook's Garden, P.O. Box 535, Londonderry, VT 05148

DeGiorgi Seeds and Goods, 6011 W Street, Omaha, NE 68117

Earthly Goods, P.O. Box 4164, Tulsa, OK 74159-1164

Henry Fields Seed and Nursery Co., 415 N. Burnett, Shenandoah, IA 51602

Garden City Seeds, 1325 Red Crow Rd., Victor, MT 59875-9713

Gardener's Supply Co., 128 Intervale Rd., Burlington, VT 05401

Garden's Alive, P.O. Box 149, Sunman, IN 47041

Garlic Seed Foundation, Rose Valley Farm, Rose, NY 14542-0149

Harris Seeds, 60 Saginaw Dr., P.O. Box 22960, Rochester, NY 14692-2960

Hastings, P.O. Box 115535, Atlanta, GA 30310-8535

J.L. Hudson Seedsman, P.O. Box 1058, Redwood City, CA 94064

Johnny's Selected Seeds, Foss Hill Road, Albion, ME 04910

Landis Valley, 2451 Kissel Hill Rd., Lancaster, PA 17601

Le Jardin du Gourmet, P.O. Box 75, St. Johnsbury Center, VT 05873

Miller Nurseries, West Lake Rd., Canandaigua, NY 14424

Native Seeds/SEARCH, 2509 N. Campbell Ave., #325, Tucson, AZ 85719

Natural Gardening Company, 217 San Anselmo Ave, San Anselmo, CA 94960

Nichols Garden Nursery, 1190 N. Pacific Highway, Albany, OR 95321

Walt Nicke Co., 36 McLeod Lane, P.O. Box 433, Topsfield, MA 01983

Park Seed, Cokesbury Rd., Greenwood, SC 29647-0001

Peaceful Valley Farm Supply, P.O. Box 2209, Grass Valley, CA 95945

Pinetree Garden Seeds, New Gloucester, ME 04260

Plants of the Southwest, 930 Baca Street, Santa Fe, NM 87501

Rayner Brothers, Inc., P.O. Box 1617, Salisbury, MD 21801

Ringer, 9959 Valley View Road, Eden Prairie, MN 55344-3585

Ronniger's Seed Potatoes, Star Route, Moyie Springs, ID 83845

Seed Savers Exchange, RR3, Box 239, Decorah, IA 52101

Seeds Blüm, Idaho City Stage, Boise, ID 83706

Shepherd's Garden Seeds, 6116 Highway 9, Felton, CA 95018

Smith and Hawken, 25 Corte Madera, Mill Valley, CA 94941

Southern Exposure Seed Exchange, P.O. Box 158, North Garden, VA 22959

Stark Brothers, Louisiana, MO 63353

Stokes Seeds, Box 548, Buffalo, NY 14240

Taylors Herb Gardens, Inc., 1535 Lone Oak Road, Vista, CA 92084

Thompson and Morgan, P.O. Box 1308, Jackson, NJ 08527

Vesey's Seeds, Ltd., York, Prince Edward Island, C0A 1P0 Canada

Walnut Acres, Penn's Creek, PA 17862

William Dam Seeds, P.O. Box 8400, Dundas, ON, Canada L9H 6M1

Willhite Seed Co., P.O. Box 23, Poolville, TX 76076

appendix IV

Suggested Reading

Adams, Bill. 1976. *Vegetable Growing for Southern Gardens.* Houston, TX: Pacesetter Press.

Arthey, V.D. 1975. *The Quality of Agricultural Products.* New York: John Wiley.

Ashworth, Suzanne. 1991. *Seed to Seed.* Decorah, IA: Seedsavers Publications.

Ball Corp. 1989. *Ball Blue Book.* Muncie, IN: Ball Corp.

Blüm. 1991. *Farmer's and Planter's Almanac.* Winston-Salem: Blüm's Almanac Co.

Boehmer, Raquel. 1988. "Better Late Than Never." *National Gardening* (July).

Burr, Fearing, Jr. 1863. *The Field and Garden Vegetables of America.* Boston: Crosby and Nichols.

Byler, Emma. 1991. *Recipes and Remedies for Plain and Happy Living.* Cleveland: Goosefoot Acres Press.

Chioffi, Nancy, and Gretchen Mead. 1991. *Keeping the Harvest.* Pownal, VT: Garden Way Publishing.

Coleman, Eliot. 1989. *The New Organic Grower.* Chelsea, VT: Chelsea Green.

Lee, Sally. 1991. *Pesticides.* New York: Franklin Watts.

Gail, Peter. 1988. *On the Trail of the Yellow-Flowered Earth Nail.* Cleveland: Goosefoot Acres Press.

Greene, Janet. 1988. *Putting Food By.* Lexington, MA: Stephen Green.

Hayes, Wayland. 1982. *Pesticides Studied in Man.* Baltimore: Williams and Wilkins.

Jeavon, John. 1991. *How to Grow More Vegetables than You Ever Thought*

Possible. Berkeley, CA: Ten Speed Press.

Klein, Leopold. 1988. *100 Pounds of Tomatoes Out of an Inexpensive Foam Box.* Valley Stream, NY: Leopold Klein.

Kline, Roger A. *Vegetable Crop Report #387.* Ithaca, NY: Cornell University.

Olkowski, William, Sheila Daar, and Helga Olkowski. 1991. *Common-Sense Pest Control.* Newtown, CT: Taunton Press.

Pennington, Jean A. T. 1989. *Food Values.* New York: Harper and Row.

Raven, Peter, Ray Evert, and Helena Curtis. 1981. *Biology of Plants.* New York: Worth Publishers.

Reynolds, Susan and Paulette Williams. *So Easy to Preserve.* Athens, GA: Cooperative Extension Service, University of Georgia.

Rhode, Eleanour Sinclair. 1938. *Vegetable Cultivation and Cookery.* London: Medici Society.

Ricketts, Harold William. 1957. *Botany for Gardeners.* New York: Macmillan.

Russell, Christine. 1990. "What Me Worry?" *American Health* (June).

Shepherd, Renee. 1990. *Recipes from a Kitchen Garden.* Felton, CA: Shepherd's Garden.

Thomson, Bob, with James Tabor. 1987. *The New Victory Garden.* Boston, MA: Little, Brown.

Wildfever, Sherry, editor. 1990. "The Kimberton Hills Agricultural Calendar 1991: A Guide to Understanding the Influence of Cosmic Rhythms in Farming and Gardening."

Solomon, Steve. 1989. *Growing Vegetables West of the Cascades.* Seattle: Sasquatch Books.

U.S. Department of Commerce. 1990. *Statistical Abstract of the United States.*

Whealy, Kent (editor). 1989. *Fruit, Berry and Nut Inventory.* Decorah, Iowa: Seed Saver Publications.

—. 1992. *Garden Seed Inventory.* 3rd Edition. Decorah, Iowa: Seed Saver Publications.

Wolf, Ray, editor. 1977. *Managing Your Personal Food Supply.* Emmaus, PA: Rodale Press.

INDEX

(Illustrations are indicated by page numbers in *italics*; charts and tables by page numbers in **bold**).